Call of the Eagle

Call of the Eagle

Dave Walker

Whittles Publishing

Published by
Whittles Publishing,
Dunbeath,
Caithness KW6 6EY,
Scotland, UK

www.whittlespublishing.com

Printed by InPrint, Latvia

Contents

Preface   vii

1 The call of the eagle   1

2 The first success   11

3 Dark days of spring   22

4 Hope after hard times   28

5 The Haweswater pair   37

6 Mating and incubation   49

7 Lakeland nestlings   60

8 First flights   73

9 Long days on the hill   84

10 Differences of opinion   95

11 Noting new behaviour   103

12 Mixed fortunes   114

13 A difficult year   123

14 A Scottish sojourn   133

15 Investigating food supply   140

16 The end of an era   153

Epilogue   162

Preface

The traditional image of the British eagle worker is of someone who endures the hardships of the Scottish Highlands; it's a person who enters the remote fastnesses in all seasons and in all weathers with a stoicism that's matched only by the bird itself. It's a person who might spend day after day tramping the hills in search of the bird or spend long and lonely nights in a hide close to the nest; someone who abseils into nests on beetling crags to ring the chicks or remove the unhatched eggs for scientific analysis; someone whose life is lived in the wildest of terrains.

While some of those elements are a part of my life, my work with eagles has followed a different route from most. I've worked extensively with eagles in the Lake District National Park where millions of human visitors impose restrictions on the birds which make it seem almost impossible that such an endangered and sensitive species should live and breed there for more than 30 years. The stoicism, the long treks and the bitter winters remain, but I'm an observer not a climber, a ringer or a photographer. I watch and record from a safe distance without causing disturbance or interfering with the eagles' lives; I derive no pleasure from going to eagle nests when I know it will alarm the birds and disrupt their lives. That way of working, initiated in 1979 during my first year with the RSPB, has stood me in good stead; it's allowed me to watch golden eagles behaving naturally across their ranges. I've seen and experienced many events that haven't previously been recorded, some of which may even seem implausible, but I'm an inveterate note-taker, recording detail down to the minutiae of when an eagle defecates, ruffles its feathers or scratches its head, so the events described in this book are presented exactly as they happened.

Working with the Lakeland eagles hasn't always been straightforward, and I couldn't have done what I've done or seen what I've seen without the RSPB and for that I am extremely grateful. I wasn't alone while in their employ, and the contract staff and volunteers who assisted with the protection duties are all an essential part of the tale I have to tell. David Woodhead, Geoff Horne and Stefan Ross also made many of my eagle days more pleasurable than they might otherwise have been. And Mike Tomkies advised and encouraged me to produce this book.

Dave Walker

Chapter 1

The call of the eagle

Slithering and sliding through the patchy snow, over sodden moss and sharp rocks that dug into my thighs, I slowly belly-crawled lower and lower towards an obscure ledge high on the almost sheer side of a Lake District ridge long before the first light of dawn began to brighten the sky. Fearful of making any sound I tested the security of any rock I might brush against until I was in place, tucked into a corner where I would await daylight and then, perhaps, wait for several hours more, chilled and wet to the bone, until I achieved my goal.

My eyes accustomed to the poor light as the gloom began to lift, and I could see below me, barely 40 metres away, the female eagle sitting tightly on her nest. I would have been far too close in normal circumstances as the nest with eggs is sacrosanct, but the call of the eagle can lure the fieldworker to difficult and dangerous locations to find another piece of the jigsaw, to answer another question that adds to our knowledge of this, the most awe-inspiring of all British birds. Even so, I would never want to be, and would never again find myself, so close to an eagle's nest that might still hold eggs that could hatch. Disturbing the bird that day wouldn't just have been an offence against the Wildlife and Countryside Act, it would have been a crime against the whole ethos of my work, to study golden eagles without causing them any distress or negatively interfering with their lives. But checking for an egg hatching was justification on this day.

The eagle was oblivious to my presence, and her mate also failed to notice me as he winged his way past the nest from time to time. The first changeover of the day isn't always early in the morning, as might be expected, even if the female's overnight stint has seen her on the nest for 12 or more hours. She turned her head to watch as her mate flew by but didn't call and occasionally drifted off into a nodding sleep, her bill resting on the front of the nest, before becoming suddenly alert as a crow called or a raven flapped noisily overhead. It was two and a half hours before the female finally stood and, without the male coming in, flew off to defecate in flight and then return to the nest. I saw all I needed to see during those few brief seconds; there in the nest lay one white egg, the first to be laid, and a tiny eaglet. It was, I believe, the first time that the second egg laid had been confirmed to hatch when the first one hadn't.

My next task, now in broad daylight with both eagles active and no matter how cold and stiff I'd become during the long wait, was to retreat to the ridgetop without the birds knowing about it. Once the female had settled again I inched away, up through a runnel and was safe, not once did she look towards me during the entire time I was on the ridge. There was a tremendous satisfaction in knowing that I had the fieldcraft to achieve such feats, to check an active nest without the eagles being aware of my presence, but that came with experience and knowledge both of the birds and of the terrain.

It wasn't always like that, this was my eighth year with the Lake District eagles, and I wouldn't have risked such an exercise without good reason or at any previous time. I was by then living within easy walking distance of the nesting valley and had followed the great birds throughout the year; long winter walks told me of the area they covered, identified the home range and helped me come to understand not only where they went but also why they'd choose a particular location in a given month. Breeding season after season enlightened me to their ways at the nest, their home life from when they began to rebuild the nest to the fledging of the nestling, and I'd followed the juveniles to witness their development from a crying baby hatchling totally dependent on its parents to a free-flying and independent golden eagle, the king of birds.

By that day, 13 May 1986, I'd been with the eagles every week since March 1983 and knew their habits well, and yet I originally had no intention of working with the species. When I was first employed by the RSPB in 1979 I was expecting to be sent to a nature reserve; I had no interest in eagles and my only experience was a handful of distant sightings made during holidays to Scotland. I'd never even seen an eagle's nest, but I was told that 'everyone starts on the eagles', and so I accepted the post I was offered and waited to hear more.

I knew of the Haweswater eagles, their presence was an open secret, and they'd appeared on television and in the press, but when I was briefed I was astonished to learn that I was being sent to a second pair in the Lake District. I had no idea that there were two pairs, so closely guarded a secret was the existence of the second, so closely guarded that even now I'm loath to name their location (even though it's many years since they were lost) and only refer to them as my first, or the west, pair. I was only given a rough idea of the eagles' location at my briefing, the name of my contact, a low-powered spotting scope by way of official equipment and told to prevent anyone from going to the nest. With that I set off to begin my days with the golden eagles.

My contact, Mike, at the local sub-post office, knew to expect my arrival, but we were both very cagey when we met; without any formal means of identification, a few pleasantries had to be exchanged before we could even mention the eagles, but even then there appeared to be a reluctance to share information. I thought it was a strange way to behave given that my involvement as the RSPB warden at the site was prearranged. Being about the same age as me, Mike wasn't what I was expecting, and, I suspect, his first impression of me was probably the same. There'd been some problems and mistakes the year before when the eagles were guarded unofficially, and I was there partly as a result of those mistakes, so I was wary of asking too many questions, but I knew I'd need Mike's help and didn't want to get off on the wrong foot. We drank some coffee and looked at the map. Mike told me some of what had happened the year before and waved a hand in the general direction of two or three valleys. I thought he was being deliberately vague, but I had every confidence in my ability to find an eagle's nest, even though I hadn't done this type of work before.

I eventually decided that it was time for me to visit the site, and Mike presented me with a scrap of paper on which he'd scribbled the route to the caravan in which I'd spend much of the next four months. Even that was unconvincing, and 30 years later, I have still to cross the second cattle grid he marked on it! I wondered if it was some kind of initiative test arranged with the office, a deliberate attempt to complicate the issue and see if I could cope, but I had no intention of falling at the first hurdle.

I found the caravan with ease; comparing Mike's scribble to the Ordnance Survey map ensured that I didn't take any wrong turns along the forest roads, regardless of how many features Mike had omitted from his map. I was in for a shock when I arrived. I'd been assured that the van was a four berth, but it was barely 4 metres long and was designed for two adults and two children, not the four men who'd be sharing it. I hoped my first official day of employment by the RSPB being 1 April was a coincidence rather than an omen. I dumped my gear in the van and set out on foot in search of my first eagle's nest, hoping they were still there. In spite of their rarity, and the threat from egg collectors, the birds had been incubating for almost two weeks before I arrived, and no one had checked them for several days.

The forest rides were deeply shaded and sodden, and when I eventually broke out onto the open hill the ridgetops were shrouded in a cloak of low cloud and drizzle. Somewhere in the valley ahead of me a golden eagle was incubating its eggs, and as I set off across the fells the responsibility of my job sank into my mind for the first time. It was my job to set up an RSPB eagle protection scheme from scratch, with no prior experience and by myself. Egg collectors were still a threat in 1979, and because someone might have attempted to take the eggs in 1978 there was a real chance of the site being targeted again. The eagles also occupied sheep country, and I was well aware of the potential conflict between eagle and shepherd, even though I'd been assured that golden eagles didn't kill lambs. I wasn't that naïve.

I waded across a wet flush and stepped onto a small rise to get a better view of the valley and, hopefully, see my first English eagle sailing against the low cloud. The sky was empty, and the ground ahead of me didn't match the image I had of eagle country; it looked unlikely to hold such rugged birds. There were no beetling crags or glacial corries, and this part of the Lake District didn't offer the remote fastnesses of the species' strongholds in the Scottish Highlands and Islands. Here was a rolling complex of glacial moraines, and while the ridgeside to my left held a few small rocky outcrops, it seemed to be one large scree and boulder field. The ridge to the right curved away from me and, from what I could see, was rounded and grassy. The coniferous plantation from which I'd emerged blanked off the ground in that direction and, in the other, lay popular hillwalking routes that would be crawling with tourists during the height of the summer. This eagle territory wasn't what I imagined, and I thought that was probably why the site had remained a secret for so long; one look at this place and it would be easy to dismiss it as being unsuitable for golden eagles.

There was also a public footpath in the valley that concerned me, but not wanting to be seen and with only a vague idea of where the nest was, I chose to avoid that and followed a sheep path along the beckside as I ventured deeper into the valley for the first time. The public footpath puzzled me as I assumed that eagles wouldn't nest close to one, and yet I'd been told that the nest was on the same side of the valley and that the path almost went below it.

Heathery mounds and low bluffs obscured my view of the ridge as I walked, but I was content that they'd also disguise my approach and lessen the risk of me accidentally disturbing the eagles if I emerged too close to the nest crag, which wasn't even marked on the Ordnance Survey map. Six red grouse flushed ahead of me, and I could hear curlews and crows; a mallard flew up from the beck, and a rabbit dived into cover on my approach, so I knew there'd be natural food for the eagles, in spite of my first impressions, and that they should only turn to lamb killing if they were absolutely desperate. There were no eagles flying, though, and the possibility of an early failure, and the end of my short RSPB career, crossed my mind.

The heather banks came to an abrupt end, and the upper reaches of the valley seemed to drop away from me, giving the strange illusion of the valley head being lower than its middle reaches, even though the water in the beck continued to flow past in the correct direction. Above the marshy valley floor, and on the right-hand ridge, two small broken crags now came into view. I settled into the last of the heather and began to scan crags that still seemed unlikely to hold an eagle. I could pick out little detail through the binoculars and so turned to the telescope for a closer look.

By sheer chance, as I put my eye to the lens to focus, the nest was in the centre of the image, and above its rim, the eagle's head was held high and alert and, for the first time, I saw that curious head-on appearance of the eagle. The dark mask of the bird's face was cowled by a halo of pale, dusty yellow-brown with an ivory triangle to mark the position of the beak as the eagle glowered down the valley towards me. But it wasn't alert because of me, it was looking for its mate, and after less than a minute the second bird dropped onto the nest and looked around, checking that its mate was happy and that nothing was close enough to the nest to cause alarm. With this confirmed, the first bird rose, and the two eagles stood side by side. The size difference told me that it had been the larger female sitting when I arrived; she looked slightly darker than her mate, but their patterning appeared to be similar. Seen singly, the size difference might not be obvious and the plumages might prove confusing, but I was confident that the ability to separate the two birds would come with experience.

The female called, stepped to the front of the nest and seemed to jump off before opening her great wings and swinging away up the valley, close to the crag and out of sight into a gully. The male settled quietly and all was calm. In my first half hour of eagle work I'd located a nest, had seen both eagles, heard one call and had seen a male taking a share of the incubation duties. I was hooked but knew that it wouldn't always be that easy.

As well as being on a crag that bore no resemblance to the popular image of an eagle crag, the nest was surprisingly close to the top of the rock. It appeared to be no more than a step down from the sloping grassy brow-top, and when they were standing, the eagles' heads appeared level with the ledge above. The nest would be easily accessible to egg collectors, and remembering the garbled tale of what might have happened the year before, when the eggs were apparently removed and then replaced, the first doubts began to appear in my mind. Could I really manage the scheme to a successful conclusion without any prior experience and so little advice?

The female returned after 10 minutes, and I saw her distinctive holed wings for the first time, holes in her primary flight feathers that she'd retain throughout the years I knew her, regardless of how many moults she completed. She called again when she reached the nest, and I could feel myself being drawn into her life. The eagles' magnetism was obvious – I was enthralled to see them undisturbed at the nest and at such comparatively close quarters without a hide. Even though the nest was still about 500 metres away it felt a great deal closer, and I thought the eagles must have been aware of my presence, and yet it didn't prevent them from behaving normally. The male stood, the female stepped over the eggs and lowered her body, rocking from side to side as she did so to settle comfortably with the eggs in the correct position. She had her head down in front of her breast as she settled, but with the male now gone, it was soon up and on the lookout. I stayed in place and started to keep behavioural notes, waiting until the light began to fade.

It had been a fantastic start to my eagle career. The size and suitability of the caravan no longer mattered as I wended my way back to the woods that late afternoon; I was too exuberant to care, and besides, I still had it all to myself at that point. I'd forgotten that it had no water supply, though, and I had to plod back through the forest to fetch some in a bucket from a stream so I could have a brew of tea and make an evening meal. It was 30 March, and it would be a cold and frosty night, but I didn't care about the inadequacies of the caravan that night, they would come to light soon enough when the other wardens arrived. The only facilities were to be found in the surrounding plantation, and it would soon become damp, infested with midges and stinking. Mike arrived with the other wardens two days later, and suddenly there was little room for the people never mind their baggage. The pressure would only be relieved once the hide was erected and we had at least one person in the valley at all times. The five of us squeezed into the van and had a cup of tea while I described what I'd seen and my first thoughts on how the scheme would work.

Suitably refreshed, I led Ken, Dave and Ron to the eagles. Wary of causing any disturbance, I didn't take them as far into the valley as when I was by myself, but they saw the birds, and my main priority was to decide a location for our hide, whenever it arrived. An obvious sheepfold had been suggested but that was impractical, it didn't give us a view of either the valley bottom or the down-valley approach to the crag, so egg collectors could have approached unseen from either direction. We settled on a very exposed position at the top of a rise that would allow us to see everything we needed to see. It also had the advantage of being only slightly below nest level so the sun's position would never be a problem, and we wouldn't struggle to see what was happening at the nest. That was all wishful thinking at the time, and until the hide arrived we had to find shelter as best we could.

The April weather was atrocious, and we sat out in storms during which the crags never came into view, freezing temperatures and days of continuous rain or snow that soaked our clothes. What little shelter we had was afforded by the sheepfold but that had no roof, and the gales drove whatever precipitation we faced straight through gaps in the walls we'd hoped would protect us. We had to walk from the van to the site before it was light and back again after dark, and thick mists made it easy to become disorientated and waste time trying to find out where you were and how you could get to where you wanted to be. I knew how to use a map and compass but without landmarks in the dark and mist it was easy to wander off course. These were the days before GPS systems that allow you tap in the coordinates of your target location and tell you the direction to walk, though they work in straight lines which can be as dangerous as being lost! The one concession to safety was a set of redundant mountain-rescue-team radios, redundant because they ate, rather than ran off, batteries, and their signal barely penetrated the forest. Having them made little difference in any case; on struggling back to the van one day after dark through a torrential thunderstorm I arrived to find the others tucked up in bed and the radio boxed and stowed under a bed 'because it was dark outside', so there would have been little chance of rescue had I needed assistance. The protection scheme was a hastily cobbled together shambles at first, and not having a hide made the conditions almost unbearable at times. Because of the lack of shelter our waterproofs and clothes were permanently sodden, and it became impossible to spend day after day out on the fells. The eagles seemed to cope all right, but we weren't as hardy as them. I devised a work roster that ensured no one was outside for longer than five hours at a stretch, but that didn't really help when little was happening, and there were days when we didn't see the eagles or their nest. We couldn't stay out overnight at that time of year either as we had neither hide nor tent, so we just concentrated on ensuring that one of the eagles was on the nest, that they were both still alive and that no humans went near the crag, even though we had yet to have a visitor of any inclination.

The situation was slightly improved by the arrival of 'the hide', though we still didn't have any means of cooking or boiling water away from the caravan. The hide itself was a standard garden shed that would normally hold a few tools, a lawnmower, an old cupboard and not much else. It arrived during the second week of April, and we eventually carried it to its position after Mike's Land Rover got bogged down in a forest ride. We struggled all day to carry the panels across the moor, stepping into hidden ditches and stumbling through the heather, but little did I realise at the time that this would become a running theme of my eagle work. We finally had the hide in place, and almost predictably, the weather improved straight away.

Some of the RSPB's Haweswater wardening team visited us for no apparent reason at this point, and a couple of days later I received a message ordering me to telephone the office. During the ensuing conversation I was threatened with the sack and accused of not keeping a full and overnight watch on the site and of going to the nest!

The Haweswater wardens had simply lied about us, but my word was believed when I reminded my boss of the problems we'd faced with no hide or other form of shelter (so we couldn't be expected to stay out all night), unlike at Haweswater where the wardens lived in a house, had a hide and a tent in the eagle valley and volunteers to help them. I also pointed out that we were supposed to be paid in the middle of the month, but instead of wages we only received phoney excuses for the delay.

What had started so well for me seemed to have descended into politics with the arrival of the other wardens, and it was a relief to spend time alone and with the birds and leave the problems at the caravan. There was barely a fortnight of the incubation period left by the time the hide was erected, and it was already apparent that we wouldn't actually be seeing very much of the eagles. The nest relief I saw almost always followed the pattern of my very first sighting, the departing bird swinging around the crag and out of sight into the gully. I occasionally picked it up again above a distant ridge and, through painstaking, inch-by-inch searching when there was nothing in view, I'd also sometimes been able to locate it perched on the opposite ridge. It always amazed me that, having flown behind the crag, the bird would appear on this perch without me seeing its approach in spite of my constantly staring and scanning the valley. And the number of times it flew and was lost from sight during the brief moment it took to make a note was ridiculous.

As the April days passed we began to look for signs of the eggs hatching. We didn't know exactly when they were laid, but we had a notion and knew how long the incubation period should be. One of the expected signs would have been the male delivering food to the nest, but I'd already seen him engage in this activity as early as 7 April. Two days later I watched the female feeding herself on the nest without even standing up. In fact, I would see most of the possibilities during that period; the male and female carrying food to the nest, both birds feeding there on food brought in by the other, both carrying food in and leaving without it and even food being delivered by the male and carried off by the female, to be eaten on a corner of the crag while the male covered the eggs.

None of these things seemed to have been well documented before, and as with the male incubating and both birds calling with some regularity, I began to wonder if any of the old eagle men whose books I'd read in preparation for my job had actually done any fieldwork! I'd seen things in my first two weeks that they didn't seem to have seen during a lifetime. They, of course, made general statements, usually from the nestling period alone, and most eagle work was, and still is, directed at the nest (either through photography or counting chicks). There are still very few people who have watched and kept accurate notes throughout the breeding season without causing any disturbance, but I'd already seen enough to encourage me to make more detailed observations. Especially as a few sources said that some of the things I'd seen simply didn't happen.

There were interesting moments to be seen around times of nest relief as well. For example, the female would leave the nest before the male arrived, but the male never left until his partner was standing beside him. After twice feeding on the nest on the

12th, the female flew off and actually stayed in view for a change. The male arrived two minutes later as the female gained height above the valley bottom and then sailed on half-closed wings. It was easy to follow a bird in the air, so I watched her through binoculars and kept the scope trained on the nest to ensure that the male was settled and still there. As I switched from one to the other a racing pigeon suddenly dashed over the nest, the eagle was taken by surprise, and I imagined a startled expression on his face. In an instant, and before he could react, a peregrine followed in hot pursuit and almost took off the eagle's head as it went by. From her position above the valley the female eagle closed her wings and fell through the air towards the intruders.

As they raced towards the hide the peregrine gained on the pigeon, and the eagle gained on the peregrine. The eagle, at first in a dive but then in level flight with tight plumage and beating strokes of half-closed wings that resembled solid muscle, thundered out of the sky. The rush of air was audible, and I could see her eyes transfixed on their target and paying no heed to the garden shed that must have been such an intrusion in her world or to me as I stepped outside to follow her flight. As they closed on each other, it was the so-called 'fastest bird on Earth' that suddenly hurtled skywards to save its life, and the pigeon escaped as the eagle continued to drive the falcon from her home. People don't realise the speed of an eagle, and there's no bird as fast as an angry eagle with a grudge to bear. Satisfied that she'd made her point, she returned up-valley within a minute, casually sailing past the hide and this time turning her head to look down at the pathetic awestruck specimen with its feet planted firmly on the ground below her. She stopped to collect some mutton from below the crag and then carried it to the nest to relieve her mate. Settling down, she wasn't even out of breath.

We were into a routine once the hide was set up, and I soon developed a roster that allowed us to take time off each week. There was no need to have long watches because the hide was within easy walking distance of the van, but it still meant that, with overnight shifts, we'd each work 24 out of 48 hours. This gave us all some time off, and it also meant that we had spare people when they were needed, and we had to safely negotiate the Easter holiday before the eggs would hatch. The Lake District can be a dreadful place when it's busy, and Easter's always a popular time with tourists, hillwalkers and climbers, so I doubled up the watches to have two people on duty at the same time. Easter was a traditional time for egg collectors to be about, so I knew there were real dangers to be expected. Readied and expectant, we awaited the rush, especially as the weather was fine and warm and most people were off work. It was a complete waste of time; the entire weekend saw us receive a grand total of three visitors, so we slipped back into the single-watcher system before it was even over. This really was a quiet corner of the Lakes, and local rumours that the eagles may have been here longer than was officially accepted had a ring of truth to them.

I wasn't disappointed by the lack of people, but I was surprised. In fact, during the entire four months we were on watch, we only had 97 visitor-days and many of those involved either David Woodhead (one of the original finders of the site) or Fred Jones, a local botanist who'd stumbled on the birds by chance. It's likely that we had fewer than

50 different people at the hide in total that year. It was just as well as we weren't set up for visitors even though those who came didn't always appreciate that fact. I was the only warden with a telescope, and the others had to make do with binoculars and the RSPB's spotting scope, but that didn't stop some people thinking we were only there for their benefit, and one time I was even knocked from my own scope by someone desperate to see the bird on the nest.

The majority of our visitors had no previous knowledge of the eagles and were delighted when we showed them off; most were happy to change their plans if they'd intended walking past the nest. It's surprising, really, given the stories we told. Because of the secrecy of the site we weren't supposed to tell visitors what we were doing and had been advised to tell them that we were engaged in a general bird survey of the area. We even specified that we were concentrating on meadow pipits and needed the telescope to follow these tiny birds as they flitted across the hillside, but the excuse became a little threadbare after a while or when a whacking great eagle then appeared above the crag, so we gave up and did a PR job instead.

Our busiest days tended to be the misty ones rather than the sunny ones, and I stopped counting the number of people I had to redirect because they'd got lost in spite of having all the equipment. The most embarrassing was a group from the local outdoor centre who weren't where they thought they were and then, having consulted their maps and compasses, set off in the wrong direction again. There was only one unfortunate incident when an elderly couple decided to picnic under the nest crag and wait for the bird to return. They were quite uppity when it was pointed out that the eagle wouldn't return with them sitting 50 metres away, but they eventually moved on, and the eagle returned as soon as they were out of sight. The thoughtlessness of some people who think they're naturalists never failed to amaze me.

With about six weeks of incubation now past since the suspected laying date, we were obviously close to the hatch, if it was going to happen, as these eagles hadn't hatched their eggs since 1976. It was difficult to know what signs to look for that might indicate the hatch, given the amount of food that had already been taken to the nest, our lack of experience and the absence of any usable advice in the books we had. The eagles' behaviour seemed to change on the 24th, and during a six-hour watch the male only relieved his mate for a minute and took three pieces of material to the nest. This was something else that wasn't supposed to happen as much as it did, but the eagles continued to collect nest material throughout the breeding attempt. Ken and Ron saw no change during their watches. The male delivered food, and the female fed herself on the nest the next day, but there was still no hatch. I was becoming concerned; I thought the signs would be obvious and seeing nothing made me suspect that the eggs might be infertile.

On the 26th, the male again flew in with food in his talons but instead of taking it to the nest he landed on the ledge above and stood looking at his mate for a minute before flying away again. This looked a bit better. The food, a lump of mutton (although eagles aren't supposed to take carrion to the chick!), clearly wasn't intended for the female.

With the eggs possibly chipping for 48 hours before hatching, the adults would be able to hear the chick calling and prepare themselves, and I hoped that that was what was happening. Perversely, I thought, not taking food directly to the nest might be a sign of the hatch. Later that evening the female jumped up to the ledge and ate before returning and settling down for the night.

She left the nest before 5 a.m. the next morning but allowed her mate only three minutes at the nest and then was off again an hour later, leaving the nest unattended for 12 minutes. I didn't know if this was a good or bad sign as it was the longest they'd been absent during my watches, and I was relieved when the male returned and took a four-minute stint before being replaced by his mate. It was another two hours before the female jumped up to the ledge to drag the food back to the nest. She tore at it and began to present slivers of meat into the nest. The first feed was at 7.17 a.m., it was as simple as that, the first egg had hatched!

CHAPTER 2

The first success

I could relax; the hatch was confirmed, and even though the wardens played only a passive role in the process, it meant the scheme had been successful and I'd soon be seeing my first nestling eaglet. It came as no surprise when we were paid as soon as I got the news to the office, the wages came without any apologies or explanations and our May wages arrived two weeks later. That problem was a thing of the past and no longer mattered.

We'd seen the female presenting pieces of meat into the nest, so we knew there was a chick but we still hadn't seen it. Ken thought that he'd seen food being offered to two different parts of the nest, suggesting that there might be two chicks, but no one else had seen this, and it may have been too soon after the first hatch to be thinking about a second egg hatching; they usually hatch about four days apart. It didn't really matter that I hadn't seen the chick straight away so long as the female continued to present food. There was no more danger of the eggs being stolen, no one would steal the chick, and it seemed that only a major food shortage could now ruin the season. I could look forward to a pleasant early summer on the hill learning about the home life of the golden eagle.

I awoke on 5 May to find the valley under 6 cm of snow. More snow blew in on a blustery north wind, so I stayed in my sleeping bag, propped open the window of the hide and brewed some tea and porridge. Spindrift had blown through the cracks in the door and around the window, but I was fairly snug and felt sorry for the tiny eaglet waking to a freezing-cold dawn on top of a pile of wet sticks. The female was brooding it, of course, to keep it warm and, to my surprise, the male was also in view, perched on a rock about 30 metres from the nest. It was an unusual place for him to be at 4.10 on a snowy morning as he didn't usually appear until much later, even on fine days. He flew after 45 minutes, and I followed his progress as he crossed the valley; gliding without a single wingbeat, he gained speed as he lost height towards the opposite slope.

He crashed into the hillside in a flurry of wings, talons and snow; there was a scuffle and as the spindrift settled an adult fox sprang away from beneath him. It ran a few metres and then turned to face him. The eagle stood upright, panting, his breath condensing on the cold morning air, and his wings were held open in heraldic fashion to increase his apparent size. That would have been a magnificent first kill to witness but that hadn't been his purpose. He stepped forward, and through the telescope, I could see that he now stood on a dead lamb he'd stolen from the fox that had killed it. He slowly relaxed and began to eat, the fox clearly having already opened up the carcass. The fox circled around him, looking for a chance to seize the meat again, but the eagle always turned to face it, and after six minutes, the fox appeared to have accepted defeat and began to move away. The eagle relaxed on seeing this, fully closed his wings and ate more eagerly. He remained alert, though, and paused when a second fox arrived to watch him from about 20 metres.

I had the best vantage point in the valley and, unlike the male eagle, noticed the foxes begin to walk in opposite directions. The vixen, which had already felt the eagle's talons, casually sauntered between the boulders to squat in front of the bird and hold his attention while the dog crept behind and below him and slowly began to belly-crawl towards him in a pincer movement. With the dog in position, the vixen stood up and drew the eagle's full attention before slowly stepping down the slope towards him. Her confidence seemed to unsettle the eagle, and with her virtually on the opposite side of the carcass and the dog fox creeping to within only a metre or so behind him, a snow flurry swept through the valley and obliterated my view. When it hit the hide I was in a white-out for 20 minutes. I couldn't believe my bad luck and now had no idea of what was happening.

When the snowfall finally cleared, I could see neither the eagle nor the foxes. I could pick out the shape of the lamb beneath its coating of fresh snow but that only confounded the problem. I'd have expected the winner of any fight to remain with the spoils and not for all three combatants to have fled. I scanned the ridgeside repeatedly throughout the remaining three and a half hours of my watch but couldn't find the eagle anywhere. There was an ominous calm over the valley, no bird called and no sheep bleated, the only movement was of the female eagle's head as she, too, scanned the valley for her mate. I began to wonder if the foxes' plan had worked, and the lamb carcass remained because they'd carried off the eagle. I gave the whole tale to Ken when he arrived to replace me at 9 a.m., and he must have been anxious as well as it was another two hours before the male eagle returned, unconcerned and in pursuit of two crows.

Ken was also the first of us to see the chick, on 7 May. I first saw it five hours later, and it was then in view for much of the time, and its calls began to reach us at the hide. The weather didn't improve much, though, and the female had to brood the chick through more rain, snow and mist. The track to the hide became a muddy stream because of our regular tramping, but even though the only luxury was a single-burner gas stove, the hide became the favourite place to be. There you could change into dry clothes and have peace and relative comfort for four or five hours at a time. As the weather grew milder, the long overnight watches became an absolute delight when stars filled the skies or when the full moon lit the valley in a silver sheen. The nocturnal sounds of snipe drumming and curlews fluting mingled with the bubbling of streams in a natural symphony, and the incongruity of it all being heard from a garden shed plonked halfway up a remote valley didn't matter at all. There were times when I didn't even bother going to sleep, so soothing was the night in the valley.

The morning of 9 May dawned as wet as many of the others, and the mist lay so thick that the view from the hide extended for no more than 5 metres, and as the hide stood on the lip of a drop, it felt as if it was on the very edge of the world with only clouded space stretching into the infinite distance. Fortunately, the mist had lifted by 5 a.m., and with the sun shining down, the female left the chick uncovered and soaked up the warming rays on the opposite slope. She zipped her long feathers through her beak to clean and prime them and ruffled her body plumage time and time again before perching with her wings loosely open and gently drying on the breeze. It must have been glorious for her after a wet night on the nest, and I looked on jealously, huddled for warmth around a cup of tea and knowing that the sun wouldn't reach the hide until after the end of my shift.

The male eagle wasn't idle during this time and visited the nest only five minutes after his mate had left it. He towered over the squeaking eaglet and then stepped into the nest cup; he leant forward, picked at the food that lay there and began to feed the chick. This was the first of only five occasions on which this would happen during 1979. And when he sat and brooded the chick, it was for the second and last occasion that year. Needless to say, feeding and brooding by the male were considered to be exceptional events by the books, but I'd seen it at my first nest and before the chick was a fortnight old. It was becoming obvious that these, and the earlier events, weren't exceptional at all, they simply weren't seen in the past because of the type of fieldwork that people preferred to do. There was, and probably still is, an attitude that says you can't be a serious eagle worker unless you visit nests and ring chicks, and that more information can be collected by doing that than by actually watching and investigating what the birds are doing without causing disturbance. I was never going to be like that, I'd rather watch birds than interfere with them at the nest. And there was more exceptional behaviour to come, and as with many of the things I've seen, the experts wouldn't believe that it happened.

I'd often read of how the adults would stand and watch while one of a two-chick brood attacked and killed the other, and it seemed odd that the adults would be so unconcerned about the fate of their own young. We only had one chick in our nest, of course, so I wouldn't see that happen, but on 17 May, I saw something that would make that disinterest appear to be very strange indeed. As was usual at such times, the chick struggled out from beneath the female and shuffled backwards up the cup and on to the rim to defecate out of the nest. Unlike small birds, the faeces aren't presented in a neat sac for the adults to remove, so they have to be squirted out to prevent the nest from becoming fouled and stinking during the 11 to 12 weeks the chick would be there. That's why the adult eagles also remove most of the old food remains that could accumulate and result in infestations of parasites and bothersome flies.

The chick lifted its stubby little tail once it was on the edge, but instead of squirting, it continued over and down the outside of the nest. It clambered a good 30 cm below the top while the female poked around in the bottom of the nest cup, oblivious to what was happening. The chick defecated but must then have realised that it was stuck. It must have called, though I didn't hear it, for the female was suddenly alert and looked around. She peered over the side of the nest and, after a few moments of contemplation, calmly leant over to gently hook her beak under the chick's tail and carefully ease it back into the nest. It seemed incongruous that a bird showing such concern and delicacy for its chick would have stood by and let one kill the other if she'd had twins.

There must have been something in the air that day as the male was afflicted in a similar way to the chick. As he approached the nest on one occasion, with a sprig of heather in his beak, he seemed to lose his sense of direction, and instead of landing neatly on the platform beside his mate, he crashed straight into the side of the nest. He received no help from the female, though, and had to climb up under his own strength and under the disapproving glare of the female. And to make matters worse, when he flew off again he dislodged the only piece of food on the nest, and the female had to fly down to the screes to retrieve it before she could feed the chick.

Wet and windy May turned into a sunny June that gradually clouded over and began to rain through the mist, but at least it didn't snow again, and we'd suffered the last of the frosts. Both we and the eagles were settled into the routine of things by now. There was no shortage of food being taken to the nest, and most of this had been killed rather than picked up as carrion. Crows, rabbits, grouse, pigeons, a curlew and small birds were all identified, and I'd even accidentally flushed the male from a grouse kill between the hide and the forest, but we still hadn't seen any kills. Ken corrected that situation. The male had been sailing by the crags when he suddenly turned on a raven that was mobbing him, caught it in flight and bundled it to the ground. Before he could administer the *coup de grâce*, though, the female flew from the nest, knocked him out of the way, completed the kill and carried the raven back to the nest, leaving the male, in spite of his best efforts, with just a pile of feathers to flick through.

While food wasn't in short supply, it wasn't always as easily available as that raven, which was killed less than 100 metres from the nest. On 10 June, the female removed an old leg of lamb from the nest and, as had become the habit, dumped it on the screes below the crag by letting it drop from her talons. This was part of the regular tidying and care of the nest that the female would often engage in for many minutes at a time. She flew around the corner and into the usual gully, and the male appeared from that direction almost at once, as if her arrival there had forced him to leave. Swinging around the crag, he stalled in flight, dropped to the screes and picked up the same leg of lamb. He hadn't seen it being dumped, of course, and carried it to the nest, arriving shortly after the female had flown in with a twig to decorate the nest. The male proudly placed the leg beside the chick and flew off, apparently satisfied that his good day's foraging justified him now taking a few hours off duty. While the male then perched and preened for 84 minutes, the female proceeded to feed the chick from the very item that she'd rejected only a few minutes earlier. Both eagles seemed oblivious to the fact that the meat had already been deemed inappropriate for the chick. While they could clearly remember where carcasses were located, the eagles seemed incapable of recognising an item they were familiar with; perhaps it was because the male hadn't seen the leg being dumped on the screes, and as she knew she'd taken something off, the female was happy to believe that the male had delivered something new.

And so the season progressed with the eagles successfully rearing a chick that grew more vocal and active with each passing day. The birds settled into more expected behaviour and would sail high above the valley or patrol the ridges when they left the nest. I'd see them leave in one direction and return via another, suggesting a long and circuitous foraging flight, even though most of the food delivered to the nest came from the north-west. While I was quite happy to meet and greet visitors, I always hoped that none would arrive and by far preferred the overnight watch that lasted 15 hours to the shorter daytime shifts. While someone might have appeared during the evening, there was little likelihood of visitors arriving before the change of watch at 9 a.m.. It wasn't that I was anti-social, but visitors disrupted my note taking. I was already sufficiently interested to want to continue the eagle work and look for information that could expand our knowledge and improve the protection schemes.

When I heard that the Haweswater eagles had failed to hatch their eggs I asked for some of their equipment to be transferred to us. All we really needed was their tent to ease the overcrowding in the caravan, but I was told that it was being used to guard peregrines. It was frustrating to know that every effort was being made to help the other wardens while we were guarding England's only successful eagles with cast-off, inadequate and second-rate equipment. It therefore came as no surprise that even our supposedly secret location was treated with some distain, and I was half expecting it when a car pulled up outside the caravan one day.

The couple who emerged from it introduced themselves as sometime-volunteers from Haweswater, but I didn't know who they were and was in no mood to be impressed by that and pointed out that they had neither permission to visit our site nor to bring their vehicle into the private woods in which we were based. They said they'd been sent with information about an egg collector, but that was an obvious ruse and they blustered when I said that nothing would still be on eggs this late in the season. To make it worse, it turned out that they hadn't even been told where we were; they'd had to find us. They said they'd been very discreet about taking directions and had only asked in the pub, the village shop and any farmers they met! They'd eventually been told of the caravan's location by a forest worker but still didn't understand the significance when he told them that he didn't know why it was there or what the occupants were doing. I asked them if that was how they dealt with all confidential information, but they could only shrug their shoulders and repeat that they thought they were being helpful. They couldn't answer at all when asked why they hadn't contacted me via the office. They wanted to see the eagles and that was the end of it, site security didn't matter.

And some people really should have known better. There was the national park officer who asked politely if he could take his dog up the valley and then spent most of the day running around after it and shouting its name at the top of his voice. They scattered sheep, separated the ewes from the lambs and generally destroyed the mood of the valley. Surely someone of his status should have had more awareness, and he must have known that his dog wasn't safe with sheep.

Perhaps the worst visitor, though, was the man who told me he'd once photographed his dog sitting on an eagle's nest. He couldn't tell me why he'd done that but went on to assure me that the dog would attack anything he told it to and that it would protect him to the death. That was just what I needed to hear; there I was alone in a garden shed halfway up a mountain with my only escape route blocked by a twit with a psychotic yellow thing tied to a piece of string and the night coming on.

It was quite a relief when the weather worsened again in early July, and these interruptions came to an end and I could concentrate on the birds. The eaglet was more than nine weeks old by 1 July and was well feathered with only its head and underwings showing noticeably white. The rest of its body was a rich chocolate-brown, almost black, but when it exercised its wings I could see the white patches that were typical of the juvenile's plumage. It was exercising more and more frequently now that it had almost fully formed wings and appeared to be very healthy and strong. It began to gain some lift, and I even saw it clinging onto the sticks of the nest to prevent its premature departure during some of the more enthusiastic bouts of flapping. It obviously didn't want to leave the nest accidentally, but its actions led me to start wondering about the first flight and which, if any of us, would see it happen. Several of the books I'd checked suggested that nestlings could fledge at nine weeks old, but this one obviously wasn't ready, though the adult male might have thought that it was.

On 2 July, the male flew across the valley from a tree near the nest and landed on the grass on the opposite side. He looked back towards the nest and saw that the eaglet was watching him. The male ran towards a sheep and a lamb in the typical hop, skip and jump gait of an eagle in a hurry. The eaglet stepped to the front of the nest and, holding its head low, scrutinised the adult's every move. The male walked a little higher, made a little jump and then a definite pounce as if to catch something. He immediately looked sharply back at the nest as if expecting the eaglet to fly off and join him, but it just stood and watched. The male pounced again and looked to the nest again, but the eaglet's interest was waning, and it began to pick at the nest material and scratch its head. The male seemed to realise that he was wasting his time, stood up fully and then flew back across the valley. Circling to gain height beside the crag, he stared hard at the eaglet as he rose past it, but it just looked at him and called to be fed. If he'd been trying to entice the eaglet off the nest he'd failed.

The male tried something similar two days later, flying straight to the ground from the nest to spend 25 minutes walking about, pouncing and looking back. The eaglet moved to the front of the nest but soon lost interest and settled down again. The male didn't repeat these actions, but it was interesting to witness what may have been his attempts to induce the eaglet to fly. The eaglet spent the next few days exercising, preening and calling. The adults visited it less and less, the female staying away for more than six hours on one day, and to relieve the boredom the eaglet began to jump about, pull at sticks and watch the pipits and wheatears that flitted about the nest.

The young eagle was 76 days old by the 11th, and I took both the morning and the overnight watches at the hide. Neither adult visited the nest during the morning watch, but the evening saw the female take a stick and spend 19 minutes repairing the damage caused by the eaglet's callisthenics. She ignored the eaglet's begging and calling and, satisfied with her handiwork, flew off and out of sight behind the crag once she was finished. The eaglet flapped its wings and called even though the adult was out of view and jumped across the nest three times, in what looked like practice pounces on prey. It would only have taken a slight stumble for it to be off the nest, but it didn't happen.

The bird's first flight was something we'd all been anticipating; very few people have seen the undisturbed first flight of a juvenile golden eagle and to see it in England would be a real rarity. At that time there'd only been seven chicks reared in England during the previous 170 years, and I suspected that some of their first flights would have been missed. I didn't see a flight on the 11th, however. At 9.14 p.m., after yet more flapping and jumping, the eaglet simply jumped to the ledge above the nest and stayed there for the next 50 minutes. It stood with its tail dangling over the nest and looked around wondering what to do next. It didn't take another step and instead spent 30 minutes preening.

The female called when she arrived at the nest and stood looking around as if she didn't know where the eaglet was, even though it was leaning towards her and screeching into her left ear. She called again, and the eaglet overbalanced and almost fell on top of her. When the eaglet jumped back to the nest the female jumped up to the ledge herself and began picking at the ground but returned when her mate arrived with food. The eaglet, as usual, dived at the male's feet to seize the food with flailing talons and slapping wings and almost knocked him off the nest. It was then his turn to jump to the ledge and look around before climbing higher and flying away. When the eaglet began to feed the female followed her mate's actions and only returned in the half-light to spend the night with her offspring. It all seemed very odd, and I couldn't think why that ledge had suddenly become so attractive. The only coincidence was that it was the ledge onto which the male had carried the first food for the chick.

I was hopeful of seeing the first flight early the next morning, and when the nest first became discernible through the morning gloom at 3.25 a.m., I was pleased to see that it was still there. And it was still there when my watch finished at 9 a.m. The female fed it for seven minutes and then jumped to the ledge above again and waited. I imagined her waiting to accompany the eaglet on its first flight, but after two and a half hours, she grew bored and flew behind the crag and, by all accounts, didn't return for another eight hours.

Ken arrived to replace me, but when I described what I'd seen I could tell that he didn't entirely believe me. Like me, he was expecting the eaglet to fly off the nest, but if I was going to lie about what I'd seen I'm sure I could have invented something a little more exciting than the tale I told. Dave and Ron didn't believe me either, and when Ken returned to the caravan he said that the eaglet still hadn't left the nest. It was still there at the end of the day, and my story began to look even thinner when the eaglet remained on the nest throughout the next day as well.

But Ken was on duty again on the 14th, and when he returned to the caravan he told me that the eaglet had jumped to the same ledge at 12.27 p.m. It still hadn't flown, but this time it didn't return to the nest either, instead it began to walk higher up the slope. The male took food to the eaglet where it stood and didn't try to entice it back to the nest. The eaglet clambered higher up the slope as the adults looked on, sometimes landing beside it but mostly just watching from a rock. Oddly, the female flew to the nest four times after the eaglet had left it and once even carried in a twig that she had, at first, offered to her youngster. The eaglet's behaviour was totally unexpected, and I began to worry about whether or not it could actually fly. At rest, the young bird pulled at the ground, stripped bracken and threw the pieces over its shoulders.

When it reached the upper sections of the crag the eaglet turned down-valley towards the perched female, and the adults' behaviour changed. As soon as it reached the female she flew lower, and she flew again when it approached again. This time she joined her mate and performed the dipping display flight, the sky-dance, and then returned to land beside the eaglet. The adults must have had a tactical meeting because, from then on, neither of them landed down-valley of the eaglet. Instead of taking food directly to it, the male landed up-valley of the eaglet and waited for it to arrive. The female also landed up-valley of it between feeds, and I realised that they were deliberately drawing it away from the lower ground and towards the safety of the valley head.

It was a deliberate action; they could have delivered each food item to where it stood at the time, but they changed its direction and forced it to walk up-valley to reach the food. While it made a few flappy flights to get itself across small streams and occasionally from a rock to the ground, it still hadn't flown, and I wondered if the adults knew that the eaglet couldn't fly and that the most they could do for it was to lead it away from imminent danger; they'd seen humans down-valley of the crag on a fairly regular basis, but only one person had appeared on the ground up-valley of it, a national park ranger who thought it would be a good idea to approach our hide by walking below the nest.

I followed the eaglet's movements from the bottom of the valley. Leaving the shelter of the hide and moving up-valley for the first time, I took cover behind rocks and lay in bracken patches when the adults were moving. They were still providing the eaglet with food and leading it deeper into the valley by landing ahead of it and making it walk towards them. The ridge from which the nest crag projected had a false top to it, and the eaglet's route took it along the lip of a broad shelf below the highest summit, through grass and patchy heather that provided no protection.

After two nights spent on the open hill, the youngster finally arrived at a rocky chair where it seemed to settle. The male delivered some sheep carrion to it and flew in later with a rook or a crow. I thought that even if it could fly there was little likelihood of it doing so after such a feed, so I left it where it stood. I was back early the next morning to see if the bird had moved, but it was still there. Mist and rain filled the valley for the next two days, and there was little to do but confirm the eaglet's continued presence on the chair. It looked as though the successful breeding season was about to come to a very disappointing end.

The wardening team was still present, but there was little point in continuing the overnight watches, so we sat out the rain in slightly improved comfort. Because of our unexpected success, the RSPB knew they'd have to warden the site again, and a second, bigger caravan was delivered in preparation for 1980. The weather conditions made it very frustrating, and I knew that something had to be done about the bird. Given that there were foxes in the valley, we couldn't just sit around waiting for something to happen as I felt certain that the young bird would be incapable of defending itself. I spoke to the office, and it was agreed that it would be a good idea to discover whether or not the eaglet could fly.

I chose 18 July, and although the day started with low cloud and drizzle the weather soon began to clear and provide acceptable conditions. I didn't want to flush the eaglet during rain when it might be waterlogged or in mist when I might lose track of where it was. I told the others of the plan and invited them to accompany me or watch from below, but to my utter amazement, none of them was interested. They'd spent the best part of four months working to achieve this moment, sitting out in foul conditions of snow and rain storms, freezing temperatures and howling gales during which the walls of the hide billowed in and out and the rocks we'd placed on the roof were shaken off, but none of them wanted to walk to the valley just one more time. They'd had their chance, so I set off alone, just as on my very first day with the eagles.

I splashed my way along the track I must have walked more than 200 times and briefly stopped at the hide to scan the hills and listen. There was nothing to be seen or heard. I crossed the beck to the opposite side of the valley to confirm that the eaglet was still on the chair and then crossed back to clamber up past the nest. I followed the route the eaglet had taken and found plenty of evidence to confirm that much of its later diet had been crows and rooks; there were piles of feathers all over the upper part of the crag and patches of eagle down and splash where the eaglet had fed and ruffled or spent the night. Climbing up to above the level of the chair, I slowly and cautiously approached to where I knew the eaglet was, constantly scanning the sky for the adults and stopping to scope known perches where they might be sitting. I assumed that they must have seen me, but I could find neither adult. I kept well back from the chair and gave the valley one final scan before moving closer.

I didn't want to blunder up to the eaglet and frighten it and realised that I should have approached from below and in full view to allow it to move in its own time. From 10 metres, I could see the eaglet half sitting and aimlessly staring out across the valley. It didn't know I was there, so I backed away until I was out of sight and coughed a warning. Stepping forward again I edged closer, but the bird was still looking unconcerned, so I coughed again. Nothing. I stepped forward and coughed loudly, and this time the eaglet turned its head to look towards the source of the sound. It moved its head from side to side to focus and try to identify what it saw, so I stepped fully into view. This time it became alert and stared hard. It then turned its head away, stepped forward and casually launched itself into its first flight. It swung away up the valley and was soon out of sight behind a bluff, but from its actions, I knew that it hadn't gone far beyond that.

I quickly dropped onto the chair, found some food remains and collected some pellets of undigested crow feathers and then made my way slowly towards where I thought the bird had landed. It saw me coming this time and flew again, this time flapping in a longer flight to land on the slopes of the valley head. I hadn't seen the adults at all during this time, so I turned to leave, knowing that the bird could fly and that my presence close by would only distress the adults if they saw me. The bird could fly, and I could begin to call it a juvenile; its decision to walk from the nest was probably simply because it could get out easily and was in no rush given the adults' ability to provide it with food. It was 83 days old before the eaglet made its first flight and that was a far cry from the 63 days suggested by some of the books or even the magnificent first flight from the nest I'd expected to see.

The female swung into view almost as soon as I'd turned to walk out and began to circle beside the nest crag. She made four display dips and then lazily swung up the valley. The male followed her, but they were in no hurry and took two minutes to drift up as far as my position. I made no attempt to hide or disguise my presence and made a point of walking openly away from the youngster. This brought me back to the chair, however, and when the adults saw me there instead of their juvenile their demeanour changed visibly and both quickly turned back down-valley. They must have known that the juvenile was safe, though, because it had started to call as soon as the adults came into view, and it was clearly audible to me, indicating both its position and the fact that it was safe. The female climbed higher and performed seven dips, but the male, egged on by the calling it could hear, powered up the centre of the valley, turning his head to glower at me as he sped past to swing in and calm the juvenile.

The female slowly turned up-valley and began to circle when she drew level with me. She circled to gain height as I stood and watched and then performed eight more dips. Diving on almost fully closed wings for perhaps 100 metres before sweeping back skywards to make a few strong wing beats at the top of the climb before tipping over the apex of the climb, or rolling over one wing, and falling again, time and again. The female was barely 100 metres away, and through binoculars I could see the colour of her hazel eyes as she slightly turned her head to stare at me at the bottom of each dive. Her talons were tightly clenched and her feathers pulled in close to make her body appear as a solid unit as she dived at a thunderous speed. The hook at the bottom of each dive must have exerted incredible G-forces on her body, and yet there was no evidence of discomfort in her expressionless face.

This wasn't typical disturbance behaviour, which, at least when the eagle is disturbed from its nest, involves one or both of the adults circling, sometimes gaining height and distance, as they keep a close watch on the human intruder. Even so, it was clear that the eagles were responding to my presence, so I decided to walk on and away from the area. I was expecting the female to circle and watch me until I was a safe distance away, but instead, she stopped displaying and swung in closer to glide beside me, no more than 30 metres away and at my pace. I could now see the colour of her eyes without binoculars, and whenever I turned my head to look at her, she turned hers to look at me. It felt as though she was shepherding me out of the valley. As well as me watching her, she, of course, had spent the past four months watching me, and I wondered if she knew that I didn't really pose a threat. Because I was moving away along the ground, and she was above the void, she must also have felt entirely safe; her chick was well, and there was nothing I could do to harm her.

An idea entered my head, and I stopped walking to see how she'd react. Surprised, she slipped ahead of me at first but swung back to sail alongside again, staring hard. It was incredible, I had a wild golden eagle almost within touching distance; she knew I was there and yet hadn't fled. She hadn't flapped her wings either, and yet had changed from moving forward to making a circle and then hanging motionless in the air beside me. I could barely feel the wind on my face, and yet with her total mastery of the elements she just hung there in the air. How could a bird that probably weighed 6 kg just float motionless on what was little more than a breath of wind?

I was awestruck but knew I had to walk on. She followed. I stopped again and this time sat down. The eagle slipped ahead and came back, and then she sailed up and started to dip-display directly above my head, coming to within 10 metres. She made six dips before I stood and walked on again, this time a little faster because I knew she didn't want me there. I started to drop down the slope and walked beneath the eagle, and on seeing the imagined danger moving away she glided ahead, made four dips and then turned to fly back up the valley to join her mate and the juvenile. It had been an exhilarating and almost unbelievable experience, just as had been much of the previous few months I'd spent in the valley, and it brought my first experiences with eagles to a more than satisfactory conclusion.

The season was at an end and all that was left was for us to dismantle the hide and wrap it in heavy-duty polythene so that it would survive the intervening winter before the next breeding attempt. The weather had turned yet again, but we saw the juvenile between showers, and when I returned on the 23rd, I saw all three birds. The juvenile was strong on the wing and flew down to land on the ledge above the nest to afford me one more glimpse of its majesty before I left the valley for the last time that year.

I'd heard the call of the eagle, and with so many unanswered questions, I was determined to work here again.

CHAPTER 3

Dark days of spring

I needed no persuasion to return to the eagles in 1980, and in that year I arrived on 14 March, before the eggs had been laid. The RSPB had woken up to the potential of the site and the need to protect it efficiently. There was just one snag, in a cost-cutting exercise they reduced the size of the wardening team from four to three, but my experience was expected to make up for the reduction. And in addition, the third warden wouldn't arrive until April. The small caravan had been removed and replaced by a larger one, and David Woodhead and Mike had erected the hide in anticipation of my arrival. All I had to do was get myself there, settle in and start work. I'd be by myself for the first few days, but that's how I liked it; I would have done the entire season by myself had it been practical.

The replacement caravan was bigger but also much older than the original one and was damp and cold after spending a Lake District winter inside a Forestry Commission plantation. There'd been no heating, so dampness had frozen and thawed half a dozen times before I arrived. The internal walls were dripping with water, the curtains were rotten and the mattresses mould-encrusted and stinking. There were holes around the windows, and the wooden trim was either hanging loose or lying on the floor. The false ceiling drooped through the collected weight of condensation and pooling rain, and rivers of filthy water dribbled down the walls onto worktops, tables and beds. The floor covering was a grime-impregnated germ trap on which I didn't dare walk without wearing shoes. It was just as it appeared, an abandoned caravan in a forest.

Into this I shifted my precious optical equipment, reference books and clothes, but they all stayed bagged and boxed in an attempt to keep them dry. This van wasn't heated by gas stove, rather by a solid fuel fire that barely put out any heat, had to be started with petrol and soon died. The fire wouldn't stay in unless constantly tended, so I couldn't even begin to warm the van through and dry out my mattress as the fire was out and everything cold and wet again by the time I returned from a watch.

To make matters worse, the spring of 1980 was much colder than that of 1979, and the hills were still white with snow when I arrived. Even so, and as ever, it was a relief to get out of the caravan and onto the hill. I followed the same route as I'd taken the previous year and was soon out of the trees. The snow cover was fairly patchy on the valley bottom, and it was a pleasant stroll knowing that the hide was waiting for me and that I had a gas stove and brew-up materials in my sack. I settled down in the hide, and before long the female appeared and flew to the nest with a bare stick. She arranged it to her satisfaction, and I could see that there'd been a fair amount of refurbishment work undertaken before my return. It was the same site as in all the previous nesting attempts of this pair, so the routine of the watch would be straightforward.

The birds clearly hadn't laid the first of their eggs, so I returned to the caravan after a few hours to try again to get some warmth into it and dry it out. It was the same the next day. I awoke with frost on my sleeping bag, dressed up to my waterproofs before having a bowl of stiff porridge for breakfast and then set out for the hide. I spent almost all of the daylight hours in the hide on 16 March but saw virtually nothing of the eagles. Neither bird visited the nest, and I suspected that they were tucked up in some sheltered nook and were probably warmer than me. Back at the caravan I lit the fire, but it was becoming a waste of time; the best I could hope for was to put some warmth into my sleeping bag in a vain attempt to dry it out and then climb inside it to keep warm.

17 March dawned grey with a thick mist and lightly falling snow. Finding my way to the hide necessitated a sixth sense; as well as the mist and snow I was also walking in the dark to ensure that I was in position by first light. I wondered if I was crazy, especially as the birds hadn't even laid an egg yet, but this was what I wanted to do and what I had to do if I was to learn about the birds. The conditions gradually improved, but the crags still didn't become visible until about midday.

The female's dark head was showing above the nest rim, and I wondered if she'd laid an egg or if she was just keeping the nest cup clear of snow in readiness for that moment. She stood and thrust her head down into the cup at one point and that seemed to be a good pointer; she also didn't stand during the male's two brief visits to the nest. When he came in again shortly after 1 p.m. the female stood up beside him, and the two great birds peered down into the nest and studied its precious contents. They stood together for three minutes before the male flew off and the female settled again to incubate the egg that I could now assume to be in the nest. The male made two more visits during the next 10 minutes, staying for seven minutes on the second occasion, but his mate neither left nor even stood up. The first changeover took place 10 minutes later and that confirmed the lay beyond all doubt. The male sat for 41 minutes before his mate returned, and then the weather closed in for the day.

After a day with the crags almost continuously obscured by clouds, 18 March proved to be the first day with good weather throughout. It was heartening to see the valley properly again, and the sunshine brought life to everything. Just as in 1979, I flushed grouse during my walk to the hide, heard curlews and saw stonechats. I was also pleased to find the female eagle still sitting tight on her nest. Although the scheme was better organised this year, and I was better equipped, I was still alone and couldn't do overnight shifts that involved spending about 16 hours in a garden shed during a freezing blizzard! It also meant that I'd have to leave the valley unguarded while I returned to the caravan for provisions. The female whiled away the day in either extreme alertness or nodding drowsiness. She stood and turned to sit facing the other way and then turned back again, presumably to relieve the boredom of probably spending 22 out of each

24-hour period just sitting on the nest. Her mate relieved her for 33 minutes, and as in 1979, she took a sharp turn off the nest and flew out of sight into the gully behind the crag. When she returned two ravens chased her, but that didn't stop her flying straight to the nest. She was relieved twice more that day, for four and 33 minutes. The eagles had also settled into their routine.

I returned to the caravan before dark that day because the first of the assistant wardens was due to arrive. He was coming via Mike, so when there was no sign of him at the van, I assumed that he hadn't yet arrived. Mike would have told him where I was, and in his place, I would have either waited at the van or wandered up the valley to introduce myself. But he wasn't there. After a hot meal, I wandered the 5 km down to the telephone to speak to Mike. He gave me the bad news: the warden had arrived, he'd called in at the shop and been given one of Mike's sketch maps. I wandered back up the forest road, quite enjoying the 10 km-round walk on a beautiful starlit evening, but there was still no one at the van when I returned. I was also lovely and warm after the walk, and so tucked myself up in my bag straightaway to get a decent night's sleep for once.

No one arrived during the night, and I even waited for an hour before setting out the next morning. I couldn't wait any longer, the eagles had to be my priority, and I had to get to the hide. There was still no sign of the warden when I returned to the van that afternoon, and it would be a few days before I discovered what had happened. The missing warden had arrived, followed Mike's map, got lost, spent 'an uncomfortable night in the woods', reached the caravan the next morning, discovered it empty (as I was in the valley protecting golden eagles!), so he turned around and went home, never to be heard of again. It meant that I'd be on my own until April.

19 March dawned bitterly cold, the coldest so far thanks to the clear skies I'd enjoyed the previous evening, and after crunching my way along the forest ride I discovered the 5m-wide beck to be completely frozen over. There'd obviously been heavy snow showers during the night as there was a good covering on the ground, and the icy wind began to whip up to gale force and brought more snow showers with it. The female eagle was sitting on the nest for most of the day, but the male did put in an appearance from time to time. I sat alone in the hide gradually getting colder and colder and not looking forward to returning to the caravan. The only time I was really warm was towards the end of the journey between the two sites, but I had to try not to sweat too much as the clammy clothes would probably have been frozen to my back after a day in the hide. Once the cold had crept from my toes to my thighs I decided it was time to head back; it was a long, stiff drag as my legs first had to thaw and then force me into the full face of the wind that was bringing more snow. I had to remain positive, though, Scottish eagles must face these conditions every year!

I could now start thinking about the second egg being laid. The female left the nest shortly after first light and spent more than an hour away. She was off twice more during the day, for 42 and 112 minutes, and during the latter I managed to track her after her initial disappearance behind the crag. She crossed the valley and circled higher before swinging out and over the ridge. It was a route that was seldom used during 1979, and it took her onto ground where there was little in the way of live prey, so I assumed she must have known of sheep carrion in that direction. The male also spent some time in view for a change, circling for 13 minutes before going up into low cloud after he'd left the nest for the final time. I didn't see him again that day, but these were clear signs that the eagles were settled. I couldn't tell if there was a second egg, though, short of going and having a look. I wandered back to the van under a clear and moonless sky, but there was sufficient light from the stars and the snow to guide me back. The wind was still near gale force, and it promised to be a bitterly cold night, but that was still better than torrential rain.

I thought I'd awoken too early the next day, so dark was it inside the van, and it wasn't until I scraped the frost from the inside of the window that I saw the truth. The darkness wasn't due to the night but to the heavy, wet snowflakes that were falling and blotting out the view of the trees that were only 20 metres away. It was near white-out conditions that, at least, meant I had the consolation of knowing that no egg collectors would be on the hills. Safe in that knowledge I, for once, had a leisurely breakfast and waited for a break in the weather before setting off for the hide.

There was a slight easing in the snowfall, so I set off along the ride. The snow didn't seem too severe in the shelter of the trees, but when I broke out onto the open hill I was hit by the full force of the wind, and driving snow blotted out any view I should have had of the valley. This was a real blizzard, and I didn't think twice about turning back to the van and waiting for another break. I probably could have reached the hide, but it would have been madness to try, the annals of the mountain rescue teams are full of people who didn't make the correct decision when they reached the point of no return, and it would probably have been at least a week before anyone even thought that I might be missing should anything have happened to me.

I tried again later that day and got beyond the edge of the forest, but I was again driven back as the winds increased and the wet snow dragged on my legs. I seemed barely able to move my feet as I pushed my way forward and had to concede defeat again. It was as well; the snowfall became heavier and more relentless and continued unbroken for the remainder of the day. I consoled myself with the knowledge that even if I'd reached the hide, the chances of me seeing anything would have been minimal.

Snow fell throughout the night on south-westerly gales, and by the morning of the 21st, it lay 50 cm deep inside the forest. It was still falling at first light, but by late morning the weather had broken to frequent heavy showers, and I prepared myself for the walk. It usually took me about 30 minutes to walk to the hide, and when the breaks between showers lengthened to 20 minutes and were filled with bright sunshine, I decided that it was time to go. It was a mistake. There was no frozen crust on the snow, and its depth and weight slowed me to a crawl. I made two abortive attempts, each time caught in white-out conditions before I made the final push.

The path was completely lost beneath the snow, but I knew the route well enough to push on in the correct direction. Even so, the streams and gullies were now only identifiable by the tops of the buried rowan trees that grew in them, and the snowdrifts were 2 metres deep in places. Because of the terrain, I was wading thigh-deep for much of the route and slowed to the point of standstill at times. It was exhausting, and I was caught in four heavy showers along the way.

It took me more than an hour longer than usual to complete the walk to the hide as I slipped and stumbled into almost every stream and had to drag my load up rises I remembered as being only slight inclines in the past. Because of its position on the lip of a bluff, the snow around the hide was windswept and not so deep, but it was still a struggle to force my way inside. And once there I sat alone staring onto a world of white and hoping that the weather would clear long enough for me to see something.

Cloud and snow still swept through the valley around the crag, but it did seem to be improving with the cloud base lifting after each shower. The sun began to break through, but it was still not until about 3.30 p.m. that the crags first came into view, or at least the white mass that I knew to be crags. There was no definition on the crag face, and the step down to the nest from the ledge onto which the 1979 chick had jumped no longer existed, there was just a continuous and even bank of snow. There was no nest to be seen, and while I stayed on watch for as long as I dared as the heavy showers persisted, I failed to see either eagle. My concern was now about whether the female had deserted the nest or was still there, underneath the blanket of snow. That horrendous possibility filled my thoughts as I ploughed my way back to the van.

The conditions were clear and frosty the next morning, and the wind had dropped, so it actually felt slightly milder than the previous day. The frozen surface made walking easier, and while my tracks from the 21st had been lost under fresh snowfalls, it seemed that no more snow would fall. Through the telescope I could see that the snow about the nest was untouched, nothing had dug its way in and nothing had forced its way out. One way or another the eagles' breeding attempt had failed this year, and it probably happened on the day that the second egg had been laid.

Heavy clouds arrived from the south, and it began to rain heavily by mid-morning, and I was soaked as I plodded my way out of the valley and then down the track to the nearest phone box to pass on the news to the RSPB office. The change in conditions was incredible, little snow remained on the lower ground, and by the time I'd returned, the snow was even disappearing from around the caravan. The rain fell for the rest of the day, all of the night and throughout the next morning. By then there was no snow left in the woods and only patches remained on the hills. The transformation of the countryside was almost unbelievable, from a frozen snowscape to a boggy morass in the space of a few hours.

So as not to waste time, I arranged for Mike to come and help remove the eggs for analysis as he had the necessary safety equipment. He arrived in the afternoon, and we made our way onto the crag. The nest was still invisible under the remaining snow even as we stood on the ledge above it. I belayed him from above, and he slithered down to the nest. So as not to squash the eggs he lay down on the ledge and swept away the snow with an ice axe. We got them out, and I had the dubious pleasure of walking out of the valley with an eagle egg in each hand. It was a dismal end to the season, but at least we knew that the female had deserted before she'd been snowed onto the nest. It was a natural failure, and we could do nothing about that. It was just so bitterly disappointing, the breeding attempt had failed earlier than I'd even arrived in 1979.

I wanted to ensure that the birds were both safe, but the RSPB wanted me somewhere else as soon as possible, so I dismantled and wrapped the hide myself (a job that had taken four of us the previous year) without seeing either eagle. A quick trip around their roosts told me that they were still in the area, but, I supposed, without an active nest there was no need for them to stay in the nesting valley. I made a brief visit to the site in April but again failed to see anything, and it wasn't until August that I saw either of the birds again.

On that day the female appeared above the nest crag and then crossed the valley to settle on a favourite perch beside a holly bush. She was in heavy moult and missing a primary and a secondary flight feather from each wing. The male, on the other hand, looked to be in prime condition when he flew from the same location about 30 minutes later. I climbed up to the nest and found that a fresh sprig of heather had been added neatly to the cup, the flowers not yet wilted. It seemed that the birds were already preparing for their next breeding attempt, even though it would be almost a year between the one failing and the next beginning.

CHAPTER 4

Hope after hard times

I didn't return to the eagles' valley until March 1981. Mike and David had erected the hide a few days before my arrival, a little surprised that it was in such good condition given my depression when dismantling it the previous year. The rotten, damp and stinking caravan was waiting for me in the woods, the weather was poor and I'd be on my own for the first week or so. Nothing much had changed.

The usual bad weather prevented me from making much headway when I first arrived, but 16 March dawned frosty and with only occasional sleet showers. I sat in the hide and scanned all the usual perches in search of an eagle, but nothing was in view. I wasn't too concerned; Mike and David had both seen the birds, and I didn't expect them to begin incubation until the next day. Both birds had also been absent the day before laying in 1980, so that wasn't unexpected. The only puzzle was that the nest didn't appear to have much fresh material on it or to have been built up during the previous few weeks. As the afternoon wore on a pair of buzzards began floating about the nest crag with impunity, and there was more than the usual numbers of crows and ravens in the valley. Two peregrines also skirted the ridgeline as if the eagles weren't there. All of a sudden the valley didn't have the right feel to it, so I decided to visit the nest.

The approach was wet and slippery, but I was on the ledge above the nest within 20 minutes and looking down into it. It hadn't been touched, the sprig of heather I'd seen freshly added the previous August was still there but now lay dead and withered; no new material had been added. It was said that eagles sometimes take a year off from their breeding efforts, but the long empty 1980 season should have passed for that, and I thought the birds would be reinvigorated and in good condition by now. There were no feathers or splash on the perches I checked and, indeed, no evidence of eagles in the valley at all. Mike and David had seen them when they erected the hide, so why weren't they here?

I returned to the hide and waited and watched. Constantly scanning the ridgetops and checking the perches to no avail, I figured that the only explanation must be that the birds had a new nest and that it wasn't in this valley. It was an age before I eventually spotted two specks in the far distance and beyond at least two ridges. Switching to the telescope, I still couldn't make out plumage patterns, but the specks were certainly eagles and the larger of the two had holes in its wings. It was the pair. The question now was were they flying close to their new nest or were they just hunting and the nest lay somewhere else? It looked like being a long search, and it was too late to start that day.

28

Mike and David were both keen to join in the hunt when I told them what I'd seen, but Mike had to work the next day, so David and I arranged to meet and reconnoitre the ground below which I'd seen the birds. We were delayed by the weather but eventually drove to what we presumed to be the best starting point and began to walk the lower ground. There was no sense in going high and close to crags as the best way to see eagles is from below, and even if one was sitting by then, we could be fairly certain of seeing the off-duty bird if we were in the right area. We'd only been walking for an hour when I picked out an eagle as it broke the skyline. It was the female. She swung out of sight almost at once but returned within three minutes before going down pursued by a crow. She reappeared and dropped again, and it seemed likely that we were close. We climbed higher on the opposite slope to obtain a better view, but the dark crags were in deep shadow, and we couldn't discern any detail. It was too late to climb up to where she was.

Mike wanted to be involved the next day, so we sent him to that area while David and I approached from the other side in a pincer movement. It would prove to be another grey day, and although we set out in the dry we were soon walking in drizzle; this became rain as we gained height and began walking in the cloud. Rain turned to snow, and at the top of the pass we were in a blizzard. Mike was somewhere below us on the other side of the ridge, but it was pointless to continue as we didn't want to risk flushing the bird in these conditions. Mike had pretty much the same experience where he was, so the nest went unfound for another day.

19 March was equally grey, and I spent a frustrating day kicking my heels in the caravan. In fact, the weather forecast for the next few days wasn't encouraging, and I was torn between wanting to find the nest and not wanting to search in conditions that might affect the breeding attempt. The weather forecast proved to be inaccurate, and the next day dawned bright and clear but with a heavy frost – ideal conditions. I stuffed myself with porridge, threw a bait-box together and drove to the new valley. David had had the same idea, and when our paths crossed we dumped my car on the verge and continued in his. Instead of following the valley floor we cut up the steep ridgeside and climbed onto a heathery shoulder, which the female had been flying towards. Crossing this we reached a corrie with near-vertical sides and fragmented crags that had been shattered by millennia of frosts and ice. The heather was deep and rank, so we settled down to scan the crags and see if there was any movement.

It was only a few minutes before the female swung into view from behind a ridge and dropped straight onto a long vegetated ledge. We watched as she slowly stalked from one end of the ledge to the other and then, almost incredibly, the male stood up beside her. She stepped past him and sat as he flew off. I didn't track his flight because I was still trying to work out how there was a nest on that ledge; there was no discernible material at all. So much for eagle nests containing a cartload of sticks! The nest was certainly there, though; we'd seen both birds sitting, so there must also be at least one egg in it. Whether or not it was much of a nest, I thought it was a good site. It was more remote and much less accessible than the previous one, and it was on much higher ground, facing north. It was still within the expected territory, though, and, as well as the ubiquitous sheep, the eagles had red grouse to hunt in front of their nest. David and I watched for a couple of hours, but there was little happening so we wandered away knowing that the nest and birds were safe.

I had to tell the office that the nest had been found and make a decision about how the site would be best protected. That was the problem; there was no chance of getting a hide to this location, and even if we could, with some well-used footpaths in the area, it would only have drawn attention to the site. The site could be protected from a camouflaged tent, but we were a long way from the base caravan, and with only three wardens, shifts would have to be very long to make them practical. The news of finding the nest was taken well, and as I thought would be the case, the decision as to how to protect the site was shifted from a full-time RSPB officer to me, a short-term contract worker.

My decision was not to run a protection scheme. I thought that the presence and regular movements of the wardening team would be more likely to attract attention to the site than afford it good protection. I felt it would be best served by a very low-key approach of regular monitoring and longer coverage at key times. I was probably talking myself out of a job, but I assumed I'd be transferred to Haweswater, as in 1980 after the failure, and would be able to undertake the monitoring here as well. It proved to be a good decision, though, because, to the best of my knowledge, no one else ever found this nest without being given precise directions.

It was clear that while Mike and David would be putting in some time with the eagles, they both had commitments that would limit their efforts, and they probably wouldn't be available during the most important phases of the season. The April weather wasn't brilliant, and even though the 1979 Easter had proved to be something of a damp squib in terms of tourist numbers, I decided to camp with the eagles. There were more, and more well-used, public footpaths around the new site, and there was a greater likelihood of the eagles being seen, so I thought it would be worthwhile to spend some time with them. It wasn't at the RSPB's expense, though, I had to finance this myself.

So as not to leave my car in a suspicious location, I arranged for Mike to drive me as close to the site as possible on 15 April. I lugged my camping gear up the hill from there and, so as not to be too conspicuous, cowered in a gully until dusk before finding a good campsite and pitching the tent in near darkness. For the same reason, I was up before dawn the next morning and struck camp to reach my chosen lookout post before it was fully light. It meant that I packed a still-frost-covered tent and had to be careful about lighting the stove to cook breakfast in a bare area surrounded by heather, but that was better than to risk being seen. I lived like this for the next two days and nights, only moving between campsite and observation post and spending the hours in between deeply ensconced among the heather. Needless to say, the Easter weekend produced very few people: I saw six hardy souls on the ridgetop and two couples strolled along the low level route, but no one came into the eagle valley.

The eagles weren't particularly active either, with just the usual round of changeovers and flying out of sight. On the morning of the 17th, I was lucky enough to locate the male still perched on his roost before first light. It would have been so easy for him to fly into a sunny location to warm through, but he just waited even though it was 40 minutes before the morning sunshine reached him. Once he was in it he intended to stay there, and he hopped onto another rock as the sun moved round and the wind changed direction. He was there for another two hours, and even though he'd been perched in full view of the female on the nest, he flew in a circle in front of the crag to forewarn his mate of his imminent departure before he left the area. It was three hours before he returned, but he then dropped straight down to the nest to relieve his mate.

It was the female's first flight in more than 15 hours, and when she returned from out of the valley an hour later she also took advantage of the sun and spent eight minutes soaking up its rays before flying to the nest. As is usual, she dropped below nest level on her approach before sweeping up and landing delicately on outstretched talons. The male stood almost at once and was off and out of the valley, this time not returning for four hours. That was fairly typical of the observations I was making; during those 10 hours, I saw about six minutes of flight, and although I always had an eagle in view, it was always the whereabouts of the other that was intriguing. I wondered where the male could have gone and what he might be doing during those long absences.

These times when an eagle was away and the inactivity allowed me to note some of the other residents of this area. There appeared to be decent numbers of red grouse here, crowing as I stowed my tent, and while meadow pipits, wheatears, skylarks and stonechats flitted about my recumbent position in the heather, I could also hear ring ouzels calling from the crags in the valley head. Dippers buzzed up and down the beck, and with one carrying insects, they clearly already had a brood of young to feed. A pair of merlins was also in residence, and they skimmed and chattered across the moor, displaying and showing an obvious interest in potential nest sites, from one of which they would go on to fledge three young.

I had to keep an eye on the eagles as well, of course, always being alert for the return of the off-duty bird and never just assuming the one on the nest was incubating happily. During one of the male's longer absences, the female's bodily functions overcame her, and she flew off the nest, leaving the eggs unguarded. She was relaxed and flew down to land about 200 metres from my position. She stood on a rock and stretched her left wing, separating each of her flight feathers, fanning her tail and stretching her left leg at the same time. She didn't stretch her right wing and leg, though, but closed up, defecated and then nibbled her breast and shoulders before relaxing for eight minutes. Returning to the nest, she turned the eggs and settled over them. She was reluctant to leave when the male arrived and stood proudly on the front of the nest. As she didn't move, he nibbled her crown feathers, and slowly, persuaded by this show of affection, she stood and flew off. No matter how reluctant she'd appeared to be, she flew straight out of the valley to return three quarters of an hour later with a bulging crop. It was as if the male had whispered the location of some food to her.

The male went to roost at 7.30 p.m. that day after making a short display flight, choosing a rocky niche only about 100 metres from where I'd pitched my tent. It was

31

useful to know that my cautious approach had worked, but it meant I couldn't move until it was pitch black that night, and I wouldn't be able to use a torch. I was up early the next day to dismantle the frost-ridden tent, and the eagle left his roost at 5.05 a.m., quickly leaving the valley for four hours and leaving me wishing that I could get up as high as he did to take in the sun's warming rays. This would prove to be a long day, and there was little to record until the afternoon when the birds decided to indulge in some nest refurbishment and hunting.

Although there was virtually no structure to the nest, the birds did add beakfuls of grass and heather twigs, and the occasional sod of earth went on from time to time. Whichever bird was off the nest this day collected material and then quartered the slopes in low-level hunting. It was odd because where they did this was mostly grass, and the grouse were in the heather. I saw no kills and suspected that the eagles would be surviving on sheep carrion at this time of year. I had made sure that the eagles weren't disturbed, and there'd been nothing to suggest that anyone else knew about the birds, so when it was time for my prearranged meeting with Mike I had no qualms about leaving the site. I returned for a quick look two days later before leaving the area, but everything was all right and I was planning on returning four days later to be around in time for the hatch, which was due to occur on about 30 April.

I was delayed, as ever, by heavy snow that this time blocked all the access routes for two days. When I finally did set out, there was still snow and ice on the major roads and overturned cars in ditches and fields. The land was frozen solid, but the sun was shining and I made good time. My car wouldn't cope with the still-snow-covered forest tracks, so Mike borrowed a more suitable vehicle, and we skidded and slid our way through the trees. We were held up three or four times as we waited for the foresters to chainsaw a route past the storm-blown trees that blocked the way but eventually started to manhandle them off the track ourselves as we always reached them first. Mike could barely keep control of the car on some of the bends, and when we suddenly hit a rut the car was jerked off the track and left with one front wheel hanging over a 6-m drop to a frozen stream that plunged through the trees to the river below.

Mike tried to reverse out with me bouncing to get some traction, but the back of the car slithered across the track, and there was a real danger that we might lose it over the edge. There seemed to be only one solution, so I clambered beneath the front of the car, wedged myself onto the banking with my shoulder under the car's wing and, with Mike under orders to steer in a straight line and keep a soft foot on the accelerator, pushed up with all of the leg strength I could muster. It worked, but I started to belly-slide down the hill as my footholds gave out, and Mike slid about 20 metres down the icy track before he could bring the car to a halt by slamming it into a forward gear while travelling backwards. We abandoned the car where it stood and left the keys in the ignition in case the foresters wanted to move past it.

I was planning on camping out again, so I hauled my gear along the track, up through the pathless trees and out onto the moor. The male merlin was calling as we broke out of the trees, but his was the only sound in a completely white scene. I felt the same terrible foreboding as I had the previous year, and no eagles were flying as we trudged across the roughest ground and onto my observation post. Dumping my sack, we stood and stared at the crag through binoculars. It was snow-bound, but unlike in the other valley there was an overhang above the nest ledge, and we thought that the bird might still be sitting. I couldn't see it through the telescope, but we wanted to be optimistic.

We needed to be certain, so leaving my sack where it lay, we climbed around the back of the male's roost crag and edged towards the lip. Belly-crawling to the edge of the drop, we sneaked our heads above the skyline and stared down. Even without binoculars it was clear that the ledge was empty; the brown form of the eagle would have been plainly visible had it been there, but it wasn't. The ledge was frozen solid, and for the second year in succession the eagles had failed because of snow. I wondered how the Scottish birds could breed successfully when they must have to suffer these conditions and worse on a much more regular basis than occurred here in the Lake District. But, when you realise how many Scottish pairs fail in their breeding attempts each year, you realise that the successful ones are very lucky indeed.

It showed what the weather could do. The 1980 attempt had failed because of snow –storms blown in from the south-west – while in 1981 the snow came on gales from the north. On each occasion the worst was over after two days, but the worst had come at a critical time. It was difficult to know which of the two failures was the hardest to bear: the first had occurred on the day the second egg was laid, and this one was less than a week before the egg was due to hatch. It would be another long empty year for the eagles, and with the Haweswater birds failing that year as well, it would be the first time since 1975 that a young eagle hadn't fledged in the Lake District.

We weren't equipped to remove the eggs, this site was a rope-job and probably required experienced climbers, so we turned around and plodded wearily back to the car and then on to where I'd left mine. I was in no mood to socialise and drove up through the other forest to spend a night or two by myself in the old caravan, not minding the hardships of that rotten and miserable place on this occasion. The weather improved, and most of the snow on the lower ground had melted by the next morning, so I took a walk into the old nesting valley.

There was nothing flying, so for no particular reason, I decided to go to the nest. The scramble was icy but safe, and I knew the route well enough not to worry about being alone. It was less than six weeks since I'd last been there and found the old sprig of heather, and the eagles had been breeding elsewhere, so I was astonished to find that the nest was now built up with heather, bracken and woodrush and that a cup had been formed as if ready to receive the eggs. This was truly a frustration nest (unless the birds had been building here during breaks in the incubation duties at the other nest) as there was no hope of the eagles laying a replacement clutch. They hadn't in 1980 when they had all the time in the world, so it wasn't going to happen this year.

The nest refurbishment raised an interesting point. We didn't know why the birds had changed nests for this season, but in spite of what had happened, the new site seemed to be better located, and it was certainly safer from egg collectors and casual disturbance. While the birds had only ever been successful in their original valley, we knew it would probably be better if they used the new one again in 1982.

I'd been transferred to Haweswater after the 1980 failure and found myself there again at the start of the 1982 season. Even though I'd already worked at Haweswater, it was like a new start for me as one of the birds had changed, the accommodation had changed and there was an entirely new wardening team as none of the previous wardens wanted to return after the previous year's failure. Being there also meant that I could put in some time with the other eagles I'd followed so closely, and I'd planned to visit them before the Haweswater birds laid their eggs. There'd been a 10-day gap between the pairs laying their first eggs, so there was little chance of my being overstretched. The RSPB had already taken the decision not to warden my first site in 1982, I assumed because it was believed that the birds would be in their new nest again, but I was surprised when they spurned my offer to spend a few days there to ensure that everything was as planned. I telephoned Mike to find out what was happening, but he seemed reluctant to talk to me. He said he'd seen the birds together in the valley but they hadn't laid eggs yet. The birds should have laid the first egg by 18 March, and it was soon obvious to me that the eagles were in a new nest and that it hadn't been found. Mike became a little more open and told me that neither the 1980 nor 1981 nest was in use. He'd seen the eagles in the old valley, and because they were active around the original nest it was assumed that it was going to be a non-breeding year. I was suspicious of this and again asked if I could take a look for myself but was again refused.

It all became clear about two weeks later when Tony Warburton, the owl man, telephoned the RSPB office to ask why the eagles weren't being protected. The nest had been found by a hillwalker in the head of the old valley, exactly where the birds were being seen! It hadn't dawned on anyone that they were seeing the birds one at a time and usually in the same place, a clear sign that there was something worth looking for. They hadn't checked the area at all because they 'knew' there weren't any crags there.

For some odd reason, when it was too late, I was then invited to become involved, and on 6 April my RSPB boss and I met up with Tony, and he showed us where the nest was, sensibly keeping us at a distance. We saw both birds, watched a changeover and then wandered out. After we left Tony, Ken turned to me and asked: 'Who would have thought of looking there?' I couldn't hold my tongue and replied that I would have because it was where the birds were being seen, so should have been the first place to look. It would become a recurring theme with the Lakeland eagles, people taking decisions without consulting those with more experience and first-hand knowledge.

My remarks didn't go down well, and that was the last official involvement I had at the site. I wasn't surprised when I was left off the list of people who were allowed to visit the nest that season but didn't dare visit it in my own time. The nest was on the ground, and the RSPB had taken the decision to soak the area in a fox deterrent. It was totally unnecessary, but needing to be undertaken on a weekly basis, it gave the chosen few a good opportunity to take photographs. In spite of, rather than because of, this, the eagles reared a single chick, and it became the first eaglet to be ringed in England when Geoff Horne did the honours in June of that year. When he did, though, he discovered that the bird had a deformed beak, the upper mandible being smaller than it should have been and twisted over the lower one. Even so, in spite of this and after the double failure in 1981, 1982 would be the first and only year in which both pairs of Lakeland eagles would breed successfully at the same time.

I didn't get to visit the site again or see the eaglet for the first time until 24 August, by which time I was no longer employed by the RSPB. It was more fun operating in my own time. I wandered up to the old hide and was greeted by the female swinging down over the crag and onto the 1979 nest. The juvenile glided down behind her and landed on the ledge above the nest. A kestrel hovered above them before the female, and then the juvenile, took off and slid down the valley towards me before crossing to the other side. The latter had an unsteady flight, and when the female swung out of the valley towards the rabbit grounds the juvenile dropped to land in a patch of bracken. I left it undisturbed and visited the old nest.

The eagles hadn't touched it, and although I picked out the male perched on a favourite old site, there were no pellets in the gully. The 1982 nest had a sheer drop on one side of it but could be approached with hands in pockets from the other side; it was a ground nest, built at the base of a rowan tree but, intriguingly, was also of some substance. I wondered if the birds had intended using it in 1981 but had been disturbed to the site they eventually used. There was no way of knowing. I collected a dozen juvenile pellets from the nest to go with seven of the firmer and smaller adult pellets. The juvenile's were composed mostly of corvid feathers, but from the nest, I collected a merlin's leg, the first I'd found as eagle prey.

I didn't know it at the time, but when the female flew out of the valley that August day, it was the last time I'd see her. Her long-dead remains were found in February 1983 on the ground towards which I'd seen her flying, and she was never replaced. The male lingered on and, having lost his mate, went in search of a new partner. He was twice in the Haweswater nesting valley in March 1983, possibly trying to entice the female away as they displayed together and disappeared into the clouds, and I saw him again in June that year. I'd heard a commotion that day and ran outside to see him, recognisable by a missing secondary I'd noted in March, flying with a buzzard behind the house and watched as he flew over me and out towards the Haweswater birds' grouse moors. I continued to check his old valley and found signs of his continued occupancy until April 1985. I collected a feather and pellets in June 1984 and found feathers and prey remains in 1985. I was told in later years that both eagles had been deliberately killed, but there was no evidence of that and no way of knowing what really became of them.

I continued, and continue, to make spring and autumn visits to the old territory, but those were the last eagle signs I found there until 1993. In October of that year I found fresh heather stems on the 1981 nest ledge but failed to find anything else. There have been occasional reports of eagles in that area, but they never filter through to me when fresh, so they can't be checked. The 1979 nest collapsed and had mouldered away by

1997, and the ledge and tree supporting the 1982 nest crashed into the gorge during the winter of 1999. The red-grouse population in the original nesting valley was extinct by 1986, and only one pair was recorded in the vicinity of the 1981 site during fieldwork for the Cumbria breeding bird atlas from 1997 to 2001, and I'd stopped seeing grouse there in about 1994. There's virtually no hope of the territory being reoccupied now, even if there were eagles to do so; you can't have an eagle territory without prey.

CHAPTER 5

The Haweswater pair

Golden eagles had been breeding in the Haweswater area of the eastern Lake District since 1969, and six chicks had been fledged from nests in Riggindale by 1979. The birds failed that year with infertile eggs, and I was transferred there from my first site when they failed in 1980. There'd been an entirely new team in 1979, and although one of them had returned as senior warden, I became involved because he didn't have a car and the peregrine protection effort would be a major part of the scheme and necessitated a vehicle. The base camp was also much further from the eagles than at the other site. Unlike the caravan, the accommodation at Haweswater was in a village about 8 km from the access point to the nesting valley.

Mike had driven me to the site because I was temporarily without a vehicle, and when we found no one at home we drove to the end of the road and set out to walk to the valley. The terrain was in stark contrast to the other site; deep valleys with extensive crag systems fed the lake with tumbling streams and provided no shortage of potential nest sites. It was a gloomy day when we arrived, with sleet and snow showers adding to the sense of foreboding that always hangs over these areas.

Mike and I had a vague notion of where the birds should be, so we set off on foot, concealing our binoculars and telescopes so as not to draw attention to our intentions in this much more popular walking area. We'd barely walked 300 metres when we spotted a lone walker coming towards us. He was dressed in the typical RSPB plumage of waxed jacket, woolly hat and big boots. It was Geoff, the warden, so we introduced ourselves, and he gave us better directions to the site, although I didn't think 'the nest is below the green bit' was a particularly helpful piece of guidance. The nest being added to wasn't the one used in the previous two years and had, in fact, only been used once before, in 1977.

A stony, and disconcertingly well-marked, track led us to the valley, and I compared it to the eagle valley I was familiar with. This one had an abundance of crags, and the southern ridge was lightly wooded with ash and rowan; boulder fields below the vertical faces were moss covered and looked treacherous in places. The valley head was rocky and precipitous with a buttress enclosing one side of a glacial corrie, and, in contrast, the northern ridge was formed by a triangular peak and a lower, rounded face, both of which held large scree fields and small outcrops before the down-valley half of the ridge transformed into a grassy bank on which red deer grazed.

The valley even held an 'Eagle Crag', testament to its past history and an attraction to eagles that went back for more than 200 years. A derelict barn stood at the bottom of the valley, and the dilapidated state of the walls showed them to have little value to the farm that lay at the far end of the lake. This was recent history; the lake, a reservoir, had been dammed barely 40 years earlier, and the old walls marked out lambing pastures and in-bye land that would have been in constant use before that time. The farm was once by the now-drowned village of Mardale with its pub, The Dun Bull, and the old Holy Trinity church. All that now remained of this community was the demolished rubble that lay on Wood Howe, the island in the lake.

The valley head was filled with cloud and showers blew by, but we soon reached an abutment to the wall and recognised it as the site of the RSPB's hide. There was no dismantled shed, though, that still lay further into the valley and closer to the nest that had been used in 1979. Within minutes, and just as at the other pair in 1979, the great form of an eagle loomed out of the murk and glided onto its pile of sticks. The nest was in a group of small trees; two small rowans appeared to hold it onto its ledge as a sheer gully slashed through the ridge beside it. A band of pillar-like rocks extended away from it, and while it was fairly close to the foot of the crag, the nest looked fairly inaccessible, certainly more so than the one I'd watched the previous year. The ridge climbed almost vertically above the nest, and the trees and outcrops would make it invisible to people walking the ridgetop path above. The eagle stood on the front edge of the nest, partly obscured by trees, and its mate rose to stand beside it. What I took to be the male then flew off, and the female sat. Although Geoff was convinced that incubation hadn't started, it obviously had, and we'd have to get the protection scheme up and running as soon as possible. It was 27 March.

With Mike away and my car unavailable, Geoff and I only had a pushbike between us. I had to walk the 8 km to the valley, starting well before daybreak, but at least that started to get me fit after the winter and allowed me to get a better idea of the terrain. The other two wardens were due to arrive on 1 April, and I'd been assured that one of them would have a car, but I kept my fingers crossed and hoped they'd both find the location and stay the course. Just as in the previous year, the watching began with us finding shelter where we could and trying to keep a complete record of the birds' activity in between rain and snow showers. At least we could retreat to the old barn during the worst of the storms here and still keep the nest in sight.

While there were no grouse at this site, the walks and watching enabled me to record a greater diversity of wildlife than there had been at the other site. There were ducks and geese, the lake also held a large gull roost, and cormorants would nest on the island; ravens and peregrines bred on several of the crags in the area, and red deer roamed the valleys and high tops. There were already wheatears and ring ouzels singing with the larks and pipits, and as the spring progressed the wooded ridges would ring with the songs of blackbirds, mistle thrushes and redstarts. I would even have the incongruous sight of the male eagle being mobbed by a spotted flycatcher as he sat casually in a tree near his nest. The semi-natural Naddle Forest lay on the opposite side of the lake, and this held decent populations of pied flycatchers, various warblers and red squirrels.

Rather than arriving with Paul, as I'd been told would be the case, the next warden, Alan, was delivered to the site by his parents on 30 March, and his first introduction to eagle work was to walk the length of the lake on the morning of the 31st. We were delayed along the way by two male goshawks displaying to a female, but we increased our speed to make up for lost time and entered the valley to cut across the fell towards the observation post. Almost at once, I noticed two men moving along the path from the car park and was immediately suspicious. Although I expected to meet many more visitors than had been the case in 1979, it was still very early on a grey and wet weekday morning, and it hadn't yet been announced that the birds were breeding again. It wasn't much to go on, and Alan couldn't see anything suspicious, but I knew at once that these were not going to be average visitors.

I'd had no training or been given any advice on how to deal with potential egg collectors, but I knew that I couldn't simply rush across and stop the men. I stopped Alan, and we waited to watch the men's progress up the valley. They passed the hide site without a second glance (so they might have been heading for the other one, further up the valley, that had been used in 1979) and walked below the occupied nest (which was shrouded in low cloud) without looking up. The 1979 hide was behind a glacial moraine, and when they slowed to edge over the rise, it confirmed to me that they weren't birdwatchers. They stopped to scan the sheepfold through binoculars and then moved in for a closer look. On seeing the hide still dismantled and wrapped in its protective plastic, the men took a quick check around the other walls and then began to angle their approach towards the 1979 nest and disappeared into the cloud.

I quickly led Alan across the slope, waded through the beck, and we tucked ourselves against a tumbled-down wall. Because the nest they approached wasn't in use the men hadn't actually done anything illegal or caused any disturbance, but I wanted to be in position in case they moved on to the occupied nest and we had to confront them. We didn't hide either, as I wanted the men to know they'd been seen if all they did was return down the valley. It was a complex situation as the men may have been acting in all innocence; if the site wasn't wardened the eagles might not have been there, and I wondered what to say if they came up to us and asked what we were doing! The low cloud was a problem as well; they could have approached the occupied nest from above, but I thought the fact it had only been used once before was in our favour.

The two men descended out of the cloud after 15 minutes and made their way down the valley, again not looking up towards, or approaching, where the bird was sitting. They reached the wall about 20 minutes later, and one just happened to look in our direction; he quickly took a second look as our presence clicked with him and spoke to his companion. They were taken by surprise but didn't come across to us and actually began to walk more slowly, stopping to admire the view from time to time, pretending to be tourists rather than egg collectors.

I was in no hurry and let them go, there was little point in challenging them and having to point out the occupied nest, and they obviously had to return to the car park.

Without transport of our own we could do little more than take their car registration number and pass it on to the investigations department at the Lodge. Once they'd turned the final corner towards the car park, Alan and I sped after them and used our telescopes to read the car number. The car didn't belong to a known collector but did, I was told, belong to someone who'd been suspected of involvement in the past. At least with this evidence there could be little doubt, and they'd both be watched for in the future.

Paul arrived with a car as promised, I regained my transport, and all we needed was to erect the hide. This would have necessitated several trips up and down the valley below the nest, so I asked voluntary helper Bernard Widowson to provide some extra manpower, and we were able to collect, move and erect the hide with the minimum of fuss. The female did leave the nest when we first walked below her, but the male flew in immediately to cover the eggs. I was expecting this, the female had probably stayed on the nest during the earlier incident because of the cloud cover, but this was a bright and sunny day and there were eight of us moving in a group in full view of her. The male flying in was also expected, and this bird would prove to be more than willing to put himself in potential danger when his mate took flight.

With the hide erected, we were able to spend nights in the valley, and because of the distances involved, we soon settled into a rote of a staggered 48-hour shift with one person being relieved each day. Just as in 1979, it was often a delight just to escape from the base camp. While it had been a cramped caravan in that year, the 'cottage' we used here was actually a disused and semi-derelict office, and while it had indoor plumbing and a flush toilet, there was no bath and the only hand basin had to be used for washing ourselves, fresh food and clothing. At least in the valley there was a clear mountain stream in which to wash and cooking on a camping stove was little worse than what we had at base. The hide also had the added advantage of being close to the eagles.

I was quickly able to note plumage differences between the two birds and how they each differed from the birds in the other pair. The female here didn't have holed wings to ease identification, but the male was by far the palest of the four birds and was easily distinguishable at almost any distance. The female was larger than the male and also appeared to have proportionally longer wings than her mate and either of the other birds. With a greater choice of potential perches available to these birds, the eagles also had their own individual favourite perches that the other didn't use. There were some shared perches, of course, and the most used of all was one of those. With a greater variety of locations in use, it was also necessary to distinguish between them, and the favoured ones (out of about 60 in all) soon became known as *the acacia tree, the cleft tree* (because of their shapes) and *the dome* (a semi-circular outcrop). Others included *the pink rock* (its obvious colour), *camouflage man* (a tree by a quartz outcrop that looked like a man in winter camouflage gear and caught out more than a few people who thought there really was someone on the crags) and *the cross tree* (again because of its obvious shape). Others were simply known by their initials, such as *hxER1*, and the most used perch of all was just *lbt*, ledge by tree, or *the ledge*. Such names would have been meaningless to the uninitiated, but they were quickly adopted, and we all knew exactly what was happening if told that the bird had spent most of the day on the *bilberry peaks*, for example.

The valley was more open than at the other site, and with the hide on the centre of its floor, rather than towards one side, the eagles were more visible and, unlike at the other site, there were days when both birds were always in sight. The male often roosted on the ridgeside above the hide while his mate was on the nest, and they seemed to survive on sheep carrion throughout the incubation period – there was no shortage of that in this valley. The female did have one habit that kept us alert, though. On leaving the nest she'd fly around for a while, sometimes finding a perch on which to shake out her feathers and defecate, but she'd then gain height and leave to the east, towards the grouse moors. That was straightforward enough, but she usually returned by coming in low over the north ridge, and you had to be alert to see her. As often as not, though, she'd usually be found perched in a favourite spot two or three hours after leaving, and it became a regular habit to keep checking these locations whenever she was out of the valley for any length of time. She was presumably away foraging for herself even when there was fresh carrion available.

The eagles were into their routine long before we settled into ours, and I saw the same differences here as I had in 1979. While I wanted to record everything I saw and see everything that happened, I was again working with someone who tried hard to emulate my record keeping, someone who edited his records to include only what he considered to be important and someone who just didn't try, always losing the bird as soon as it dropped below the skyline or claiming that it had flown behind the ridge when it hadn't. It didn't matter how much I emphasised the need for completeness, there was always an excuse not to watch the bird away from the nest, and yet they missed so much by not looking. It also raised my concerns about the effectiveness of the warden-ing scheme.

I was on watch with Geoff on 12 April, and as the light was fading that evening I noticed someone moving through the trees and boulders on the ridge above the hide. I quickly grabbed my jacket and suggested that Geoff do the same, but he just said: 'What can we do?' I told him in no uncertain terms that we could find out what the person was doing, but as I went after the intruder Geoff stayed at the hide. I lost the man in the gloom and complex terrain, but I knew I'd made him turn back down the valley and when I returned to the hide in total darkness it was to find Geoff tucked up in bed with the door locked. This didn't fill me with confidence, and it was shortly afterwards that I took over as senior warden at the site.

On 7 May, I was shown how the eagles' instincts could cause a conflict of inter-ests. The male swung down-valley in pursuit of a peregrine, but when she saw them the female abandoned the eggs and joined the chase; on seeing his mate off the nest, the male quickly broke away from the pursuit and dropped down to cover the eggs. This was typical of these birds – the female almost invariably left the nest to deal with peregrines, but she usually allowed her mate to handle the buzzards and ravens that en-tered the valley. The female chased away the falcon but was joined by a buzzard as she turned back up the valley. Constantly harried, she sought safe haven on *the pink rock*, but the buzzard continued to stoop at her, and she flashed her wings as it approached but failed to scare it away. After seven minutes, she decided to give chase and pursued the buzzard down-valley past the nest. When she stopped to circle, possibly expecting her mate to take over from her, the buzzard regained its composure and stooped in at her again. The male sat tight, he wasn't going to leave the eggs for something as trivial as a buzzard.

The female cocked her head to look down at her mate and up at the buzzard and clearly had a conflict of interests; she wanted to be on the eggs but couldn't lead a possible danger to the nest. She tried to stoop in when the buzzard circled higher, and the male stood ready to leave, but she had to pull out again as the buzzard dropped to follow her. The male, his instincts telling him to give chase but also not to leave the eggs, settled again and watched intently as this was repeated twice more. The third time, he even stepped to the edge of the nest in readiness, but again the buzzard stooping right past the nest dissuaded the female from landing and caused him to sit.

Once more the female swung away to gain height, her tormentor stooping at her all the while even though she rolled to slash with her talons as it neared her. She circled higher and higher, gaining more than 500 metres of height above the ridgetop, and then, after 22 minutes of constant mobbing, the female tipped over one wing and dived headlong towards the nest. I could hear the rush of wind from where I was, almost a kilometre away, as the fractured air tore at her feathers, and I could barely keep her in the telescope's field of view so fast was she dropping. She arrived at the nest in an incredible flurry of wings, dust and feathers; braking hard with tail fully fanned and wings feathered against the rushing air, she somehow managed to avoid her mate and the eggs. The male stood when he saw her dropping and was off the moment she touched down, but not before. The buzzard pulled out of its dive when it saw the male and used its momentum to swing out across the valley, but the male, in level flight and from a standing start, closed in with every oaring beat of his wings. By mid-valley the buzzard was screaming with fear, and when the eagle arrived, the hawk began to make terror-stricken jerks and stalls to avoid the flashing talons as the eagle swooped past, rolled and came in time and again. As the eagle stooped once more, the buzzard somehow managed to roll and reverse its direction at the same time and raced back over the hide and out of the valley. The eagle had made its point and followed more leisurely to settle on the crags, fully satisfied with his retaliation on behalf of his mate.

Incredibly, the buzzard was back the next morning, both my and the male's attention being drawn to it by the female calling from the nest, but on seeing the eagle's approach, this time the buzzard turned tail and was out of the valley before the male could arrive.

I knew the hatch date to be approaching by now and looked for any sign of its arrival. The female defecated from the nest on 8 May and in doing so left a white streak on it. This was unusual as the male was in the valley at the time and a marking like that could identify it as an occupied nest to any potential predators. I still thought that it could be a good sign, though, as it suggested that she was reluctant to leave the nest, and that she might be able to hear a chick calling from the egg. She also didn't allow her mate to incubate at all that day. I expected the hatch to have been confirmed in my absence, but when I returned to the hide in mid-afternoon the next day the male was in his third stint of incubation that day. No food had been taken in, and there was no ceremony when the female returned three quarters of an hour later. I began to wonder if something had gone wrong.

The wind had turned from a cold north-westerly to a milder south-easterly by the next morning, and the clouds rolled back to allow the first of several bright days; the first spell of good settled weather we'd had all season. I hoped this would be a good omen, and while the female was standing for the first time that day, the male flew onto the stick platform beside the nest with a clump of woodrush. The eagles looked at one another before the male flew off, and the female sat again. He might have been checking on developments in the nest.

At a few minutes after 5 o'clock that morning, I noticed some foxhounds in the valley-head corrie, and by a quarter past the full hunt was running across the slopes. The hounds scurried around the corrie, and the male eagle left his perch to circle above them. The hounds worked their way over the buttress, through the big screes below *lbt*, across the valley head and out past the old nest crag. The eagle circled and watched, but once the hounds were out of the corrie, he dropped into it and out of my line of sight. The valley was soon quiet again, but knowing where he was, I kept watch on the corrie. It was almost 2 km away, and even a bird as big as an eagle can easily blend into the background at such a range.

My luck was in – the eagle flew into my field of view almost as soon as it was possible, 20 minutes after he'd gone down. He was carrying a lamb. The lamb was obviously freshly dead as I could see blood on it through the telescope, but I didn't know if he'd killed it; it seemed likely that it had been separated from the ewe by the hounds, and the eagle had grabbed what was effectively an abandoned lamb. The eagle carried his prize around the valley head in a heavy glide to land on top of the other nest crag. He panted heavily as a result of his exertions, and his breath condensed on the cool morning air. He didn't feed from the lamb, a good sign, and started down-valley with it after a few minutes rest. His first flight took him out of sight into a gully but he re-emerged six minutes later to continue down and past the nest. He turned back up-valley when his mate called from the nest and performed three display dips while still carrying the lamb before turning in to land on a ledge above the nest.

The male began to pluck the lamb after he'd caught his breath again and ate a few choice morsels before looking around, dragging it to a lower ledge and then flying again. This time he carried the lamb to the centre of the ridge, and when the female stood to look into the nest, the male took off to display and then came back down to the lamb. I wondered why he didn't just take it to the nest and get it over with! During the next 90 minutes, the male carried the lamb back and forth along the ridge, his mate calling from the nest every time he passed by. He landed, flew and relanded, picked at

43

the carcass and made three more display flights. When the female stood again, for seven minutes, he left the lamb high on the ridge and flew to his favourite perch as if that was all he needed to do.

This was confusing, had the egg hatched or was the male just going through the motions? Three quarters of an hour later the female left the nest, and the male flew to join her circling in front of the other nest crag, a kilometre from the one they were using. Was this good or bad? They both turned down-valley, the male arriving at the nest a few seconds ahead of his mate; they stood looking into it and then the male flew off. He flew straight to the lamb, seized it in his talons and then flew with it to the stick platform beside the nest. He left it, flew to a favoured perch, and after calling, the female jumped up, grabbed the carcass and dragged it into the nest. She immediately began to tear at it and present pieces into the nest. There was a chick!

The similarities between the final actions and what I'd seen the previous year, the male not taking the food directly to the nest and the female having to retrieve it from an adjoining ledge, were amazing. But here it had taken the food two and a half hours to arrive from the moment the male disappeared into the corrie. And after all of that, the first feed lasted only four minutes. It would be another two and a half hours before the next feed (10 minutes), and the third and final one of the day (eight minutes) began at 3.30 p.m. The female only left the nest once after the food arrived, allowing her mate to cover the chick for seven minutes.

Most of the early feeds I recorded were of only four or five minutes, but things suddenly changed on the 16th; the female presented food for 16 minutes from 5.25 a.m. and did so for 19 minutes about two hours later, and again, after another hour, she presented for a quarter of an hour. There were three more feeds that day before I went off duty at 4 p.m., and I began to wonder if the second egg might have hatched. The feeds seemed too long for one chick, but I couldn't see into the nest from the valley floor and couldn't be certain. I couldn't go and look either, the nest was hidden from above without getting far too close, and I effectively couldn't leave the hide because of the number of visitors we were receiving. This was a much better known location than the other eagle site, and by the end of the four months we would have seen almost a thousand visitors coming specifically to look for the eagles.

I continued to see the longer feeds during my next watches, and on the morning of the 19th, I allowed Brian, a volunteer at the scheme, to wander up the opposite ridge. He only had binoculars but was certain when he returned that he'd seen two chicks in the nest. I didn't waste a second, there were no visitors in sight, so I grabbed my telescope and charged up the ridgeside, going higher than Brian and settling among some rocks. Watching with 40 times magnification instead of eight, I willed the female to stand and let me see what was in the nest, and she did so after five minutes. With the bright morning sun illuminating the nest I could clearly see two chicks lying in the cup. The female flew off, but the chicks didn't move and didn't do so when she returned either. The female cocked her head to look at the chicks, stepped over them and gently lowered her body, rocking from side to side, to cover and protect them. It was the best news, and I had, for the first time, the opportunity to see two chicks fledge together from an English eagle nest.

I dropped back down to the hide, and at 10.21 a.m., as luck would have it, a chick raised its head into view. The female offered it a tiny sliver of meat, and when she flew off it stood shakily surveying the valley through bleary eyes before collapsing back into the cup and out of sight. The joy I felt at seeing another chick and knowing that I'd have another full season with eagles was immeasurable. With the male taking his turns at brooding the chicks, sometimes staying on for over an hour, they were well protected, and I didn't begin to see both of them from the hide until a couple of days later. I knew they were both alive, though, as the clear actions of the female presenting food to different parts of the nest indicated that both were being fed in turn.

In the excitement of having two chicks, I hadn't lost track of one of the curious features of golden eagles and their related species, that of sibling aggression, the Cain and Abel syndrome as it was called after Seton Gordon's experiences in Scotland, where one chick kills the other. Its cause or purpose still isn't understood: it's been suggested that it was a result of food shortage but, even with my inexperience at the time, that seemed unlikely to be the case; would the adults really be incapable of finding enough food for chicks of less than two weeks old? If there were food shortages one would simply die; the other surely couldn't recognise the problem at that age, they seemed barely capable of standing, and the amount of food they required must have been so small as to make shortages unlikely to be an explanation for the aggression.

Both the chicks became visible from the hide on the floor of the valley during the next few days, and I was able to watch the aggression for myself. Shortly after the male delivered a fox cub to the nest on the 22nd, first one and then the second chick raised its head above the rim of the nest. The smaller of the two, Abel, turned to look out over the valley and was immediately attacked about the head by Cain, but the two quickly disappeared from view while the adult female stood and watched. The chicks next appeared at 9.15 a.m. the next day, and Abel was flattened again. They were back in view at 11.25 a.m., and Abel was soon knocked over and lay prostrate on the edge of the nest while Cain rained blows onto its body and pulled at its wings. Through the scope I could see Cain drawing blood from Abel as it lay undefended by its parents and not retaliating. This wasn't a fight, it was an unprovoked attack by a bully.

I couldn't sex the chicks from where I was and had to assume that the larger of the two was the first hatched, but, even then, I wondered if a male chick would have no chance of surviving if the first hatched was a female bulking up quickly during the three or four days before the second egg hatched. There were four more attacks that day, and even though I spent the next 24 hours in the valley, I didn't see Abel again; Cain had won, and its sibling had lived for no more than 10 days. I was pleased to have witnessed the event with my own eyes but saddened to have seen an eaglet being killed when we needed all the eagles we could get in England.

The surviving chick grew well after that, fattened on a selection of lambs, corvids, a number of smaller prey items and even a badger cub, but without a nest-mate to attack, its activity declined for a while and it spent most of its time dozing between meals or being sheltered from rain and soaking mist by the female. The lambs on the nest were a real concern at Haweswater, and while I saw the eagles collecting ones that were obviously dead when found, I also saw the eagles killing some of the lambs they fed to the chick. The adult birds used a variety of techniques to claim their prey, but only rarely did I see a long plunging stoop to make the catch. The lambs presented too easy a target for that to be employed, and the eagles, more often than not, simply waited for a ewe to wander away from its sleepy lamb before gliding down to make the strike, sometimes almost parachuting onto the unsuspecting creature. With such a slow approach, the kill wasn't instant, and many lambs escaped before the bird could find the correct grip to either squeeze the life away or puncture head or vital organs with a hind talon, and many an onrushing ewe saved its lamb by attacking the eagle during these moments. One lamb did succumb to its injuries beneath the ewe, and the eagle had to wait another 50 minutes before it could fly back, retrieve the carcass and carry it to the nest. It was a life lost, but it helped the much rarer eagle to survive.

The adult eagles' lives revolved around the chick; they provided shelter, protection and sustenance for it, drove other birds of prey, crows and ravens away from the nest area and collected nest material to maintain the soft cup in which it would spend 11 or 12 weeks. And so it was surprising when, at 6.47 p.m. on 2 June, the female flew to land on another nest, the top nest as it is known, the one used in 1970 when eagles first bred in this valley and again in 1979. It was more than a kilometre from the nest with the chick, and I assumed that it was just a passing visit, but the male then joined her, and the eagles stood together for two minutes, looking in and out as if assessing it at the start of a breeding season. The male was back there again the next day, though, and collected and carried a bunch of heather to it; on the 25th he took a stick as well. It was what I would have expected if the breeding attempt had failed, the birds turning their attention away from the abandoned site in a type of displacement activity, but the chick was strong and healthy and calling most of the time to ensure that it wasn't forgotten about.

The chick grew stronger as the days passed; it fed itself for the first time on 21 June and within four days was pulling and tearing at meat left in the nest by the adults. There was no shortage of food, but there were occasions when the adults had to just accept what was available. When the male found a lamb in the valley-head screes it looked as though a fox had been on it first, but he still ate for 11 minutes and was immediately replaced by the female that ate for 22 minutes. She then plucked and tore at the carcass and, an hour later, ate for another 12 minutes. She plucked and cut again and, two and a half hours after arriving, gripped the carcass with her talons and flew to below the top nest. She stood panting before dragging the lamb up the slope, heaving it up with one foot until she was high enough to fly directly to the chick, the lamb hanging limply beneath her. She immediately fed the chick for half an hour, by which time she'd been with the lamb for 183 minutes. It was a pattern I'd see repeated many times over the years, an eagle claiming a carcass and not leaving it until the chick had been fed, no matter how long it took to carry it to the nest.

The chick was virtually fully grown and fully feathered by July; it was more active, jumping about the nest and exercising its wings and, it seemed, constantly calling for its parents' attentions. The adults spent more time away from the nest to lessen the calling and harassment they suffered, and when they arrived the chick always pounced on them, whether or not they carried food, and no matter how small the item was. On one such occasion, the male arrived with a vole in its beak, but, as usual, the chick pounced at his feet with wings spread to mantle and defend the food. The adult tried to avoid it but was pinned down and in some obvious discomfort. He raised his wings but almost toppled backwards from the nest and had to flap hard to regain his balance. Once the chick had realised there was no food it released the adult and backed away, it looked up as it did so, saw the vole and pounced again. It leapt with flashing talons and thrashing wings, grabbed the vole, swallowed it and bowled the male cart-wheeling out of the nest in one action. And as the male turned away the chick started to call for more. That was the fourth vole it had been given that day, so the chick was probably frustrated at the lack of a proper meal, but the violence of the assault didn't deter the adult, and the male was back with another vole almost immediately and was assailed yet again.

Just as seemed to be happening in 1979, all of these voles might have suggested that the adults were trying to starve the chick from the nest, but that wasn't the case. The chick had survived on voles for the first 16 hours of the day, but the female then arrived with a grouse. Two and a half hours later the male caught and delivered a crow and later still that evening the female did likewise. The chick ate them all, and rather than being starved from the nest, it would by then have been too fat to fly!

The adults were back on the top nest the next day, 21 July, the female arriving at the end of the fourth dip of a display flight, and when she flew again the male swept in and they performed two flight-rolls with touching talons in a fast ground-hugging chase close to the crag. The female then went to a ledge, and the male went on to the top nest. After picking at the sticks, he flew towards the female, and as he arrived the female sprang up, performed a backward flip, locked talons with the male and rolled him off to the ground beside her. A flight-roll on the ground! It would be 23 years before I saw another between adults. Interestingly, the eagles would later carry sticks to the ledge on which the first was performed. They were back on the ledge less than an hour later, but this time stood bowing to each other, their beaks almost touching the ground. It was another first, and I could find no reference to such behaviour in any of the books, nor think of a suitable explanation.

Everything suddenly changed the next afternoon when I was off duty and away from the valley. I'd learnt the previous year not to expect a magnificent first flight from the nest, but at least the 1980 chick didn't just walk off it: this one fell out backwards. It didn't come to any harm and, in a similar vein to 1979, spent the next three days more or less where it had landed. It wandered about, stripped bracken, threw turf and called almost incessantly. The male provided its food, and it eventually made its first flight, unassisted by me, four days after it fell from the nest, 77 days after hatching. It was the seventh eaglet to have fledged in this valley since the species had returned to England.

I closed the scheme down fairly quickly after that, under instructions from the RSPB (my contract only ran until the end of July and the fledging was seen as the end of the story), and could manage only two more visits that year. I discovered that the eaglet was still present towards the end of August and watched as it flew along the ridge to settle on a ledge above the nest. Its crop bulged from a good feed that morning, and I quickly found the male perched on *the ledge* and the female on *the pink rock*. Nothing else happened before it was time for me to leave and make plans for the next year.

Chapter 6

Mating and incubation

1981 proved to be a pretty disastrous year all round. My first pair of eagles failed because of the April snow, and the Haweswater birds failed around the time of the hatch.
The RSPB sent me to Wales to warden a little tern colony after the first eagles had
failed, instead of Haweswater, but a developing illness made me abandon that and a
later Welsh contract I was offered. I only managed a few days with the eagles that year,
and the timing of my illness couldn't have been worse. News came that the first national
golden eagle survey was to be undertaken in 1982, and I desperately wanted to take part
in that. The RSPB offered me a contract to cover the Scottish islands of Islay and Jura,
but I reluctantly decided that I had to turn down the offer, fearing that my illness might
compromise the results.

With none of the 1981 team wanting to return to Haweswater, I was offered that
job again in 1982 instead and was only too pleased to accept it. I'd thought that I'd
also be involved with the other eagles but that proved to be wrong, which irritated me
at the time, but the Haweswater birds provided me with an opportunity that had to be
grabbed with both hands. When trying to check my observations with the available literature in 1979 and 1980, I'd come to realise that there were big gaps in our knowledge
of golden eagles in spite of what was claimed, and I was in a unique position to fill some
of those gaps. I was already the RSPB's most experienced eagle warden, and my detailed
note-taking gave me a record of behaviour that wasn't going to be surpassed.

Eagle work in Scotland has traditionally been linked to breeding performance and
population size, with only the old boys such as H B MacPherson and Seton Gordon
writing about the intimacies of behaviour, but even their work was conducted at the nest,
using hides from which they could see little else. Lea McNally had written about his
observations, but his work as a stalker and ranger kept his involvement largely to breeding checks and incidental contacts with the birds away from the nest. But 1982 would
see the publication of another eagle book, this one written by Mike Tomkies. While he
too had spent long hours in cramped hides next to nests, he'd also recorded and tried to
interpret his observations of eagles away from the nest. He'd made a tremendous effort,
had monitored the breeding performance of a population of eagles in more than 800
sq km of the Western Highlands of Scotland (returning to the same pairs year after
year and recording their breeding attempts), observed his birds the whole year round
(not just during the breeding season) and worked to change attitudes towards a species
that has long been seen as a threat to sporting and farming interests. He'd also sampled

many of the aspects of eagle ecology that I wanted to investigate, but that was encouragement to me not a deterrent.

One of the biggest gaps in our knowledge was what became of juvenile eagles once they had left the nest. No one really knew how long they stayed with their parents, if the adults taught them to hunt or even if, at the end of their adolescence, they were driven away from the territory as had been suggested by some sources. Assumptions were made about these aspects of the eagle's life, but there was little proof to support them. The brief observations I'd made of the 1979 and 1980 juveniles revealed no flying or hunting lessons, and the concern the adults showed in 1979 by leading the walking juvenile away from the low ground and to the safety of the valley head suggested that being driven away would be a tremendous change of behaviour in the adults, and one that seemed highly unlikely.

I would only learn the truth through watching the eagles, and for that I needed them to breed successfully. But I had no delusions about the amount of work that this would involve; it would have to be a long-term project. Observations of one bird would be insufficient, and to make a detailed record of the movements and behaviour of three, or possibly five, juveniles could take seven or eight years. While I was happy to be involved at Haweswater for that length of time, the RSPB might not have been, and of course, the eagles might have stopped breeding or producing young before I'd collected sufficient data to really understand what happened. The one thing I was sure of was that I wouldn't be competing with other fieldworkers, if no one had thought of undertaking such a project before then it was unlikely that anyone would be starting one at the same time as me, especially with a breeding survey in progress when everyone would be concentrating on the nests.

The first thing I needed was for the Haweswater eagles to breed successfully in 1982. That meant the protection scheme had to be reliable and that depended on my coworkers as much as it did on myself. In 1982 we were down to a three-man team; Chris and Alan were young, keen to have a successful season and willing to learn. With three cars at our disposal (including one from the RSPB for the first time), we were better prepared than in any of the previous three years and in a position to amend rosters and schedules without having to take account of wardens who couldn't drive or who weren't willing to put in the hours. There was still a learning curve, of course, and when I first took Chris to the nesting valley, I had to explain about discipline and disturbance after, having stopped to watch through the telescope, he asked if we could go closer to the nest. It wasn't what I wanted to hear, but he'd not done this type of work before and quickly understood what our role was in the valley; we were there to protect the eagles from robbery and disturbance, not to take advantage of an elite position of being able to go closer than anyone else.

At that stage in the season, my main concerns were ensuring that we still had a pair of eagles and that they weren't disturbed in the build-up to egg laying. It quickly became apparent that, having used the middle nest for the previous two years, the eagles had moved and were concentrating on refurbishing their top nest. This meant that I'd be carrying a garden shed about the Lakeland fells for the third time in four years, but at least I wouldn't be carrying it below the occupied nest this time. Even though we would be better provided with voluntary help than in any previous year, I wanted to get the hide erected so we could start the watch, and so, once Alan had arrived, we set about carrying the sections up the valley. There were two hides now, a second had been bought in 1981 so that one could act as a visitor shelter while the other provided the wardens with some privacy, but the second proved to be too small and could only be used for storage.

It was as well that we acted promptly. I was expecting the first egg to be laid on or about 27 March, as had been the case in 1980, but when I went to the valley on the 23rd, I realised that the laying date had changed. The weather, as usual, was hampering observations, but the female arrived at the nest at about 7 a.m., sat, stood and sat several times, pulled at the nest material and then stood looking out from the nest. The male arrived at 7.13 a.m., and the female flew off a minute later. He watched her go, looked into the nest, checked the valley and then, to my surprise, five minutes later, he sat rocking his body and began to incubate the first egg. The female had laid it but hadn't sat, and the male took the first stint. The female allowed him 31 minutes before returning to replace him on the egg.

I don't think that anyone else has confirmed the male eagle taking the first stint of incubation; as is the case with so much about golden eagles, it's just assumed that the female lays the egg and then sits on it. Incredibly (or perhaps typically) it was the male that took the first stint of incubation in 1983 as well. On that occasion, the male made the first nest visit at 8.20 a.m. but didn't stay long and was almost immediately replaced by the female on the nest rim. She was on for a minute, off for two, on for one and then back almost immediately with a stick that she built into the edge of the nest. She was on for nine minutes; she sat and stood a couple of times, seemed about to settle but then stood fully, turned around, looked into the nest and then out, and I assumed that she was making the final preparations. The male was flying with two peregrines, and when she noticed that she flew off to intercept at 8.39 a.m., as would become her habit. The male broke away on her approach, dropped to the nest and sat to incubate, the female flying in 10 minutes later to relieve him of his duties. With the watches extending from pre-dawn to post-dusk, I knew these to be the first nest visits of the day on both of these occasions, and it was the male which took the first stint of incubation.

Nothing had been mentioned to me, but the earlier laying date in 1982 suggested a change of bird, and after contacting Paul from the previous year, I discovered that she'd also laid early in 1981 and 'looked more ragged' than she had in 1980. There'd almost certainly been a change of bird at some point, but no one had noticed and no one had bothered to tell me about the change of laying date. It was soon clear that the female was a new bird – once we were settled into the hides and the roster was working I was able to note both plumage and behavioural differences from the bird I'd watched in 1980. This bird appeared to be heavier bodied but comparatively shorter winged than her predecessor, and she was also darker of plumage, a sure sign of a young adult. And she used different perches to her predecessor: the 1980 female's favourite perch, *the cross tree*, fell into disuse and was replaced by *the hole* perch, which I hadn't seen used before then. The almost daily flights of the 1980 female towards the grouse moors ceased as well, and one final indicator was the behaviour of the male.

He was definitely the same bird as before, but unlike in 1980 with his established mate, this year he called almost every time he landed. He called on landing after leaving the nest, when he returned from outside the valley and even when he arrived at his roost, almost 2 km from the nest. He was clearly educating his new mate to his habits, and the location of his favourite perches and his calling were so predictable that I was able to stop visitors chattering when I saw him approaching a perch just in time for them to hear what the books describe as the 'usually silent' golden eagle. The calling gradually declined over the years as the female's assurance increased until, by 1985, it had stopped altogether.

I moved to live close to the eagles in the spring of 1983, to allow me to follow them throughout the year, to study their winter habits and to witness the build-up to egg-laying, when, it was assumed, most display flights were made. The birds returned to the middle nest for the 1983 season, but I realised as early as February that they'd be in the top nest again for 1984, and that I'd be carrying the hide for the fifth time in six years. The onset of nest refurbishment proved to be a casual affair with only a few sticks and heather stalks being added in the first week or two of February before the effort increased and the eagles began to rebuild in sessions of an hour or more that saw 20 to 30 items being added. The nest top was gradually tightened-up as the material was interwoven and then, with about three weeks to go, bracken and soft material were added for the platform and topped with grasses and woodrush for the soft cup that held the eggs. The female formed the cup like a small bird, by pushing her breast into this soft material, only two or three days before the first egg was laid. The process could be affected by the weather, though, with storms delaying the building and fine weather often seeing the nest fully restructured after a few concerted sessions.

The male did the bulk of the collecting while the female stayed on the nest to arrange the material he delivered and rearrange the less perfect efforts he made during her absences. It was fascinating to watch the process and the care and determination needed to position a 2m-long stick into the correct location; clods of earth were stuffed in to bulk out the nest, and bunches of heather dragged from side to side until a satisfactory shape was achieved. The eagles collected sticks from the ground or by breaking them from trees; dead sticks were easily snapped from trees but live ones had to be bounced on until they broke or were tweaked at with the bird's beak. But even though the bird was often on the wrong side of the break, the branch never fell to the ground; the eagle used its weight to make the final break and then just swept into flight as the stick broke free. Very occasionally, though, the branch didn't break when the bird expected it to, and on a few occasions, I saw an eagle dangling upside down from a tree like an acrobatic parrot.

Heather, bracken, woodrush and grass were usually collected by the bird gripping tightly with its feet and then launching itself backwards into flight, again with the occasional example of the roots not giving way and the eagle dropping onto its tail.

An eagle often picked up loose material with its beak, and it wasn't uncommon to see the material transferred from beak to feet in flight, although the bird did often arrive at the nest with smaller items still held in the beak. The eagles also often accidentally dropped material in flight and twisted down to catch it before it struck the ground; they'd retrieve it if they missed the catch. I watched all of this during February 1984 and also found evidence of the female spending time perched, and possibly roosting, close to the nest, just to remind me that I'd be carrying the hide again.

As well as nest refurbishment, and rebuilding if it had been damaged during the winter storms, the eagles also had to mate before laying their eggs and, appropriately, the earliest mating I recorded occurred on 14 February 1984. After circling with her mate beside the nest ridge, the female dropped to land on a ledge, and the male descended to land directly on her from flight. They were together for 20 seconds and then spent half an hour building the nest. Not all matings were to fertilise the egg, of course, and I couldn't tell if they actually connected on these occasions. Although I would go on to see such attempts in every month of the year, most were seen in March, and the couplings that fertilised the eggs probably only occurred in the last day or two before laying. They were usually performed without any ceremony, but on 1 March that year, with the pair perched together on a ledge, I watched the male sidle towards his mate, and then both began to bow until their beaks almost touched the ground. The male mounted the female for 12 seconds before they stood side by side and called with an unusually high-pitched note. So what had so puzzled me that day in 1980 now had an explanation, it was a resurgence of the breeding instinct just when the juvenile was about to leave the nest.

I didn't actually see any matings before laying in 1983, but another feature that appeared at this time was the eagles' habit of disappearing from the valley in the days before laying. The birds had access to a grouse moor that I knew they'd visit if there was a shortage of carrion in the core area of the territory, and so on 15 March 1984 I decided to take a speculative visit to the moor to see if there was any activity. It was a bitingly cold day and I was glad of the 5-km walk-in that put some warmth into my legs and body. I moved through incised streams, seeing a small group of twite and some winter thrushes, but there was no sign of an eagle, so I settled into a sheltered corner I knew from before that gave me a good view of the rolling heather and even allowed me to see the tops of the nesting valley ridges, even though they were almost 12 km away.

I waited, getting colder and colder until, at 2 p.m., I picked up the male eagle approaching as if directly from Riggindale. He was chased by two crows, flew past me and circled before slipping below a bluff and, presumably, starting to hunt. He was back in view four minutes later and spent five quartering the heather without flushing a grouse. He settled onto a grassy knoll and surveyed his surroundings. The rolling moors provided good hunting, not just because of the grouse but because the terrain allowed the eagle to move about small areas without alarming the entire grouse population and gave him the chance to sweep over a bluff and catch a grouse unawares. A trick they used was also to land below the top of a bluff and then walk over it, partly concealed by the heather, to view the next area to be hunted without alerting potential prey. The bluffs also meant that I kept losing track of the male that day, but after a few bursts of activity he eventually reappeared with his mate, which I hadn't even seen arrive.

They hunted together, with the female about 100 metres ahead of the male, but only flushed two grouse and caught neither before they settled onto the stones of an old cairn. They stayed there for half an hour before taking flight as one and flying with more determination, the male this time taking the lead. They were about 10 metres above the ground, and when a group of five grouse were flushed, they were onto them straight away. In a tight group at first, the grouse began to scatter as the eagles closed in, one was singled out, and the male eagle followed every twist and turn the grouse made. I half expected the grouse to dive into cover but it didn't, and its fate was sealed when it crossed a hollow. The male was up to it and half-rolled and flashed his talons to pluck the grouse from the air. Throwing back its wings, the eagle quickly landed on a bank and began to tear at its prey while the female continued the chase but soon broke away to drift off in search of easier prey. The male ate for 30 minutes and then made his way back towards the nesting valley, heedless of the success or failure of his mate's attempts to find food. It had been a long cold day for me but a satisfying one, not just because of the kill but also because the hard work I'd done in previous years had allowed me to identify the foraging areas and be in the right place at the right time.

In 1984, a surprise was in store before the breeding season got under way. The birds had laid their first egg on the 23rd in 1982 and on the 22nd in 1983, and they were in the valley when I arrived on the 23rd in 1984. They flew out to the next valley shortly afterwards, however, and I had a two-hour wait before they returned. They went out, came back and went again, so I decided to see what was so interesting in the next valley. It was only a short walk of about 20 minutes, but the eagles could have flown anywhere in that time, even perhaps returning to the nest site and performing activities that are still a mystery to me. I was fortunate, though, and both birds were still there when I arrived. I was surprised to see them dip-displaying in unison in this valley as most such displays were seen in or above the nesting valley. There were old nests in here, though, one that had been built in 1969 by neither of these birds but also ones they'd partly built themselves. After perching for a while, they were up to chase two peregrines before the male displayed again and then flew to settle close to the location of one of their out-of-season nests, those partly built in the autumn. These were usually abandoned once breeding time returned, but the same sites were often added to over several years, perhaps providing the eagles with a late replacement site should something happen to one of their favourite nests.

The male displayed again and this time called when he landed, giving four very immature-sounding yelps. I'd lost track of the female, but she replied from somewhere on the crags, and when the male dropped out of sight, I moved to get a better viewing angle of the crags and gullies that covered the ridgeside. I could see neither eagle nor nest, and when the female reappeared, she made six more display dips and called 12 times when she landed. The unseen male replied with five of his immature calls, and I really was now wondering what was happening. He flew out from the crags, the female took off to join him, and both performed two dips, dealt with a peregrine and then landed on a branch on top of the crag that held the unused 1969 nest. As I'd learned with the other pair in 1981, eagle nests can be very small and insignificant when they're first used, so I scoured the crags through the telescope while I knew where both birds were but could find nothing. The male gave 12 yelps and was up with the female behind him; he called again, and both circled to gain height and chase peregrines in what appeared to be clear nest-area defence behaviour. The male then dropped to land in the same tree he'd left and gave 20 of the immature calls before jumping to a ledge.

I didn't curse at losing track of the female because I knew that the male was always likely to return to a nest before the female when peregrines were about, but when he moved it was only to a nearby fallen tree. I scanned the crags in vain for the female or a nest, and when the male flew, he left the valley and moved even further away from the established one. I was uncertain of what was happening but had the consolation that no one else would know of the possible new site. I could safely leave the bird sitting to take a roost watch in the other valley to see if one, both or neither eagle returned that evening. I gave it another half hour and then plodded back to the sheepfold in which we'd been about to construct our hide. My old mate Stefan was waiting and wondering why I wasn't there. We compared notes, and I discovered that, far from sitting on a new nest, the female had returned to Riggindale and spent time adding material to the nest we expected her to use! The male flew in a little later and that was the end of that interesting, if inexplicable, episode. The first egg was laid in the Riggindale nest the next day, and we had to move the hide again. It was back to the old routine.

The three incubation periods 1982–84 progressed without a hitch. We received increasing numbers of visitors as the years passed, and there were occasional incidents of disturbance, but the culprits were always birdwatchers who wanted to take a closer look at the nest rather than egg collectors. There was one nice little episode in 1982 that reminded me of what I'd read in Seton Gordon's books. As well as a change of female at the site, there'd also been a change of farmer since I'd worked here in 1980. The new one, Hugh, changed the shepherding regime; he'd reduced the size of the hill flock in the valley, had taken the ewes off the hill to lamb and had introduced supplementary feed blocks to see his sheep through the late winter period – activities that would eventually reduce the amount of food available to the eagles.

It was the feed blocks that caused the initial upset. Before incubation had begun, Hugh contacted me to say that the blocks would be dropped from a helicopter into the sheepfold in which the dismantled hide was lying and that I'd have to move it if I didn't want to find half a tonne of sheep food on top of it. While we stopped visitors from progressing up-valley beyond the hide, we obviously couldn't stop Mac, the shepherd, from performing his tasks, and at some point he would have to go past the nest crag to check the flock and distribute the next set of blocks. He would have to do this fortnightly, and fortunately I was on duty the first time it happened and was able to record the hill-shepherd in action.

Mac and I exchanged pleasantries at the hide, and then he set off deeper into the valley. Going via the nest crag wasn't the most direct route to the next set of blocks but what could I say? The argument would be that he had to check the sheep, and I had no intention of initiating a confrontation with someone who was likely to have cause for complaint himself if the eagles killed lambs the way they had in 1980. Apart from which, I wanted to see how the eagles would react to a human below the crag during incubation (most of the birdwatcher disturbance came from above, on the ridgetop paths). I was ready, though, and if the eagle left the nest and stayed off, I was prepared to go and move him, whatever he was doing.

The female eagle was incubating at the time, and she became alert almost as soon as Mac had left the hide. I could see through the telescope that she became more unsettled the closer he got. Mac was never going to reach the crag, it was too far above the valley floor for that, but the eagle was inexperienced and clearly didn't like what she saw. She stretched her neck to peer over the nest rim as he walked and reached her crisis point when he was only about 300 metres in front of the hide, only about one third of the way to the nest. She stood, paused and then abandoned her eggs. The male had been watching developments from a favourite perch, but now he also flew and joined his mate in circling above the valley head, the typical response to human disturbance. The shepherd had certainly disturbed the eagle, and I was about to set off in pursuit when the male suddenly broke away from the female and stooped directly onto the nest to incubate the eggs, even though Mac was still getting closer.

The eagle settled tightly into the nest, apparently flattening himself into the cup and not poking his head up to watch or be seen. The behaviour was totally unexpected, and I put it down to his greater experience at the site compared to the youth of his mate. I relaxed and waited. Mac didn't continue on to the blocks at first but instead (and convincing me that he'd also read some of the old eagle books) stopped to have his lunch below the crag. I waited; I knew the eagle was on the nest and knew that it was covering the eggs and not simply standing above them, and as long as that continued I was prepared to let Mac do what he wanted. Whether it was because of my apparent lack of concern or the fact that he knew he shouldn't be there, Mac's lunch turned into a quick snack and he went on his way. No harm had been done, the female returned to the nest a short while afterwards, and the actions weren't repeated. A quiet word the next time I met Mac ensured that.

The intrusion in 1983 was of a different kind altogether and occurred on the day that incubation began. The day had started normally; I'd seen the activity to confirm egg laying, and the eagles had quickly settled into the routine that would last for 43 days. The female later left the nest to join the male and two peregrines, and he dropped down to cover the eggs as expected. The female disappeared into the murk of the valley head, and it was 38 minutes before I saw her again as she dip-displayed along the cloud base. The first sightings were often with the naked eye, but when I lifted my binoculars, it was to see two golden eagles displaying along the cloud base! I immediately looked through the telescope that was kept trained on the nest not believing that the male could have left and joined the female since I'd last checked. That would have been almost impossible, the nest was kept under almost constant scrutiny, especially when the female was away.

I hadn't missed his departure from the nest; the male was still sitting and was very alert. That was hardly surprising; in fact the surprise was that he was still there, given that his mate was flying with another male eagle. The two birds circled together, and I noticed the intruder was missing a secondary flight feather from his left wing – it was the male from my first pair. He'd lost his mate over winter and had found his way to Riggindale in search of a new partner. The two birds made two dips in unison and then turned away into the low cloud and rain. It was 20 minutes before the female returned, but when she did so it was to fly directly to the nest to relieve her mate, which then flew off as if nothing had happened.

The male returned to the nest at 1.45 p.m., delivering a clump of woodrush, but he had to leave again as his mate refused to stand. He flew up-valley and began to circle higher, and once he was above the skyline I put down my binoculars to watch with the naked eye and catch up on the note-taking, glancing back at him every few seconds so as not to lose track of him and prepared to raise the binoculars again if he dropped towards the ridge. When I looked up again it was to see a second eagle crossing the valley towards the nest. As before, a quick check through the scope told me the female was still sitting and that the intruder had returned. The female was alert and staring at the third bird and began to stand as it neared the ridge. The resident male had also seen it and was now speeding down-valley to intercept. The intruder slowed as it reached the ridge, and the female left the eggs unprotected to quickly circle higher with strongly beating wings, buoyed up by the blustery wind.

On seeing the eggs unattended, the resident male dropped to the nest in spite of the other male, and with the female closing in, the intruder began to display, performing a 'pot-hook' version of the dipping display. The female was almost with him by then, but the intruder turned away over the ridge and out of my sight. Oddly, instead of chasing it from the home range, the female swung back in and dropped down to the nest. The pair stood together and called before the female tweaked some sticks and sat. The male didn't leave, though, and stayed beside her for four minutes before relaxing and moving on. I thought it strange that neither resident had pursued the intruder, and it seemed as though the fact it had left the valley was enough to satisfy their territorial defence, even though it remained in the heart of their home range.

The eagles generally survived on a diet of sheep carrion at that time of year, supplemented by crows and ravens they caught in flight and by small birds and mammals they usually caught on the ground. There was usually plenty of carrion, but they seldom missed the opportunity to kill fresh prey when it presented itself. The male often ate first thing in the morning and again last thing in the evening while the female ate when necessary. The laying day in 1982 saw the male feeding from a carcass for 25 minutes in the evening, and the female was off the nest early the next day to feed from a second one. I hadn't seen the male eating that morning, so after 50 minutes on the nest, I expected him to fly straight to the food, but instead, he flew to a favourite perch and seemed to stare at a carcass before changing perches and only then dropping to the food. I was astonished to see a magpie fly from the carcass as the eagle landed. It was the first magpie I'd seen in the valley and was surprised that the eagle was beside it before it left; carrion crows and ravens would have been up and calling long before the eagle arrived.

The magpie didn't fly far, and once the eagle was feeding, it hopped back in to grab slivers of meat. It became bolder and eventually stood to feed on the opposite side of the carcass from the eagle, barely 50 cm away. It even dipped down and inside the carcass, completely out of sight of the eagle, and it seemed an easy target for the eagle to catch by jumping to that side, but the eagle didn't react at all, and the magpie four times flew away and returned without the eagle taking any notice. The two fed together like this for 30 minutes before the magpie eventually flew off and didn't return, leaving the eagle to eat alone for another seven minutes.

It was an odd sighting as the magpie must have presented an easy target for the eagle, and while I did occasionally see crows snatching bits of meat while an eagle ate, they were never as bold as the magpie and always grabbed and ran. The magpie flapped its way up the valley and below the perched eagle the next day, and the latter simply watched it go by. It even approached the nest that day without either eagle responding to its presence, and subsequently, magpies continued to be ignored whenever they were in the valley, even though they're known to be taken as prey by eagles in other areas.

Other species weren't so lucky or tolerated in that fashion. After feeding from a sheep carcass for 22 minutes on 1 April 1983, the female approached the nest to relieve her mate. Most unusually, the male stood as she approached and, perhaps surprised by his actions, the female stalled and circled before approaching again. The female was still several metres from the nest when the male flew off, and this was the first and only time during my years of close observation at the nest that a male eagle left the eggs for a changeover before its mate arrived. He crossed the valley in a fast glide and swung down the opposite ridge in a contour-hugging flight to flip over the only notable tree on that side, flush three pigeons and catch one of them as if he was an enormous sparrowhawk. He landed immediately and spent 19 minutes feasting on his prize. For him to leave the nest as he did and make a direct, though disguised, approach to make the kill I can only assume that he'd been watching the pigeons, about a kilometre from his nest, for some time and must have been willing his mate to return before the pigeons left the valley.

Almost three weeks later, on the 20th, I watched as the male left a perch on one side of the valley, and I assumed that he was heading off a raven and peregrine above the nest crag but then realised that he wasn't gaining any height as he crossed low above the hide and in towards the ridge. There was a flurry of wings, and once again, he snatched a pigeon from the air. He drifted down to a grassy knoll and began to pluck his prey, turning the carcass to clean both sides, even removing the smallest of feathers with a deft tweak of his beak. The entire process took about 10 minutes, and he then grasped the pigeon with one set of talons and took off to fly up towards the nest. I was interested to see if he would carry it to the nest as, unlike at the other pair, I'd never seen food taken in during the incubation period at this site. He flew straight past the nest, though, watched intently by his mate, and disappeared into the murk that would prevent me from seeing him again that day.

Six centimetres of snow fell overnight, and my first view of the female was when she stood on the nest to shake off what had accumulated on her back as she covered the eggs. The male relieved her shortly after 8 a.m., and the female flew directly to feed from a sheep carcass in the valley head, and although I didn't see him feeding after he'd been relieved of the nest duties, the male appeared later on with a bulging crop. He was dip-displaying at the time, and the third dip took him straight to the nest. His mate wasn't interested even though he spent 10 minutes standing there, and he eventually flew off to land in front of the top nest crag. When he flew again I was surprised to see that he was carrying a plucked, medium-sized bird, and I wondered if it was the pigeon from the previous day. He flew back down-valley, made a half-hearted stoop at a passing crow, and landed on the nest with the prey. The female stood and flew off with the bird. It was yet another of the questions the eagles would pose for me over the years. Was it the pigeon? I hadn't seen him kill anything that day, so if it was fresh why hadn't he taken it to the nest on his first or second visit, or directly after killing and plucking? If it was yesterday's capture, why hadn't he taken it to the nest then and why had he been feeding from another source? There's only one sure thing about working with eagles, you never have all the answers.

Chapter 7

Lakeland nestlings

As we entered May we could hope that the worst of the weather was behind us (although I'd see snow falling in July in some years); the days were lengthening and were warmer, and, of course, I could look forward to the eggs hatching. The dangers posed by egg collectors were over by then and, although there were more tourists on the hill who might deliberately or inadvertently cause disturbance around the eagle nest, what happened next was entirely in the hands of the birds themselves. If the eggs were fertile they'd hatch, if not they wouldn't, and I wouldn't be able to carry out the plans I'd so carefully formulated during the spring.

Incubation had begun on 23 March in 1982, so I was expecting to see evidence of the hatch 43 days later, on 5 May. To welcome us into the time of summer migrants and regrowth May started with constant rain and hail falling on a brisk northerly wind. The wind had turned southerly by the next morning, and although it was frosty at dawn, it augured well for a settled period of good weather just when it was needed. We had a double shift change at 4 p.m., and by the time John (the volunteer) and I had reached the hide the southerly wind was near gale force and rain fell heavily and constantly. We couldn't see the nest crag let alone the bird sitting there, but I expected the weather to clear during my 48 hours on duty and hoped to see signs that would at least point towards the first egg hatching.

We settled into the hide as best we could. I'd never felt comfortable in these garden sheds and always preferred to sleep in a tent when I could. The rocks on the roof of the hide might have given some confidence, but if it came to the crunch, I'd rather be wrapped up and blown away than be caught underneath a fallen roof. Even so, as the wind turned to a full gale I must have felt more secure than the eagle up there on the crag in a nest that seemed to be held in place by wishes rather than physics. The hide was tightly enclosed by the dry-stone walls of a sheepfold that rose to almost 2 metres on the blind sides and more than a metre in front. In fact, we couldn't fully lower the window shutter during the day, so close and high was the front wall. The only real gap in the defences was to allow the door to open but, again, even that couldn't open fully, and we had to squeeze through the gap to get inside. The hide was held together with durable coach-bolts and six-inch nails, had a roof weighed down by a variety of rocks and its walls were nailed down and weighted to the floor. The contents, plus our body weights, gave it an air of stability. By contrast, the other shed stood outside the main walls but was still enclosed by the sheepfold, and the tent lay in its lee.

John and I sat on the bench seat and peered at the window because we couldn't open it due to the force of the wind, and the falling rain made it impossible to see through it. From a full gale the wind increased to severe and still the rain fell, it found every crack in the woodwork, and John and I sat in full waterproofs and rubber boots to stay dry while inside the hide. Lashed by the rain, the hide came alive and breathed with the wind, gusts bowing the walls inwards and lulls allowing them to exhale again. Rocks slid from the roof, whether from the vibrations or the amount of water I couldn't tell, but I eventually stopped braving the elements to replace them and, instead, sat waiting for the next one to slide and plop into the mud that now surrounded us. The hide took such a buffeting that tinned food rattled its way from the shelves and crashed to the floor. The floor itself was too wet to leave anything on it, and there was no safe place to stow anything above floor level. We clung on with our bags of clothes and sleeping bags on our laps, the gas stove on the bench seat and all perishables hanging from nails in the walls.

The day was prematurely dark, and footsteps outside the hide made my heart sink. I'd seen some dozy visitors in my time, paddling up the valley in rain and nil visibility to bang on the door with the opening gambit of: 'Are they flying?', but this wasn't people, it was sheep. You know the weather's bad when the hill sheep desert their hefts and head for the lower ground. And they did just that; peering through the glass I could see lines of them filing past on their way to the comparative safety of the lake-shore. By 7 p.m. we were sitting out a full storm. Knowing that it couldn't get much worse was little consolation when you had to shout to make yourself heard against the noise of the rain and hail battering against the hide. I started to feel uncomfortable when I noticed that the hide was actually twisting on its base, the whole structure, weighed down by us, our equipment and rocks, being slowly edged around the sheepfold. The coach bolts and nails were twisting and tearing into the wood, and the constant movement of the walls pulled the panels away from their struts in creaking groans that sapped the confidence.

The rain grew heavier and hit us in walls of water rather than droplets as the wind howled about the valley, and even though we were on the sloping valley floor, the hide seemed to be an island within a lake. A lull and then a swirling roar heralded a mini-tornado, and we braced ourselves for the impact, but it went straight past and missed us. It didn't miss the storage shed, though, and an explosion of splintered wood crashed from only 2 metres away. Glass smashed against the rocks, and as I stared through the window, an entire wall went flying up the valley and disappeared into the murk. Planks and debris bounced off our hide, and the stored equipment clattered against the rocks. I stood in awe as a surge of wind delivered the flying wall back to us to be smashed against the rocks only a few metres away. There we were, in a garden shed about 5 km from the next human, with no means of communication with the outside world and soaked to the skin by staying inside. I sensed an expression of relief on John's face when I said it was time to go.

I left the decision to the very last minute, not wanting to desert my post or the eagles. We were already dressed and packed, not having changed our clothes since our arrival, so I thought we could have a few minutes salvaging the bigger remnants of the other shed and then just enough time for a slower than usual walk back to the road to meet up with the other wardens as they did the evening drive around the peregrine sites, assuming they'd bother doing it on such a night. We stepped outside, forced the door closed, wedged it with a rock and surveyed the devastation that lay around us. Where the smaller hide had been lay only splintered matchwood and shards of broken glass. Planks had been scattered to the four winds, and torn shreds of roofing felt littered the sheepfold, only the floor remained in place, weighed down by the heavier equipment and its selection of rocks. I quickly gathered the larger fragments and weighted them down to prevent them from damaging the hide or the tent and stood back to survey the sorry pile they made.

John leant on a corner of the remaining hide as I stooped to place a final rock on the pyre, and the wind struck again. The shed suddenly imploded causing John to fall in with it and then blew out, with John reeling away and the roof tipping over the highest wall. The shed's walls were folded like a pack of cards, thrown up against the wall and then collapsed in a heap. Rocks and wood went flying, the wall panels split as struts were snapped like twigs and coach-bolts and nails were wrenched through the wood. One steel bolt I later retrieved was bent at right angles to its length so great had been the force. If the shed had blown backwards it and the retaining dry-stone wall would have been on top of me as I piled up the other remnants, but fortunately, neither of us had been hurt. A two-minute delay, however, in my decision to leave would have seen us both inside the hide when it collapsed.

We couldn't delay any longer, and there was no question of our collecting this debris, so we set off out of the valley. There wasn't a dry footfall to be found as we splashed our way along, buffeted and blasted by the wind and weather that forced us into an uncontrolled stumbling run at times. We were grateful to have the wind behind us until we turned the final corner to face it head-on. Weighed down with equipment and walking in rubber boots we were exhausted when we reached the end of the road, but the timing was perfect, and to their credit, the others had made the peregrine run and were turning the last corner towards us as we arrived. We slumped onto the wall but then had to jump up and flag down the car as the driver didn't look like stopping.

I was in a sombre mood on the drive back to base, and I hardly slept that night. The memories of the two failures because of the weather at the other site were still fresh in my mind, and I doubted that the female eagle would sit through such a storm as this. I had premonitions of the nest collapsing from its rock and smashing the eggs, and it was with some trepidation that John and I set out the next morning to complete our watch. The weather had somewhat improved by then, but we still took a drenching on the walk and couldn't see the nest crag when we arrived at the hide. There was debris everywhere; the main hide was just a pile of broken panels, and even the tent had collapsed, its waterproof groundsheet holding the water in rather than keeping it out.

The cloud had lifted by 8 a.m. to reveal the nest crag, and through the telescope I could see the nest and then the female's head surveying the scene around her, unfussed and relaxed. It looked good, but I didn't know if she'd been on all night or if she'd returned at first light. I joined her in scanning the valley for the male, but it was four hours before he arrived at the nest to relieve her. By then she must have been sitting for at least 22 hours, and yet she was only off for six minutes, just long enough for her to perform her ablutions, stretch her wings and shake out the stiffness from her long vigil. I hoped it was a good sign and kept watch for more during the next couple of days, but my mood blackened on the 5th. The eagles were calling, gathering and delivering nest material, and they left the nest unattended for eight minutes while they perched together near the high point of the opposite ridge. Would they leave a newly hatched chick and an unhatched egg alone like that or were they just winding down the breeding attempt because it had failed? I'd changed the wardening roster because there was now no means of sheltering overnight in the valley, and so left at lunchtime and missed the first food being taken in that afternoon. The first egg had hatched in spite of the storm.

There were no such problems with the weather during the next two years, and for the sake of my planned study project, it was fantastic news that the birds would breed successfully in three consecutive years. I'd be able to follow the chicks' development to and beyond their first flight. I'd already seen two successful breeding seasons through to fledging, of course, but there were still new things to be seen and new situations to address, and the post-fledging period was the most important of those as far as I was concerned.

I was on duty when the first food went to the nest in 1983. I'd followed the male to his roost the previous evening, on this occasion using a ledge rather than his favourite tree, a ledge on which he would begin to build a new nest in 1989. He was still there when the lightness of the morning allowed me to check, and he didn't fly until 4.11 a.m. He made his way past the nest crag and straight to a lamb carcass in the valley head. After studying the carcass he began to pluck, cut and eat it. Through the telescope I could clearly see him using his hooked beak to rip through the skin and flesh and see him pushing backwards for a greater purchase and heaving up with powerful neck muscles. It was 69 minutes before he began to drag the carcass higher, grasped in one set of talons as he flappy-hopped through the rocks. He struggled with the lamb's weight and stopped and rested for long and often; panting hard his breath condensed on the cold morning air.

It was another hour before the eagle had gained enough height to attempt a flight, but he landed heavily after about 80 metres to catch his breath and rest before plucking a few more beakfuls of wool from the lamb (as if that would reduce its weight!) and then beginning to make a series of short flights that brought him around the valley and onto the centre of the nest crag. He was obviously aware that the lamb's weight was too great for him to carry it directly across the open valley, and by following the ridgeside, he'd made the distance without losing any height. Meanwhile, the female had left the nest and was by then perched on a ledge with her wings wafting to dry on the breeze. When she saw her mate approaching she gave eight yelps, and the male replied with 24. It was a conversation; she gave four and the male five, her three to his six. She returned to the nest after that, and the male flew to a tree; it was the first time he'd left the carcass in three and a quarter hours, but it still wasn't at the nest. In fact, it was another 90 minutes before the female flew across to it, grasped it with her right talons and hauled it to the nest. The chick's first feed began almost immediately.

I also saw the first food delivery in 1984. That hatching day was heavily overcast at first, and it was difficult to see the nest, but my first sighting of the male was of him swinging out from the ridgeside pursued by two crows and carrying what appeared to be a third. He swung away from his pursuers, landed, called and began to pluck. After eight minutes he pulled off the crow's legs and ate them before resuming his plucking. When he flew I assumed that he'd go straight to the nest, but he turned to perform six display dips while carrying the crow, with the last dip taking him to a higher perch. He looked around and flew about 150 metres closer to the nest and called from a rock. He jumped into a tree, still carrying the crow, and called again. He took off, displayed, landed and called before soaring away, this time leaving the crow. I couldn't know whether there was a kind of ritual to the first food being delivered, or whether it was because the eagles knew the hatch was imminent, but they seemed to go through this palaver every time they bred successfully. And, as in previous years, the male carrying food to a ledge near the nest proved to be the best indication of the hatch. But I still couldn't answer why he didn't just take the food straight there!

Even though I was satisfied that an egg had hatched, I made my way to a distant ledge the next morning from which I knew I could see into the nest without the disturbing the eagles. I had to make the peregrine run first, of course, and so didn't arrive until about 6.45 a.m., but the female was on the nest and sitting with her wings partly open, presumably to take some of her weight. She was relaxed and either hadn't seen my approach or was unperturbed by my presence. I was still about 500 metres away and in front of the crag, so she could keep an eye on me if she wasn't happy. There were no problems, though, and the male flew past about 40 minutes later and didn't even turn his head to look at me. Beside the female lay an emaciated lamb, it wasn't bloody and so had been dead when the eagles found it, almost certainly a stillbirth. After watching the male go by, the female began to pick at the lamb without standing and pulled off two pieces of meat, snippering each in her beak, almost as if she were drinking. I was reminded of the old tales of eagles drinking the blood of their victims, but there was no blood in this lamb.

The female stretched her neck to peer beneath her body and then stood. Picking up the lamb with her hooked beak, she moved it easily to the front of the nest and got a better grip with her talons. As she began to tear the meat, the tiny chick wavered into view for the first time; barely able to hold up its head it wobbled from side to side before reaching up towards the adult, its black bead-like eyes still full of sleep, but it knew what to do. I couldn't hear any calling because of the distance, but the female also knew what it wanted. She pulled a snippet from the lamb and then did something I'd never seen before.

At first I thought she was just getting the morsel into the correct position, but through the telescope I could see her manoeuvre it in her beak, I could see her tongue pressing it against the roof of her mouth as if tenderising it or perhaps even adding moisture as the chick, obviously, had no opportunity to drink while on the nest. She pushed the sliver to the front of her beak and tenderly tilted her head down and to one side to present the meat to the chick. She did this with all six pieces she offered to the chick and showed incredible patience. Even though the pieces she offered were tiny the chick was tiny as well, and it struggled to swallow them. The adult, however, wouldn't tear off another piece until the previous one had been swallowed, and she watched and waited for each piece to go down in case the chick choked. Fully sated after this minuscule meal, the chick slumped back into the nest cup, and the adult carefully stepped over it with open talons and slowly settled down to brood, rocking from side to side as she lowered her great body down to warm the chick.

Watching the eagles preparing their food was always fascinating, be it the chase and the kill or just the butchery of a carcass. On 26 May 1983, the female managed to catch one of the four lambs left in the valley after gathering. It was 6.38 p.m., and the eagles had been circling together before the female broke away to snatch a lamb that had wandered from the ewe and carry it to a lower ledge. The male made three display dips as the female mantled the terrified victim and took the prescribed four minutes to kill the lamb. She then released her grip and began to pluck the carcass almost immediately, and I, to the amusement of Keith, the volunteer, began to count the pieces she tore off.

In the first seven minutes the eagle tore off 347 pieces of wool, cleaning one flank of the lamb. She cut through the skin and spent four minutes eating intestines and then 25 feasting on the internal organs. She plucked again and removed 129 pieces of wool, pulling each off with a twist of her beak and discarding them with a flick of her head. She dragged the carcass higher and, after resting, removed another 113 pieces and then stepped away. She flew to a tree without the carcass and wiped her beak on a branch, deliberately cleaning the edges of both mandibles; she defecated, pulled off but dropped a twig, tweaked off a second and flew to the nest with it. After spending five minutes arranging the new twig to her liking, she looked around and then sat to brood the chick for the night; she'd been at the lamb for a minute less than an hour. Having watched his mate make the kill, the male made brief visits to two old carcasses, feeding for 14 minutes, but he flew straight to the fresh kill as soon as his mate had left. He took his turn and removed 163 pieces of wool and then ate for 11 minutes before going to roost.

The female left the nest at 3.30 the next morning and flew straight to the carcass. She wasted no time in plucking or feeding, but having looked around to check for intruders, she gripped the lamb with both sets of talons and flew straight back to the nest, where she fed the chick for 15 minutes. It was interesting that the eagles were happy to leave the carcass unattended overnight in a valley where there were both scavenging foxes and badgers, and that again, in spite of the fresh food being on the nest, the female flew to feed on one of the older carcasses two hours later.

This suggested that the eagles knew the chick needed fresh food more than they did although, of course, they could kill fresh prey if they needed it. There were many opportunities for them, not just with the lambs; crows and pigeons provided a substantial meal and there were titbits as well. The Haweswater male became well known for his taste for ring ouzels, and I watched him farming many an ouzel nest. He'd follow an adult by sight or pick up on the location when he was mobbed. Going in he'd remove the chicks one at a time, sometimes taking them to his own nest at regular intervals but also treating himself to a chick if he was peckish. He did the same with meadow pipits and field voles that could have offered no more than a taster. It always seemed that the eagle chick received the best that was available (even grouse were delivered from time to time), but that changed in June 1983 when the eagles suffered what proved to be their most severe breeding season food shortage.

The female delivered part of a lamb to the nest on the 19th, and after feeding the chick for 35 minutes, she fed herself for 10. There was nothing unusual in that as the female consumed a large part of her diet at that time of year by sharing with the chick, but 11 minutes after she left the nest the male arrived and ate for 18 minutes. He totally ignored the chick that called and begged beside him and then flew off. He hadn't even arrived with a token twig, and it was the first time I'd ever seen a male feed on the nest in this way. He delivered two ring ouzels the next day but later returned without prey and fed himself from the carcass again. A larger prey item reached the nest in my absence on the 22nd, and the male was back to feed shortly after his mate had left, for 20 minutes, and he returned to feed again only two and a half hours after that. The food shortage was clearly biting hard and, for the first time, I began to wonder if the chick was receiving enough food to survive.

Apart from a dry lamb on the 27th, I was seeing little more than voles going to the nest, and Chris and Ken had similar tales to tell: there'd be a large item one day but then nothing. The female was feeding the chick when I arrived on the 28th, and the male flew in to feed once she'd left. This was becoming routine, but seven minutes later the female returned. I wondered what would happen, had she failed to see the male stealing the chick's food on the previous occasions but was now about to defend the food? To my amazement the male didn't defend his share of the food, he simply dragged it to one side and continued to feed. The female fed the chick a few morsels but then began to feed herself, and I had the unique sighting of two adult golden eagles feeding themselves on the nest while ignoring the screaming eaglet that stood beside them. This was also the longest I'd seen the adults at the nest together, and it was the nearest I ever came to seeing two adults feeding simultaneously from the same carcass.

It was a worrying time, and yet although this was by far the worst example, there seemed to be some degree of food shortage during most of the Junes in which I made detailed observations. It's perhaps why, in later years, I would find six- or seven-week-old chicks dead in a number of Scottish nests. It was easy to see why, having survived the battering they receive in the first couple of weeks of life, the younger chick of twins often succumbs at about that age. They can cope with the most foul of winters, but eagles seem to suffer their hardest times in June as it coincides with a decline in carrion and is before live prey becomes fully available.

Fortunately for this chick, it was the only one, in good health and the food shortage seemed to pass shortly afterwards; I didn't see the male feeding on the nest again. The question of how twins would have survived didn't arise in 1983, but we may have come close in 1982. After briefly seeing twins in 1980, I had high hopes for 1982, and sure enough, both eggs hatched that year. Just as in 1980, however, the second chick's greeting to the world was a battering from its nest-mate. There was plenty of food at that time for the tiny chicks, and the feeds almost seemed excessive. Feeding times of 40 minutes were commonplace with the chicks less than a week old, and by two weeks of age there were feeds of 61 minutes in the morning followed by one of 58 minutes shortly after midday. Such feasts didn't stop the beatings, though, and provided further evidence to show that the attacks had little to do with food supply.

Watching Cain's attacks on Abel were as tragic in 1982 and they'd been in 1980. Cain stood by as Abel was being fed and then attacked as soon as the feed was over. The attacks seemed more vicious than in 1980, and again, the adults appeared disinterested. After a repeated pounding, Abel eventually flopped onto the nest front and lay unmoving. When the female sat to brood Cain after feeding she showed no interest in Abel, and I thought its life was over, and yet 10 minutes later Abel managed to crawl underneath the adult. There were more attacks later that day, and with feeds of only 13, 25 and 10 minutes the next day, I imagined that the end had come.

Incredibly, and even though I hadn't seen it for two days, the second chick then reappeared, and the chicks sat side by side apparently happy to watch the adults as they dealt with a peregrine above the ridge. Abel looked battered but had survived for 16 days; I had hope after all, but it wasn't to be. That was the last time I saw Abel and was, in fact, the last time I'd see two chicks in a Lakeland nest. I had mixed emotions: it was tragic to lose an eaglet in that fashion, but it was fascinating to watch, not least because golden eagles don't kill prey with their beaks.

There are many reasons why 1982 proved to be an interesting year. To start with, the breeding success resulted in golden eagles being ringed in England for the first time. The RSPB had prevented me from having input with the other eagles, much to my frustration, so I missed the very first ringing, but on 13 June, I was in Riggindale for the great event which would, of course, also see me at the nest for the first time while it was in use. Geoff Horne couldn't give me a precise arrival time, and we had no means of communication, but I was in the valley overnight and knew enough not to get caught out by his early appearance. Geoff was the peregrine man but had also been one of the first people to see an eagle egg in England for almost 200 years, photographing the first egg to be laid in March 1969.

I was half expecting Geoff to arrive fairly early in the morning and come up the valley from the lake, but I knew he'd be ringing a brood of peregrines before coming to the eagles so I kept a watch on the ridgetop just in case. It was a dull overcast day, so visibility wasn't great, and I missed him crossing the ridge. In fact, he, John and Bob sneaked through a hollow and were already moving as fast as they could towards the crag before I spotted them. I never asked if he was testing our response, but it was a good exercise to see how quickly we might react to egg collectors, so I set off at once to see if I could reach the crag in time to stop the 'robbery'. It was about 500 metres across the slopes for them and almost a kilometre uphill for me, the final approach being through boulder fields and greasy rocks. Geoff had to unpack his ropes and find a belay, of course, and I reached the foot of the crag just as he landed on the nest. It was clear that, if the wardens were alert, we could have stopped the robbery, although it would have been interesting to try the experiment with some of the other wardens who worked here!

I waited at the foot of the crag while Geoff examined and ringed the chick before he abseiled down to join me. I couldn't see a great deal as I was underneath the nest, but it was fantastic to see the bird ringed. Geoff had been hoping to ring the eagles from the first hatch in 1970, but he'd been prevented from doing so; he'd missed nine opportunities, but now he'd ringed two in one year. I had a request for him before he left the nest, though. Information had come through that an egg collector had planned to target the Lakes birds, and I had to ask him to look for a fishing line. It seemed that the plan had been to attach the line above the nest so that it could be found in the dark. It seemed a bit far-fetched, and there wasn't anything to be found either here or at the other nest, where I'd already looked. I further distracted Geoff on his way down as, and again for the first time ever, I'd been seeing the eagles taking food to a cache in a niche just around from the nest. Again there was nothing to be found, and when he eventually joined me Geoff gave me the bad news.

The chick had a deformed beak; the upper mandible was undersized and twisted to one side. Even worse, he told me that the chick at the other pair was similarly deformed. Once John and Bob had gathered the ropes and joined us, we talked about it all the way back to the hide without reaching any conclusions. The most obvious explanations were food shortages and inbreeding, but while I couldn't comment on what was happening at the other site, I'd seen no evidence of food shortages at Haweswater. It was a similar situation to sibling aggression; at the time of the fights or deformities the chicks were simply too small to be affected by food supply. If the adults couldn't find sufficient food during those first days the chicks wouldn't survive to be ringed at six weeks of age. The other possible explanation for the deformities – inbreeding – just didn't seem credible. Given the breeding histories it was, however, possible for all four of the 1982 adults to be related (they could all have been brothers and sisters), and it was actually possible for the 1982 Haweswater female to be either the daughter of the male to which she was paired, to be his sister or his cousin. It was also possible that none of the four adults were in any way related, of course. There was no way of knowing, and because none of the earlier chicks had been ringed we didn't know if they'd been deformed as well.

A possible clue revealed itself a few years later when I read a paper about similar deformities in waterfowl in the USA. The cause there was believed to be relatively high levels of selenium in the food chain. Coincidence or not, the farmers in both eagle valleys began providing supplementary feed blocks for their sheep in the winter of 1981/82, and these contained additional levels of selenium. I wondered if this had become con-

68

centrated in the late winter sheep carrion and if its sudden appearance in their diet had taken an immediate effect on the eagles. We would never know.

I was able to witness the ringing at close quarters in 1983, and to see for myself that the bird wasn't deformed. In fact, none of the subsequent chicks showed any visible deformities (though there may have been internal abnormalities), so the mystery of 1982 will remain forever unsolved. With the birds using the middle nest in 1983, the easiest access was from below, so I went along with Geoff and got to perform the 'eagleman's leap'.

It was a straightforward scramble to the nest ledge with the only tricky move being the final step up from a lower ledge. This necessitated stepping up and across a triangular chimney (and slightly round a corner at the same time), and the handhold was a pressure grip made by thrusting your arm between two slabs of rock and opening your fist until it locked into place. Getting there, with the adrenalin pumping, was easy enough and watching Geoff handle the docile chick was enjoyable (this one just sat and allowed him to pull out its leg, slip on the ring and push the leg back again) but turning round on the narrow ledge and getting back to the lower one was a different matter altogether. It was, quite simply, easiest to jump across the chimney, round the corner and land on the lower ledge, without a safety rope, and hope that you stopped before you slid over the edge!

There were more new records in1982. I'd heard the female at the other pair make a peculiar call in 1979 and heard the same thing from the 1980 Haweswater female, but the 1982 bird took it to excess. It was very similar to the nestling's call but was much more raucous, and it seemed to resound about the valley with anger and viciousness. I would hear it again in Scotland in 1987, but these seem to be the only records of its use. Although there were no food shortages at the time, the call was definitely linked to food, just as it is with the nestling, and the best example was in June 1982 when I was on watch with Edna, a visiting Israeli ecologist.

The female had roosted away from the nest the previous evening, and her first visit of the day was to remove, rather than deliver, food. The male came to the nest shortly before 4.30 a.m., without food, and as he left and crossed the valley, the female gave the call from her tree perch, an evil-sounding 'wee-yow'. She screeched at the male for two minutes and then less intensely for three more, and he seemed to understand the message as he gained height and left the valley. I expected him to return with food, but he was back a minute later to ignore his mate and land in a tree near the middle nest, more than a kilometre from the female. When he drifted back up the valley half an hour later she screamed at him again but then went into displacement behaviour. With no food available, she delivered six pieces of material to the nest, grasses, heather, a dead stick and a leafy twig, before finding her way to a high perch. When the female saw the male visiting the nest she quickly joined him, but he hadn't carried food, and she followed him off to circle beside the crag. Frustrated, she broke away to stoop at a lamb but it evaded her, and after flying towards another that ran back to the ewe, she flew back to the high perch. The male continued to circle and gain height and then turned out of the valley.

The female could see out of the valley from her perch and became very alert at 9.01 a.m. She flew to circle higher, perhaps to get a better view, and then dropped to land close to her last perch and gave three of the screaming shouts. I knew the male must be carrying food, and after the female gave two more of the calls, he entered the valley about 300 metres from her perch. He'd been away for 87 minutes. The male quickly dropped up-valley, possibly losing height because of the weight of his prey, and as he did I tentatively identified what he carried but didn't mention it to Edna as it seemed so improbable. When he landed on a short buttress the female gave six more of her screeches, impatient that he hadn't flown straight to the nest. The male flew again and I was certain of his prey, a black cat. Edna wasn't convinced, but there it was, its tail streaming out behind the eagle, it couldn't be anything else.

The female gave another 11 screams when the male landed and continued to do so when he flew again. When she realised that this flight would take him to the nest she took off and, screaming all the way, followed him to thump onto the nest and screech in his ear. The male was away at once with the female screaming until he was well on his way to his favourite perch. The eaglet had pounced on the male's arrival, and once it relaxed the female fed it for 27 minutes. As a postscript to this, when I went round the perches after the chick had left the nest, as well as the remains of two foxes and four red deer calves, I found the cat's palate, with all the teeth still in place, to confirm the identification I'd made while the bird was in flight.

There was another unusual prey item in 1984. It was 2 July, and I was expecting to see something of interest as I'd watched the male hunting for voles the previous evening and the female collecting nest material. At shortly after 5 a.m., the male performed five display dips and then landed down-valley of the nest. He was up almost immediately and down again to land on a large badger cub. It was already dead but was in an odd place for a dead badger to be lying, so I wondered if the eagles had killed it and carried it the previous day. It was possible, in 1980 Paul and Alan had seen the bird kill a badger cub. The eagle began to pluck the badger but soon stopped to grip it and look around. He took off down-valley with it in his talons and then swung back up, his momentum gaining him some height as he turned into the breeze. He began to circle higher but was dragged down by the chunky weight of even quite a small badger to crash into the ground and stand panting hard from his exertions. The female arrived to drive away a peregrine that circled above the male, and after plucking off two or three beakfuls of hair, he flew again. He struggled to gain sufficient height to reach the nest but managed it and thumped down to be greeted, as usual, by the screaming, flapping, pouncing nestling that was, by then, almost as big as himself. The eaglet mantled over the food as the male left and continued to do so when the female arrived, but it soon relented and, with the chick now 57 days old, allowed the female to feed it for 64 minutes. It then decided that it could feed itself and ate for a further 14. But it then accepted food from the female for another 28 minutes. That gave a total feed length of 106 minutes, the longest I'd seen.

Life at Haweswater wasn't all to do with learning new things about eagles and being able to spend hours, days, weeks and months in their company, there were also the people. Tourists were a constant source of frustration: they had to be entertained, informed and shown the birds even though this was a protection, not a public, scheme, a fact of which I was repeatedly reminded. In spite of the illegality, there were disturbance incidents every year, and a classic came just six days after the badger went to the nest. I was approaching the end of a fairly uneventful 48-hour watch when the eagles started to circle and swoop in an obvious disturbance display. It was a Sunday, and I had 27 visitors at the hide with me. I explained what seemed to be happening, but it was another six minutes before two men suddenly appeared at the top of the nest spur and began to descend towards the nest face. They obviously weren't egg collectors but both carried sacks that were large enough to hold climbing gear, and I assumed they were trying to photograph the chick.

I set off from the hide as quickly as I could, leaving the visitors to keep watch and act as witnesses. Having covered the route only a couple of weeks earlier to meet Geoff, I knew I could get to the crag in time, but it was still a lung-bursting dash, made worse by the knowledge that I was doing it for real this time. The men reached the top of the nest face and began to peer over the edge, moving about to get a better angle and demonstrating that they were looking for the nest; a single look over the edge would have told them that there was no route down from there. The men were as close to the nest as they could be, but fortunately, it was set back in a recess and was out of sight from above.

I called them off the crag, and one of them clambered back up and quickly found the route down to me, but the other seemed determined to find the nest, and he was the one with the camera around his neck. I directed him from the crag and then led them both down to the hide, calmly explaining what I was doing as we walked and trying to extract some information without direct questioning. They seemed to relax and told me they'd been fell walking in the area for more than 20 years but had only heard of the eagles the previous evening. They had no more than a passing interest in wildlife and it was just a coincidence that they'd entered the valley over the eagle crag (instead of down the grassy slope in front of the crag). They weren't carrying binoculars, but their story didn't ring true, and their expressions changed when we neared the hide and they realised how many people had been watching them. It was then that I asked for names and addresses, and they became quite flustered, probably not daring to refuse with so many genuine birdwatchers surrounding them.

I'd been here before, and just as I'd done with Alan in 1980, I let the men walk away down-valley and then followed them. I didn't know if the addresses they'd given me were correct, so I aimed to reach The Rigg in time to read the registration number of their car and pass that on to the RSPB. To my surprise, when they reached the end of the track they didn't turn towards the car park but walked in the opposite direction and then stopped. They looked around to see if they were being watched and then removed binoculars from their sacks. I was right to be suspicious, their claims of disinterest were lies, and they turned to scan a peregrine crag. I watched as they moved on, and once I was certain they weren't going on to the crag, I returned to the hide.

I reported the incident, but in spite of the RSPB's determination to counteract illegal interference with birds of prey I heard nothing back from them. When I eventually asked, I was told that the men had been sent a stern letter of condemnation asking them not to do it again. This would become a running theme. No matter how many known egg collectors or illegal falconers I caught, no matter how much disturbance I prevented or confronted, both in Cumbria and in Scotland, with eagles and peregrines, none of the cases would ever reach court. My efforts seemed pointless, and I wondered if I shouldn't just react like the other wardens I worked with, the ones who just ignored any interference that occurred. In later years, I'd visit the hide and see people camped in the head of the valley and walking out past the hide without stopping and without the wardens even talking to them. I often wondered why I bothered to make all the effort I did, but then again, any day now, an eaglet would make its first flight from a nest in England.

The West Cumbrian nesting valley was not my idea of golden eagle country.

My first eagle nest was on little more than a rocky outcrop.

The 1981 nest crag was in a more remote and rocky location – the nest was no more than a pad of soft material.

left: *The last breeding attempt here was in a ground nest in 1982.* top right: *The 1982 nestling was found to have a deformed beak (courtesy of G. Horne).* bottom right: *Curiously the nestling reared in the eastern Lake District that year was similarly deformed (courtesy of G. Horne).*

Riggindale, by Haweswater, better fitted the image of eagle country.

As well as being the first person to ring a Lake District eagle Geoff Horne was also on hand to photograph the first eggs in 1969.

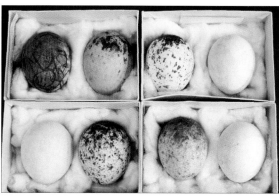

The unhatched 1985 eggs illustrate why eagle eggs are so highly prized by collectors (courtesy of G. Horne).

Other unhatched eggs (including those from 1969 – top left with scribbling to deter collectors) are held in Tullie House Museum, Carlisle.

The 1985/86 winter was one of the most severe I saw.

Ringing the 1986 nestling allowed me my closest view.

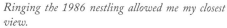

I was later able to stalk this bird after fledging.

The middle nest before it was destroyed by egg collectors.

I followed the Haweswater female from her arrival in 1982 until her death in 2004. She remained the darkest adult golden eagle I have seen.

The handsome male was already at Haweswater when I arrived and survived until 2001.

The last photograph of the female, taken less than an hour before my last ever sighting of her.

CHAPTER 8

First flights

Unlike the 1983 bird on the middle nest, the 1982 and 1984 eaglets found their develop-ment very restricted on the top nest, which had no ledges or trees alongside onto which they could venture and explore. These eaglets often knocked great lumps of material from the nest as they exercised and sometimes came close to falling out at the same time, just as had happened in 1980. There hadn't been a first flight in 1979 or 1980, and while I had high hopes of seeing the fabled event, I began to have doubts about it happening. The 1982 chick, in the top nest, and the 1983 bird, in the middle nest, both simply jumped out and parachuted to the ground below. By then I really was wondering if the first flight was a legend, and if those reported were the result of disturbance or were actually a later flight by a bird that had returned to the nest some time after fledg-ing; or perhaps they were just a flight of fancy.

When I arrived at the hide in 1982, Alan and a volunteer announced that the eaglet had flown. It had, apparently, left the nest and then, a little while later, flown again to pursue two ravens down-valley past the hide (only narrowly failing to catch one of them in a rolling, talon-flashing lunge) and then returned to circle over the nest crag before settling to roost in the valley head. They hadn't seen the adults at the time, but when I looked through the telescope they'd fixed on the bird all I could see was the adult female. I switched to the nest crag, and there, in the bracken where it had landed on jumping from the nest, stood the eaglet! I had high hopes for the 1983 bird, and its activity seemed to say that it was brave and game for anything. It had spent days dashing from the nest to the ledge and then back across to the stick platform; it pounced, jumped and flapped from one to the other and ran with raised wings as if to gain momentum, but it wasn't to be – it stopped, looked over the edge and jumped to the ground below. Four out of four nestlings hadn't made a first flight from the nest.

With the top nest again in use in 1984 there seemed to be another opportunity for a first flight, and I returned day after day in the hope of seeing it fly, but this bird didn't seem in the slightest bit interested in leaving the nest. The fledging period obviously varied in length from bird to bird, with the youngster of 1983 leaving the nest only 72 days after it hatched, but they averaged about 76 days.

The eaglet was still in the nest on Day 84 in 1984 and fed itself at 6.30 a.m. before taking a short nap prior to beginning its daily exercises. Flapping its broad wings and shouting at the top of its voice, it stomped about the nest and picked and pulled at the nest material. It engaged in long sessions of pouncing (as if on to prey), gripping (as if to kill) and throwing (as in plucking) various bits of the nest and food remains and did so continuously until 9.30 a.m. when it got bored and slumped down with its beak resting on the front of the nest. The male delivered food an hour later, was knocked backwards from the nest by the charging chick (as usual), and the chick ate for eight minutes and then fell asleep again. Even at this late date there was no suggestion of the chick being starved from the nest.

When it awoke again at 6 p.m., the chick didn't even bother to stand but just lay there shouting whenever an adult came into view and for several minutes after it flew out of sight again, presumably just in case it returned. After half an hour of this, it climbed to its feet and began exercising on the front of the nest. It flapped its wings three times at 6.37 p.m. and then made 12 flaps, and two more. At 6.40 p.m., it opened and closed its wings, and at 6.41 p.m. it leant forward, nodded its head twice and jumped off the nest. A first flight! What could now officially be called a juvenile eagle flapped awkwardly, lost height, skidded across a flat-topped rock, came to a halt and looked around. It had flown all of 30 metres. Not quite the majestic master of the skies the books might have led me to expect, but it had made a first flight, there was no doubt about that.

The next few weeks in these years were some of the best of my eagling days. Three consecutive successes meant that I could collect enough information on the juveniles not only to satisfy my own curiosity but to write about and publish my findings. I'd realised in 1979 that virtually nothing was known about the post-fledging period; just as it was assumed that the first flight would be a thing of great significance and distance, so it was assumed that the juveniles would follow the adults about the home range, be taught how to kill and eventually be driven away from their birthplace to seek out a home of their own. These were the events I wanted to see, and I was prepared for the long days, the long walks over hill and valley and the frustrations of losing track of the eagles as the adults led the juveniles about their range.

I'd seen the 1979 adults redirect the juvenile's wanderings to lead it to safety but was still surprised to see something similar in 1982. There were many more people walking the Haweswater hills than at the other site and, with the nest below a well-walked ridge, there was the potential for greater human disturbance here, and so, as in 1979, these adults guided their juvenile to a safe place. For the first couple of days off the nest all the juveniles I'd seen stayed where they landed, they didn't fly but just wandered around a little and spent most of the time calling, sleeping and stripping vegetation. It was satisfying to see this because if they'd behaved differently there'd be no pattern to their behaviour and no sound conclusions could be reached, but they were the same when they were first off the nest, regardless of how long it had taken them to fledge.

One of the first things I noticed in 1982 was that the male delivered all the food to the juvenile, and this continued throughout the later years. Not once did I see the female deliver food to a youngster after it left the nest. The female's involvement was passive, to say the least, and the only close contact she had with any of the juveniles was with the 1982 bird. I would see her twice feed it beak to beak, but of course, this juvenile had a deformed beak. I worried about its survival chances, but I'd seen it plucking, tearing and eating its own food on the nest, so there was no reason why it shouldn't continue now that it was on the ground.

The male at first delivered food to where the juvenile had landed, either directly under the nest or to the 1984 bird's landing strip. I was then amazed to see the adults behave towards the 1982 juvenile just as the other pair had towards their juvenile in 1979. The male started to land with food 10 to 20 metres away, drawing the juvenile towards him and on a course towards a safe perch, *the dome,* some 300 metres away. Once it was there the male delivered its food directly, and the female kept her distance to dissuade it from moving any further. 1979 had taught me not to be too concerned about the lack of proper flights from the juvenile, but the deformed beak was always in my mind, and in 1982 the behaviour seemed to be continuing for longer than in 1979, although I caused that bird to fly, of course. Now, only three years later, I was confident that (apart from its beak) the juvenile had no problems, and there was nothing to worry about.

To my delight I saw exactly the same behaviour when the same nest was used in 1984; the juvenile was at first restricted to its landing site, it was then led into the valley head and introduced to the safe perch. As with the other pair's *chair,* it was a 'safe perch' because the location provided a cryptic backdrop and an uninterrupted view of all the approach routes. If danger threatened when the adults were absent, the juvenile would have ample time to move away.

The behaviour in 1983 was the reverse of what I'd previously seen, and I was a little puzzled by the changes at first. The male always took food to below the nest in this year and waited for the juvenile to claim it, even when the latter had wandered away a little. The female either kept her distance or settled above the nest, and the male used the lure of food to prevent the juvenile from wandering too far, but there was a reason for this. While the top nest, used in 1982 and 1984, was on a bare rock face, the middle nest, used in 1983, was surrounded by trees, ledges, lush vegetation, boulders, overhangs and outcrops and was, in spite of being more accessible, much more cryptically positioned. It was well hidden and easily missed, and even though, by jumping out, the juvenile effectively found itself at the foot of the nest rock it was still among boulders and bracken and trees that would disguise its position. The adults clearly recognised this as a safe location on a par with the safe perches and used their influence to prevent the juvenile from wandering either along the ridge or towards the valley floor.

With the juveniles on their safe perches it was now a case of waiting to see when they decided to fly. I was in the valley by first light on most mornings and could almost invariably find the bird where I'd left it the previous evening. When I couldn't it was because it was still asleep or had walked behind a rock, but a passing adult soon caused it to call and reveal its position. The calling could be deceptive, though, and there were many occasions when I was fooled by the eagle's apparent ventriloquial skills. The juvenile turning its head or standing behind a rock when calling could bounce the sound around the valley, and my head was often turning when I first heard them call. My efforts to locate them also weren't helped by my determination not to disturb the eagles, forcing me to watch from a long way down-valley of where they were. I was often recording from more than 2 km away, but I soon learned the trick of listening-back to the sound and realised that where I last saw the bird on the previous visit was usually the best place to start looking on the next visit, no matter how many hours had intervened.

I didn't expect to see the juveniles leave their safe perches because I wasn't on watch all day every day, but I wanted to see the first flight from the valley and didn't know if the two events might coincide. It was only August, so the days were still long, and because my RSPB contracts ended on 31 July, I also had to earn a living of sorts to finance what I wanted to do, so there were frustrating times wondering what I'd find when I next returned to Riggindale. The juvenile's advance towards the safe perch included a few flappy-flights and no real distance was covered, but I was still surprised to find the 1982 juvenile attached to the safe perch for so long. It was, in fact, almost three weeks before the bird made a serious flight out over the open valley, everything before that had been ridge-hugging. And that pattern was repeated in the subsequent years, even the strong 1984 bird struggled at times, not least because of the weather.

August 1984 was exceptionally hot, so both adults and juvenile suffered. While the golden eagle can be found in arid locations, the British bird is more used to cold and damp than hot and dry. I'd seen the adults panting through exertion when dragging food, but in this month they panted to keep cool and sought the shade of leafy trees. But it was the juvenile that suffered the most. It was so hot on the 22nd that the young bird made its way lower down the slope and began to walk about the boulder field. At first I thought it was vole-hunting like the adults (I'd seen the first flight and thought I might be about to see the first kill), but it walked up to a large boulder and then crawled into the shady hollow formed by a wash-out beneath the rock. It lay down, put its head on one side and gasped for air. As the afternoon sun moved through the sky the shadow of the ridge was eventually cast over the rock, and the juvenile struggled out to flap heavily into the valley head and even deeper shade.

The heat wave continued, and all animal life suffered. The woolly sheep flopped down from where they stood, and the red deer sought out the higher slopes to rest and chew the cud where what little breeze there was would drift by and perhaps take the edge off the heat; heads were stretched along the ground and they lay oblivious to events around them. Tourists walked the ridgetop paths barely 100 metres above them, but the deer paid no heed, and the unobservant humans went by without seeing. A week after it had been under the rock, I watched the young eagle make its way to the adults' favourite perch, *the ledge*, at some 700 metres above sea level. There it flopped down almost at once and lay prostrate, its head and neck outstretched, its tail fanned and one wing hanging limply over the edge. It was suffering from heat exhaustion, as was I; it was stifling on the valley floor without a breath of air and in the full glare of the sun. I was frazzled, and I wondered just how bad it was for the bird as it didn't move for almost four hours, and when it did, it was just to twitch its wing.

As I waited I noticed two people on the ridge above the bird. That wasn't too unusual even though the path was set back from the edge at that point, but these two were walking towards the edge. They began to descend the near-vertical drop in a stony shoot that passed close to *the ledge*, but they seemed unaware of their route or the bird. I'd been there myself on many occasions when collecting pellets and knew the best path through the outcrops, so I also knew that the route the men had chosen became even steeper as they went down. Eventually realising this themselves they sat and began to slither down some small screes, kicking loose stones and causing some slides. The eagle heard the noise and stood up slowly and stiffly, dragging itself upright to strain its neck and stare in the direction of the falling stones. Just then the men dislodged a proper rock that went tumbling down the slope, and alerted and alarmed, the eagle took off and swung straight past the men. They were taken by complete surprise, stumbled and almost fell as the great bird almost touched them with its wings as it flew by on its way to seek a perch near the nest crag.

That was only the second time I'd seen anyone enter the valley via that route and, incredibly, the first occasion had only been a fortnight earlier, when the adults were disturbed in an almost identical fashion. The third time I knew of the route being used came in the following winter when someone enjoying the snow on the high tops glissaded over *the ledge* and landed in Newcastle General Hospital!

The temperatures were oppressive that year, and the lack of rainfall saw the water levels in the Haweswater reservoir drop alarmingly. The area became a tourist attraction with tales of the drowned village of Mardale emerging from the waters. There must have been some disappointment because all the buildings had been flattened and all that remained intact were an old tennis court and the bridge over the main beck. One pile of stones marked the old pub and another the site of the church, and there was little more than that to be seen, but it didn't stop the publicity or the people from coming. The valley-head car park was big enough for about 20 vehicles, but there were days when the line of parked cars stretched for more than 3 km along the lakeside; traffic jams formed on the single-track road, and ice-cream vans appeared to cash in on the bonanza as the area became a tourist trap. There were times when it was pointless driving to the eagles, I could get there all right in the morning but returning could take hours, so if I didn't walk I took to leaving the car and cycling up the road, crossing the old bridge and then pushing the bike up the valley. There must have been thousands of visitors in the area at the time, but virtually no one else visited the eagles. I had the valley to myself, and people just stood and watched as I cycled past. It was a relief that so few people came and not just because they'd disturb me and disrupt my observations.

The main concerns of the RSPB protection scheme were to prevent disturbance at the nest and stop the eggs from being stolen, but disturbance didn't only occur at the nest. I was once watching the juvenile on the ridge above the middle nest when I noticed two people on the ridgetop. The footpath was visible from the valley floor in places, but I realised that these two people had left the path and were slowly edging lower down the slope. I assumed they'd been attracted by the eagle's calls and, sure enough, one suddenly pointed as the juvenile flew and turned back past them. That should have been a good enough view for anyone, but they scampered after the bird and disturbed it again, making it fly back to where it had started. But that still wasn't enough, and they chased it again and made it fly again. This time it flew away from the ridge before dropping out of their sight, but I watched the people and they still tried to follow it. It could be argued that the second time they flushed the eagle was deliberate disturbance of a Schedule 1, specially protected, species, but if I couldn't get egg collectors prosecuted, there was little point in me trying to do anything about these idiots. They'd had brief glimpses of a frightened eagle, but if they'd been on the valley floor they would have seen the bird flying freely and without alarm.

Another sign of the August heat was the amount of bathing performed by the eagles. I'd seen the adults soaking in wet moss and flushes from time to time over the years, but on 27 August in 1982 (36 days after fledging), I possibly became the first person to see eagles bathing fully in the wild in Britain. It wasn't as hot as it would be in 1984 but it was bad enough, and as the juvenile perched on the shady south side of the valley I watched the male skimming the opposite slopes. A steeply running stream exits the corrie on that side, and the bird dropped to land on its banks, fortunately for me, just below where it came out of the corrie. Eagles weren't supposed to bathe, but the male seemed quite happy to step into the flow and duck himself for a few minutes. He was almost out of sight and I couldn't quite get a clear view, so I was pleased when the juvenile flew across to land lower down, by a steeper stretch of water.

The juvenile stood and looked at the water (a short stretch of level surface between some rapids and a waterfall), stepped closer and nervously tested it with one toe. A little more confident, it tiptoed into the middle of the stream and squatted down, soaking its body feathers. The bird didn't seem at all happy and stepped in and out of the water a dozen times before settling in midstream again. It looked round as the adult finished his toilet and flew across the valley but then began to bathe fully. Dipping its head and fluttering its wings it looked like an enormous blackbird in a garden pond. It hopped in and out of the water and then splashed about some more. Dipping and flapping, it sat on its tail and appeared to be enjoying the experience, but with its head down, it suddenly lost its footing, slipped and was washed over the waterfall. It scrabbled about and just managed to grab hold of something to hang upside down in the flow for a few seconds before it pulled itself out and leapt to the shore. I'd guessed that it and the adult were trying to keep their flight feathers dry when in the water, but the juvenile was thoroughly drenched by now and shook out its feathers before flying heavily to perch near the male to dry out and preen.

Seeing the juvenile bathing felt like a once-in-a-lifetime achievement, and yet on 14 August the next year (Day 30), I saw the 1983 juvenile fly to and bathe in exactly the same place as in 1982. I may have missed earlier bathing, of course, but the adult wasn't present the second time (and had been higher up in 1982 in any case), so I didn't know if the juveniles had been shown this location or if it just attracted them as eagles. The 1983 bird was also much more confident; it flew straight to the stream, stepped in and bathed fully for 69 minutes. On finishing, it jumped out and onto a rock to preen. It took great care to zip every feather it could reach through its beak and rub its face on the preen gland and then over its shoulders to ensure that its plumage was in tip-top condition before flying again.

When I reached my observation post on Day 31 in 1984 I checked the perches and found the female, but there was neither sight nor sound of the juvenile. My experiences of the two previous years implied that it wouldn't have left the valley and, on a hunch, and instead of laboriously sweeping the vastness of the valley for a juvenile eagle that might be hiding in a bracken patch, I turned my binoculars straight onto the bathing stream. There, on the bank, in exactly the same position as in 1982 and 1983 stood the juvenile with wet feathers. Had I checked there first I would have seen that bird bathing as well, but it had clearly done so during my walk up the valley.

The coincidences of time were almost unbelievable, but what I saw in 1982 was often repeated in 1983 and 1984, and it usually happened about the same stage in the juveniles' development. With each passing year, I learnt that what I saw wasn't unusual at all, it was typical behaviour that simply hadn't been noted before. It was easy for me to see these things because I was seldom away from the place and that was mainly because, even by that Day 36 in 1982, I still hadn't seen the juvenile leave Riggindale, return to it or even give the impression of having been away. I never failed to find the bird soon after I arrived, even though it grew stronger on the wing with each passing day and by that time had given up the safe perch and was likely to be anywhere. In 1982 I still wondered why it hadn't left: I hadn't seen the long first flight from the nest or seen the youngster following the adults about the home range or being taught to fly or hunt, in fact, none of these three birds made much effort at all to fly during their first two weeks off the nest, but I couldn't believe their behaviour could be so different from the birds in Scotland. The eagles were no different, and the adults were either Scottish themselves or born of Scottish parents.

It was the same with food provisioning (the male collecting all the juvenile's food) and care of the youngster; what I saw didn't match what the books had led me to expect. And the male's increased role was matched by a decline in the female's: the male did most of the material collection for nest repairs before the eggs were laid and the female then effectively spent six weeks lying down in the nest, 12 weeks screaming at the male to find more food and then she just avoided the juvenile whenever she could. Her only role seemed to be to lead the juvenile from potential danger and then fly out of the valley as soon as the male returned. It didn't seem fair.

In 1982 I still didn't know if any of this was normal behaviour or the result of the juvenile having a deformed beak. When I saw the female feed four snippets of carrion to this juvenile I was certain it was because of the deformity; all items the other juveniles ate were freshly killed and delivered by the male. The female was already feeding when the juvenile arrived beside her that day, and I watched as it sidled up to her with its head held submissively low. With the juvenile screaming in her ear, instinct got the better of the female and she offered the first of the pieces of meat. They were greedily accepted, but the female then turned to eat (for 42 minutes) and the juvenile joined her in the feast, feeding for 50 minutes. Not only was this the only carrion feed by a juvenile during these years, it was the only beak-to-beak feeding after the first day off the nest, and it is still (after 30 years of eagle work) the only occasion on which I've seen two eagles feeding from the same carcass at the same time.

A few voles were given to the youngsters, but most of their food was medium-sized birds such as corvids that were easy to catch. With the fledged and inexperienced young of all species now on the wing, the male had little difficulty in catching prey, especially when the corvid flocks were close to the valley. In these years there could be flocks of more than 2,000 crows, rooks, ravens and jackdaws roaming the fells in search of leatherjackets and other invertebrates, and there were a few occasions when I watched the male leave the valley to hunt and be back with prey before I could settle down to await his return. He'd literally flown over the ridge, caught something and returned such was the surfeit of available prey and his prowess as a hunter, not that the juvenile always appreciated his efforts. On 18 August 1983, I found and tracked the juvenile to a gully where I could see it playing with bracken. It didn't call when the male arrived with food, and the adult landed a couple of times and looked about, but he didn't call to attract the juvenile. After a while, as the juvenile hadn't claimed the food, the male wasn't going to waste it and ate it himself instead.

That was another common factor, little food ever went to waste; it either went to the juvenile or the male ate it. The only exception came on 22 August 1983; the male had caught a small prey item in the valley head and then flew over the nest crag to land above where the juvenile was perched and calling. The latter walked and scrambled higher, it scratched its head, slid off a rock and then, six minutes after the male had landed, it made a bounding hop, skip and jump to grab the food from the adult's beak. The male left immediately, and the juvenile watched him fly to a safe distance and then turned its attention to the food. I couldn't identify the prey but could see that it was small enough to be swallowed in one gulp, but instead of that the juvenile spent nine minutes playing with it. It picked it up and threw it away before hopping after it to pick it up, drop it, call and climb higher with it to throw it away again. It pounced on the prey as if it needed to be killed, snatched and gripped it with its right talons and repeated and repeated the actions before dragging it higher, looking round and then flying off without it.

I waited a couple of hours to be happy that the food had been abandoned and then climbed up the ridgeside to examine what it was. I was surprised to find the fully plucked body of a ring ouzel, even the smallest of feathers had been removed from its head by the male to leave the naked, pink thrush only identifiable because of its bill. The skin wasn't broken, but the bruising showed that it had been killed with a lethal squeeze. That was the only prey item I ever knew to have been rejected in its entirety.

But still none of the juveniles had left the valley by this time; the 1983 bird played with the ouzel on the narrow ridgetop path and could easily have crossed into the next valley but it didn't. There were no long first flights from the nest, and I was seeing nothing to suggest that the adults taught the juveniles to hunt. The juvenile's life revolved around food, which was always delivered, and they just sat and squawked until the male arrived. The young birds didn't seem to learn very much at this stage, but the subtleties of behaviour are easily overlooked. When the adults warned the juvenile of a potential threat, including me on sorties to collect pellets and check food remains, they circled just as they would if a threat approached the nest. The juveniles clearly understood what the adults were doing and followed them away, but what separated those flights from circling to gain height or from circling just to have a look was indiscernible to the human eye.

When I arrived in the valley on 20 August 1984, I found the juvenile perched near the top nest, the female was perch-hopping in the valley head and the male was away foraging. When the female reached the ridgetop, the juvenile flew up and stood beside her calling and begging, but after a few minutes the adult grew disenchanted and flew into the next valley. As ever, the juvenile didn't follow her, and after watching for a couple of minutes, it flew back into the nest valley causing the adult to return when she saw it being chased by a raven. The male returned with a crow, and while the youngster ate its breakfast, the adults dealt with a succession of crows, ravens and peregrines that invaded the valley. They must have been getting frustrated by all these intrusions because, at 11.18 a.m., the adults broke away from two ravens to gain height and then turn their attention to a buzzard.

The female led the way to chase and stoop at the buzzard, each eagle taking its turn at diving and flashing its talons at the hapless buzzard, just as they did when chasing prey as a pair. The female charged in again, and as the buzzard flight-rolled to defend itself, the two, eagle and buzzard, locked talons and fell through the air. The female released her grip, and her partner dashed in to grapple and fall with the buzzard. The male caught and released it three times before the female returned for more as all three slowly dropped, cartwheeled and tumbled hundreds of metres past the crags. The male grappled the buzzard again and this time only released its grip when they were 10 metres from the ground. The eagle swept away as the buzzard crashed into the hillside, and I awaited the denouement. I'd never seen an eagle kill a buzzard, but I thought that was about to change. The eagles perched together above the feeding juvenile and ignored the motionless buzzard in the grass. After an hour, I decided to retrieve the buzzard, which I felt certain must have died from the impact or the stress caused by the eagles' attacks, but, incredibly, it was still alive and suddenly took off to fly down-valley when I was about 10 metres away.

In 1982 I was still intrigued by why the juvenile hadn't yet left the valley. I knew this bird had a deformed beak, but it was capable of feeding itself, and a misshapen beak wouldn't prevent it from killing its own food as almost all of an eagle's prey is killed with the talons. It was possible that the adults were overprotective, too attentive in their provisioning of food, meaning that the juvenile had no need to leave (perhaps this was why the adults might indeed drive the juveniles from their range at some point), but a pattern was beginning to emerge, even in that first year.

Food was taken directly to the juveniles when they first left the nest, and the male could influence the juvenile's position by taking food to the safe perch, but the youngsters had scarcely wandered any distance at that time. I soon started to note that the male began to land with prey away from the juvenile, even if it was on the safe perch, making the youngster come to meet him to claim the food. The distances increased, and as they did so, the juvenile soon saw the male's approach and followed him to the ground. It then flew out to meet him and follow him, but then I saw the 1982 juvenile follow at a distance and make what appeared to be a flight-roll even though it was nowhere near the adult and there was nothing else in the air. To some extent it looked as though the juvenile had a fit, but it was a flight-roll, and over the next few days, it repeated the action and performed the roll closer to the male as he carried food. I saw this entire sequence, which could have been the development of flight skills, in each of these three years, but in 1982 I saw something that I'd never imagined and something that I knew had never been recorded before.

It was 1 September, and all was as normal when I arrived in the valley. The female was perched in the valley head, and the juvenile was playing with bracken on the slopes near the top nest. I couldn't find the male, so I assumed he was away hunting. I knew his flight-lines and his habits and knew that the longer I waited the closer I was to seeing him return, so I waited, kept a check on the two birds I could see and scanned the male's most likely approach route with monotonous regularity. It was a long wait, but I eventually spotted him just as he rose above the skyline of a ridge about 4 km from my position. Through the telescope I could see that he was carrying food, and I knew from his flight-line that the food must be a red grouse.

The eagle's leisurely glide carried him across the lake and into the valley. The weight of the grouse was no hindrance to him, and he scarcely lost any height as he sailed along the ridge and began listening for the juvenile to call him in. It took him two minutes to cover the distance from the far ridge to be opposite my position, an average speed of 120 km per hour, or 75 mph, in a relaxed almost horizontal glide; the size and grandeur of the eagle are deceiving and betray no trace of its actual speed. I confirmed the identity of the prey as grouse as he approached, and then I waited.

The juvenile saw the adult as soon as he was opposite me and began to call, but instead of flying to it, the male, as had become the practice, swung out above the valley head, and the juvenile flew in pursuit. It was a hard chase, even though the adult wasn't trying to escape, and the juvenile beat its wings forcibly to make up the distance. Even so, it was only seconds before the juvenile was onto the male, but instead of the two dropping down to the ground as had been happening, the juvenile flight-rolled with legs and talons extended and grabbed hold of the grouse. The two eagles were momentarily linked, adult above juvenile, each holding the grouse, before the male released his grip, and the juvenile swung away to land close to its previous perch. The juvenile mantled over the prey with half-opened wings as it waited for the adult to reach his favourite perch before plucking for 10 minutes and then feasting on fresh grouse for 21 minutes.

The entire action seemed to be over in a flash, but it was the most exhilarating sight I'd ever seen. Even though its significance wasn't immediately apparent, the food pass was the culmination of the male's prey-delivery service – what had started with him delivering prey to where the juvenile stood now ended with the juvenile meeting him and seizing the food in flight, just as it would when killing a bird. It was a sequence of events that had taken fully six weeks from the juvenile's first day off the nest, and I wondered if that marked the end of the juvenile's dependency. The adults knew that it was strong on the wing, that the juvenile was capable of a fast pursuit and that it could catch and hold prey while in flight. The juvenile seemed to know all that it needed, and if it was to be driven from the area by the adults, this seemed to be the most likely time for that to occur. Although there were still rich pickings to be had, with the grouse population at its peak in the autumn, it would soon be winter, food availability would quickly decline, and the adults would need their entire range and the food it provided to survive that winter and recover their condition in preparation for the next breeding season. If this was to be the end, I'd been delighted, if somewhat astonished, by what I'd seen in my first full post-fledging period, but I still had to confirm that it was the end.

Little else happened that day, and I was back in the valley shortly after dawn the next morning. It was very quiet, no eagles were flying, and I feared that the bird had flown the previous evening or, after digesting its meal, had been chased away at first light that day. I spent the time painstakingly checking all the known perches, all the potential perches and it felt like every rock and tree in the valley, but after two hours of constant searching I finally tracked down the juvenile. It was perched deep inside what was now *the new cross tree* perch, a slight movement or ruffle of the feathers fortuitously coinciding with my looking at the tree from more than a kilometre away. With one bird found it was suddenly easy to find the others: the female was perched sheltering from the sun in the canopy of a tree near the middle nest and the male was peeking out from behind some rocks high above the juvenile's position. Nothing had happened yet.

The juvenile called twice at 11.05 a.m. and took off down-valley to circle between the nest sites. The female looked round sharply when she heard the calling, but the male was more relaxed and just kept a weary eye on his charge. The juvenile gained some height on the wind and thermals and then suddenly changed direction and flew over the ridge. It was out of the valley for the first time, and the significance of the aerial food pass became clear; it wasn't a sign for the adults to drive their offspring from their home, but for the juvenile to make its own move.

The female barely twitched with the juvenile's departure, but the male was quickly in the air and in pursuit. I was packed and ready to follow and looked on enviously as he sped across the sky and was out of the valley in a matter of seconds to see what was happening beyond the ridge. By contrast, it took me 20 minutes to cover the 1.5 km and gain 300 metres of height to reach a position from where I could view the next valley, and while I couldn't see either bird on my arrival, I was relieved to hear the juvenile calling and to know that it hadn't travelled on to an unknown location. Not seeing a long flight from the nest no longer held any importance, what I'd just witnessed was the real first flight of a juvenile golden eagle.

CHAPTER 9

Long days on the hill

I was amazed that it had taken the 1982 juvenile fully six weeks to leave the nesting valley, but the events of that year were mirrored in each of the next two years. There was near symmetry in the timing of the main aspects of the juveniles' development with the first open flight over the valley floor, the first use of the adult perches, the bathing and others all taking place within a day or two of the median date. The gradual development of the juveniles' skills was uniform and could be recognised even if I missed a few days of observation. Just as I'd missed the 1984 juvenile bathing by a matter of seconds, I knew it had occurred, and while I didn't see the aerial food pass repeated in later years, the whole sequence that led up to it was recorded in 1983 and 1984, and I knew when to expect the first flight from the valley. It had taken place on Day 42 in 1982 and was on Days 41 and 44 respectively in the next two years. The question was now, what happens next? There was no hint in the literature that the juveniles' development might progress in this manner, so I had to prepare myself for anything and most of all, I thought, for some long days on the hill.

I eventually tracked down the 1982 bird to a jumble of rocks near a deep gully by following its calls and fixed the telescope on the location, assuming that the male would be perched nearby. I tried to find him through binoculars, but the shadows were too deep, so I sat and waited. I had plenty of time to kill as it wasn't until 2.15 p.m. that the juvenile flew again, and when it did the male appeared and followed it back to the nesting valley. I packed up and retraced my steps, unaware at the time that this would become a running theme. The young bird was in a tree by the middle nest when I reached a viewpoint, and it stayed there for the next four hours. The juvenile had obviously had enough excitement for one day, but it would now spend time away from the valley for the remainder of its days.

The youngster still wasn't travelling far on these initial flights, and I spent a good many hours running back and forth from one valley to the next. I was lucky in that I could use the lower ground towards the valley mouth for access, but then again, had the juvenile been leaving over the valley head I would have secreted myself somewhere along that ridgetop and have less distance to travel. I would do whatever was necessary to learn about the juveniles. The first flights of all three of these birds had been to the same valley and that would remain the case for about two weeks. This was useful because I could reach it on foot from the village and often took afternoon and evening watches there instead of in the nesting valley.

I was putting in longer and more circuitous walks as well, hoping to meet the eagles on fresh ground but also to ensure that I wasn't simply recording the eagles when they came to me. There was also Stefan, of course, who preferred to be in Riggindale and who often informed me that he'd had the youngster in view while I was searching for it elsewhere. This didn't concern me at all, it was a good way of knowing that the bird still hadn't ventured far from home, and the same sequence was repeated in 1983 and 1984.

In 1982 I was fascinated to discover that it was still the male that played the greater role with the juvenile. It had always been assumed that both adults were involved with the juveniles' development, but while the male followed the juvenile, the female appeared almost confined to the nesting valley and, just as in the first part of the period, would often leave when the others returned. And the male did follow the juvenile, just as on that first exit flight in 1982; it was a rare event when the juvenile followed the adult.

On 13 September 1982, the adult female was being constantly pestered by the juvenile calling and flying to her to beg even though she hadn't fed it for eight weeks. When the juvenile flew from the valley I remained in place, and the female changed perches and found her way to a well-concealed perch as if trying to hide from the youngster. She'd just settled when the juvenile returned, and she sat and watched as it spent 20 minutes flapping about the valley, calling continuously and obviously searching for one or other of its parents. The female flew again when the juvenile left once more but this time appeared to be trying to draw its attention by circling over the ridge it had crossed. The juvenile reappeared with the male, and the two adults quickly turned away down-valley, with the juvenile calling and following. Uniquely, all three eagles then flew out of the valley mouth together, across the lake and began to circle over the ridgeside that lay between the valley and the grouse moors, and I wondered if the adults were about to take the juvenile out there to teach it to hunt after all.

The local pair of peregrines then appeared, and the juvenile followed the female to the ground and stayed when the latter immediately flew to join the male with the falcons. It seemed slightly odd that she should land rather than lead the juvenile away, but what was happening soon became clear. After only two minutes of aerial combat, the adults turned away and quickly recrossed the lake to settle on the first rocky outcrop they reached, leaving the juvenile grounded and at the full mercy of the furious falcons. Their attacks were steep and severe, but the adults didn't move to offer assistance. The juvenile's calls became increasingly desperate and were clearly audible to me more than 3 km away, but still the adults didn't move. If this was a lesson in how to fend for itself the juvenile was certainly learning the hard way.

The young bird took flight and laboriously gained height by flapping and riding the wind, while being continuously bombarded by the falcons, their angry *kekking* and flashing talons causing it to take evasive action as the peregrines dived in again and again. But not once did the eagle flight-roll in defence or retaliation, it simply called, ducked and gained enough height to break away and cross the lake. It left the falcons behind, and I expected the juvenile to land with the adults and cry, but as it approached them, the adults took flight and the three eagles circled together. As if nothing had happened at all the juvenile then led the male into the next valley, and the female made her way into the valley head, where she drank from a stream before making her way to the perch on which she would spend the night. It was another hour and a half before the others returned to do likewise.

With only a little competition for food between eagle and falcon, this seemed to be an odd piece of behaviour, the eagles dominated the social standings and the falcons were potential prey rather than potential predator, so there didn't seem to be much point to the action other than to teach the youngster a lesson. Those events occurred on Day 53 in 1982, and the 1983 juvenile received a similar introduction to the harsh reality of life on 7 September that year, Day 55 after it had left the nest. With the juveniles obviously more active and prone to be absent from the valley at this time, I'd often get there in time for first light, if I hadn't been there the previous evening to check on whether or not the young bird had roosted in the valley. There was some activity from the adults on this morning, but I'd been on watch for five hours before the juvenile raised the effort to join them in circling by the nest ridge. With the male then settled on his favourite perch, the female and juvenile made their way to the ground beside the bathing stream, but instead of stepping into the water, the juvenile took flight again and swung down-valley close to the ground. To my amazement, it landed beside a fox that stopped its progress up the slope, and the two predators glared at one another: the eagle, the fox's only natural predator, and the fox, probably the juvenile eagle's main competitor and threat, each wondering how to react.

The eagle took flight and stooped straight at the fox as if to catch it, but the fox jumped and the bird landed on the grass. The young bird then walked towards the fox. It broke into a bouncing trot and bounded up to jump and strike at the fox with both sets of talons, but instead of retreating the fox struck back, jumping forward to meet the assault with bared teeth. The eagle was bowled over backwards by the impact, and with thrashing wings and slashing talons its attack turned into desperate defence. The fox made savage, snarling lunges and bit onto the eagle's forewing but was beaten back by the bird's swiping talons. It dived in again and again at the eagle's wings, grabbing hold on at least two more occasions, but it could never quite take the grip it needed. Enraged by the young bird's tenacity and temerity, the fox seemed to alter its approach and leapt at the eagle's legs and once bit hard into the right one. The beating wings and strikes and clawing by the free talons forced the fox away, but after a pause it tried again to control the striking talons. After a flurry of wings and tumbling, however, the eagle emerged on top, with one set of talons on the fox's muzzle and the other on its shoulders, the killing pose. But this advantage was only momentarily held, and with a twisting roll the fox was free and pressing home its own attack.

The titanic struggle waged on and amply illustrated the ease with which these natural-born killers procure their food: how could a rabbit or a grouse protect itself against this venom? I felt sure that the victor here would make a meal of the vanquished. They broke free of one another, took a breath and dived back in headlong. This wasn't a fight for survival – one wasn't trying to escape the other – this had turned into a grudge match, killer versus killer. They were finely matched, the fox probably only slightly heavier than the eagle, and so I could only pray that the eagle would win. The fight intensified with the combatants wrestling, snapping and slashing as they rolled on the ground. Inquisitive sheep approached but backed away as the furious spitting ball of feather and fur rumbled towards them. But then the eagle lost the fight. After another minute of flying dust, the bird broke free and retreated in a panicky flight for survival, the fox running behind jumping and snapping at the eagle's tail as it struggled to gain height. But the eagle wasn't quite finished after all and, having gained some momentum, swung back to slash at the fox. Rather than cowering in fear, the fox had pressed its body to the ground to gain extra spring and leapt up at the passing eagle, only just failing to grab its tail. Encouraged by the advantage of height and speed, the eagle turned in again, but the leaping fox kept it at bay, and the eagle flew to land beside its parent for a soothing word of support.

The juvenile called and called, but the adult ignored it, perhaps disappointed that an eaglet of hers couldn't dispatch a fox. After three minutes the youngster flew at the fox again to slash from flight and then landed to run in and renew the battle. The two struggled for a couple of minutes with neither gaining the upper hand, and it was again the eagle that disengaged. This time it moved right away and vented its anger on an innocent sheep, raking its hind talon through the fleece before landing, apparently none the worse for its encounter with the fox, and wandering about the hillside. The fox watched for a moment and then trotted away up the slope, its tail raised high as a flag of triumph to show all and sundry that it had defeated its mortal enemy.

I'd always kept contemporaneous notes with the eagles, usually timed to the half minute or more precisely for the finer activities, and did so automatically, almost sub-consciously, while enjoying or concentrating on the actions before me. The times in my notebook were accurate for this fight, but my writing had become a scrawl by the end, so engrossed had I become, and it wasn't until the struggle ended and I consciously checked the time that I became aware of the facts; the battle had lasted for 40 minutes!

Neither of the adult eagles had intervened in the fight and, in fact, neither even moved from their chosen perches, not even when the fox held the eagle by one wing. Was this, as with delivering the 1982 juvenile to the peregrines, the one lesson taught by the adults? Fight or flight? The juveniles certainly did have to learn to distinguish between an easy meal and a dangerous foe that could fight back with vigour and aggression. It was the difference between death and survival, but even so, the fox was still a potential meal, I'd seen the adult eagles kill foxes as well as their cubs.

There was another lesson the juveniles needed to learn about food, and it was the 1982 bird that learned the hard way. After having provided them with all their food during their confinement to the nesting valley, the male stopped catching and killing for the juveniles as soon as they flew beyond the ridgeline. I watched all of the juveniles catching and trying to catch a few small prey items, such as voles, but the 1982 bird's first attempt on more than a snack ended in defeat when a pine marten out on the high rocks of the second valley fought back rather too strongly for the bird with the bent beak. That was a lesson in itself, another dangerous species that could fight back and another sign that attacks didn't always result in a meal. These three juveniles turned to carrion once they were out of the valley, and fortunately, there never appeared to be any lack of dead sheep on the Lakeland fells in those days.

On the day after the peregrine incident, I watched the male fly to the top nest with a twig in his beak, and after joining him there, the juvenile flew off and led the way out of the valley, juvenile eagle, adult male and me (lagging some way behind no matter how fit I thought I was). This had become the routine, even by then, and I walked to the site fully expecting to be led about the fells to a point distant from my car, had I used it. It was an 8-km walk from my house to my observation post, but that was just the shortest route, I often found myself on the high tops or walking right around the lake at ridgetop level or doubling back on myself time and time again in pursuit of the birds. It was frustrating at times, the eagles capable of flying from one end of their range to the other in a couple of minutes, a journey that could take me three hours given all the ridges and valleys that had to be traversed. I knew the best routes, though, and at this stage could reliably predict where the birds were going, so I quickly made my way to the top of Castle Crag.

This was where I found myself at the end of this bird's first flight from the nesting valley, and it proved to be an ideal lookout post. Just as on that day, I could hear the juvenile calling when I arrived and quickly located it circling in the valley head with the male. The youngster three times attempted to engage the adult in a flight-roll (another behavioural feature that became prominent at this stage in all years), but the male wasn't interested and found his way to a perch. As I settled back to watch, the juvenile entered into a long sequence of seemingly pointless perch-to-perch flights.

There were buzzards and peregrines active in the valley, a place where the eagles regularly built or began new nests but where they'd never bred; ravens had nested below where I sat and *cronked* about the crags, and red deer lazed in the sun on the grassy slopes opposite. A fox worked the screes and boulder fields but wasn't attacked, and there wasn't a single human to be seen. It was two hours before the male eagle flew again when he glided directly down to a sheep carcass. The juvenile quickly followed him, landed nearby and then stalked closer, head down and calling to be fed. The male flew as if he'd led the juvenile to the food, but after feeding for two minutes, it joined him in circling by the crags. The adult returned to the sheep but after four minutes stopped feeding to stare at the approaching juvenile, its legs down and talons spread in a long drop. Whether or not the adult interpreted this as an attack I don't know, but when the juvenile arrived, the adult jumped, rolled over backwards and talon-grappled the juvenile away, throwing it to one side. The male did relinquish the food, though, and flew a short distance to drink from a stream. The juvenile followed and was grappled and thrown away again to stand watching as the male returned to the carcass to feed.

The juvenile appeared to have got the message and took off to circle higher and higher, but then, after 14 minutes, it furled back its wings and stooped in once more.

The adult must have heard the rush of air and looked up just in time to jump, roll and grapple the juvenile for a third time. This time the juvenile did get the message and shuffled away to stand on a rock and watch and wait disconsolately. The female arrived a couple of minutes later, and I had the rare sight of seeing all three birds on the ground together. The male's hackles were up by then, and he crouched in an aggressive defence posture as his larger mate approached him, but after stopping to reconsider, she flew away, the juvenile learning another lesson, and the female keeping to the rule that eagles don't feed together once they're off the nest – each has to wait its turn, even if it's the female waiting for the smaller male to finish eating.

After the six weeks in the valley and about two weeks making short excursions such as these, the juveniles became more elusive, and I spent many full days walking the fells in search of them. The walk to the nesting valley took me past the two next most important valleys, so I'd check these en route and scour the lakeside ridges as I walked. The birds were often in one of these locations, but as the days rolled by it was obvious that the juveniles were wandering further afield. They were still based in the nesting valley, though, and the male/female roles hadn't changed. If the female was there I could be fairly certain that the male and juvenile wouldn't be, and if they were there it was usually obvious. The male was still accompanying the juvenile, which made them easier to locate when they were elsewhere, but I had to go high now, attaining vantage points that allowed me to see beyond the nearest ridge. I'd often see the male circling and chase him down, knowing that the youngster would be in that vicinity, and as I neared its calling would keep me on track. But not all the days were successful, and I spent many in a fruitless search of valley and fell, suspecting that the birds were back in Riggindale but wary of going there the next day, not finding anything and suspecting that they'd be where I'd been the day before.

It could be frustrating at times, but knowing that the female wouldn't be with the others gave me two targets and the encouragement to press on. The two valleys, the lakeside ridge, Riggindale, up on to the tops, around the head of the lake, out to the grouse moor, back again, over the secondary moor, through the woods and back home. I often found myself walking upwards of 30 km on consecutive days, with many hundreds of metres of climbs and descents thrown in as well, but the records I obtained allowed me to map the home range as well as study the juveniles' development, both elements of the eagle's life that hadn't before been studied in any detail. By following the birds and recording their locations over a series of years I was able to see that, in spite of having no near neighbours to restrict their movements, the Haweswater birds had a definable home range beyond which they seldom travelled. It was the area that provided them with sufficient food to survive the winter, reach breeding condition and supply and feed a nestling and then a juvenile. The seasonal food sources were in different locations but the nesting area was the most important, and it seemed to me that the nests had been located in the area that provided the most reliable year-round food supply. The eagles ranged over about 50 sq km, and the female probably never left that area for more than a few minutes after forming a pair.

I was engaged in this kind of search activity on 25 September 1984 when I spied the female hunting the slopes to which she'd taken the juvenile to ground for the peregrines in 1982. It was easier in 1984, the lake was at its lowest level, and I could cut the corner and walk across the lakebed to access the hills where she was. I soon lost sight of her but continued onto the ridge to scan the distant grouse moor. There appeared to be no activity, so I pressed on for the secondary moor, an area that wasn't managed for grouse, was overgrazed but still held a decent grouse population on which I'd seen the eagles preying during the previous two years. These grouse proved to be more than an asset for the eagles, it was the nearest population to the nesting valley, and I'd seen the male returning from that direction with a grouse on many occasions both during the nestling and the post-fledging periods. It was, however, an asset they'd soon lose; by 1986 the grouse had gone and would never return.

As always, I settled into a convenient observation post, tucked into the rocks before I reached the heather and with a view of the approaches. The juvenile came into view almost immediately and drifted along the heathery ridge but flushed no grouse. Two buzzards came out to meet it, taking turns to dive in, but the eagle took little heed, it tilted its wings and half-heartedly flicked out a set of talons and that was enough to dissuade the buzzards from repeating the attacks. I watched the eagle as it drifted along, and as it turned away over a small valley and on towards the main grouse moors, it dawned on me that by then I'd walked about 20 km to see an eagle that was less than 2 km from where I lived!

The juvenile was wandering alone on that day, and I knew from the previous two years that it would soon become even more difficult to locate and follow. By then, at about nine weeks off the nest, even the adult male had largely abandoned the juvenile and, apart from some excursions to follow or seek out the juvenile, now spent almost all of his time with his mate. The change coincided with the juvenile roaming outside the adults' home range, and the male being apparently unwilling to spend too much time away from home. In fact, the adults now tended to keep to the nesting area, to act as a pair and appeared to be avoiding the juvenile. The tales of adults driving the young away from the area simply weren't true – just as with leaving the nest it was the juveniles themselves that chose the moment to move on.

Even though they'd been abandoned, all three of these juveniles were still essentially living in the adults' home range, so there was still the opportunity for me to learn more about their habits, but they had to be found now and not just bumped into. As well as walking to intercept the birds I cold-searched neighbouring valleys and closely examined potential perch and roost sites. I found some, the juveniles' signature being the type of feather left at the site and the pellets that were still sufficiently distinctive to separate them from those of the adult, but these roosts were scattered in and around the home range and suggested that the juveniles rarely used the same place twice when they were outside the nesting valley. They probably just settled at the closest suitable location. This was almost certainly why my contacts with the juveniles had become less frequent, even though I'd never been fitter than I was by the end of 1984 and searched the area repeatedly.

I spent innumerable hours and walked myself over every blade of grass in the home range to discover not just where the juveniles went but also what they were doing when they were there. And I was usually travelling at some pace in order to reach the birds' location before they moved on. Walking around ridges became tiresome, so I searched out, found and used routes that took me straight through the steepest sections of crag to cut corners and save time. I was constantly on the hill and on the move because it was the only way to learn. My curiosity had been originally aroused by the lack of available information and the number of assumptions that were published as facts, so I couldn't just scratch the surface like everyone else, I had to collect all the data I could. My results were eventually published in *Ibis*, the journal of the British Ornithologists' Union.

I set off before dawn on 10 October 1984 for another long day. I hadn't seen the juvenile since that day it was close to my house, so my intention was to reach the secondary valley as soon as possible, gain some height and then wander the high fells, looking into each of the radiating valleys for sight or sound of the young bird. Seeing the bird was all that mattered, and there was no more satisfying manner of seeing an eagle than during a good high-level hike on a fine autumnal day. It didn't work out like that, though, as so few planned trips do when you're at the mercy of the whims of a golden eagle.

I crossed a major side stream after 20 minutes of walking, and as I did the young eagle swung out of the side valley and began to drift along the lakeside ridge in the direction I was travelling. Fortunately for me the eagle wasn't in a hurry, it had almost certainly roosted in that valley and was probably now looking for breakfast. I ploughed on behind the bird with the contours of the hill working in my favour and enabling me to keep it in sight as I charged along the woodland edge to minimise disturbance. I looked on as the eagle hugged the ground, so obviously hunting, and rolled at a red deer calf, sending it into a panic and dashing for the protection of the hind. The eagle glided on serenely while I followed as best I could. After another kilometre the bird stooped and rolled at a fox, but it was in no mood for a fight and dived into a jumble of rocks. The eagle kept on going and swung into the next valley. I'd recognised its flight-line and was by then running to keep up, but the eagle slipped ahead and managed to turn the corner and was out of my sight while I was still trying desperately to clamber over a steep shoulder of hill so as not to lose track of it altogether. I was quick enough to follow its unseen path and smart enough to start my scan ahead of the bird and work backwards to meet it rather than try to catch up with it by sweeping the binoculars in the direction it was travelling. My view crossed the eagle's path and latched onto it just in time to see it dive and roll at a sheep.

The bird seemed to be in a very belligerent mood; it didn't have a hope of catching and killing any of the animals it had attacked, but nothing was going to escape its attention or fail to afford it the opportunity to practise its skills. I've seen attacks similar to these described as the desperate efforts of a starving eagle, but they are clearly little more than games, and I've seen juveniles riding sheep and deer they couldn't possibly have mistaken for potential prey. Two crows were next in line to be maltreated, but they avoided the eagle by dropping to the trees as the big bird circled to gain height in one corner of the valley and turn away over the ridge-top. The juvenile was out of my reach this time, it had made it to the high ground and could easily have been 50 km away by the time I reached the top of the ridge, so I pressed on to the nesting valley instead and spent the day with the adults.

As the October days rolled by it became increasingly difficult to see the juveniles, and this was largely because they were rapidly approaching their full independence. There were no spectacular fights between juvenile and adult to coincide with this because the young birds simply began to wander further afield. They'd also stay away for longer (perhaps for several days before returning) and at times paid no attention to the adults when they were in the range. It was a slow process but one that fitted in well with the development I'd recorded during the period when they left the nest. The juveniles' development to independence involved learning by experience and adventure. By this stage, wandering far from home, they had to fend for themselves and were abandoned by the adults, even by the male that had expended so much time and energy on their survival.

The adult eagles were in the process of leaving their roost when I arrived in the valley shortly after dawn on 16 October 1984, and they circled to gain height before making for the valley head. There was an unusual amount of high circling that morning, and on one occasion the birds flew so high that they became invisible to the naked eye. I watched through the telescope and, at what may have been more than 1,000 metres above me, saw the female perform five display dips. Such a high display at such a time must have been advertisement behaviour and had there been other pairs of eagles in Cumbria it could have been seen as establishing their dominance of this particular patch of ground. There were no others by then, of course, so I assumed that it must have been for the benefit of the juvenile or else a display to demonstrate that the young bird had gone. The female's last dip saw her fall through the void and land neatly on her favourite perch, and the male followed her down.

When they flew 22 minutes later the pair took off as one, but rather than challenging an intruder, as was so often the case when they took flight in unison, the female dropped straight to a sheep carcass, and the male simply crossed to a different perch. The female commenced what would become the longest single feed I ever saw her take, feasting without interruption for 79 minutes. At one point two foxes approached her, but they didn't dare try to share the feast; they circled her to size up the opportunity, but an attack would never have worked. The female was in her youthful prime, probably only eight years of age, and was heavy bodied, dark coloured and had piercing yellow eyes that if seen up close would deter any approach. The foxes only stayed for four minutes before moving on in search of easier pickings, but two crows arrived almost at once. The female flashed her wings to scare them away, but they remained in the area until the male arrived to spend 20 minutes keeping them occupied while his partner ate her fill.

The male chased the crows in flight but also on the ground and didn't give them a moment's peace. After one final stoop at the crows the male landed beside the carcass and stood opposite his mate. He held his wings open and raised above and behind him as he stood on long legs. The female looked, stood upright, stretched and, leaning backwards, she too opened and raised her wings so that the two birds stood as in a mirror, holding the pose of rampant heraldic eagles. This was something I'd never seen before.

The posing was clearly meaningful, even if the male had simply grown tired of waiting for his turn to feed. As eagles don't feed from the same carcass at the same time, the female turned away after 10 seconds and flew off; the male closed his wings, watched her go and then began his own feed. Perhaps upset by her mate's impatience, the female didn't defend the male from interference, and he had to feed under the close attention of up to 14 crows. Two of these jumped in to steal snippets of meat as he ate, but he was too hungrily devouring ripe flesh to take any notice. Because of the length of the female's feed and the male's impatience to take over, I expected him to engage in a long feast as well but it wasn't to be. Thirty minutes into the feed he suddenly looked round and called. The female was still perched, and I couldn't see a reason for his behaviour and apparent anxiety. The pair again took flight almost as one, even though they were perched far apart on this occasion, and as they did so I heard the juvenile call; they'd obviously heard or sensed it before I had.

While the female made short, perch-to-perch flights, the male circled and flapped up and down the ridge as the juvenile glided up the valley below him and called from time to time. The female worked her way across the valley head, and the adults then followed the juvenile before all three circled in front of the middle nest. The female turned to land on the *camouflage man*, and the juvenile sped across to the carcass, scattering the crows as it arrived and immediately commencing to feed voraciously. The male swept back and forth along the ridge, landed beside the juvenile and then joined his mate, now circling above the juvenile. The adults were clearly unsettled by the juvenile's presence and were uncertain how to react to it at such a late date. They circled, perched, flew, perched and swept every corner of the valley for 43 minutes before the female left her mate to deal with the juvenile, just as she had throughout the post-fledging period, and flew out of the valley. For his part, and again just as before, the male settled on a favourite perch to watch and await developments. If ever there was evidence to show that the adults didn't drive away their young, then this was it.

The juvenile, oblivious to the confusion it had caused, ate on. It gobbled down the mutton, organs and skin, and I even saw it swallowing bones it wrenched from the carcass. I'd never seen an eagle feed with such desperation. Crows hopped in and out to grab pieces of meat with impunity, and six times I saw a crow hop on and off the eagle's back without the predator even reacting never mind retaliating. This was obviously a hungry eagle, and nothing was going to deter it from feeding.

The juvenile ate rapidly and continuously for two and a quarter hours, by far the longest single feed I ever recorded. In its desperation to find food, the young bird must have forsaken its independence in favour of the one place it had known to be a good source, the valley in which it had been born. There are many tales of eagles eating too much to fly, including a 1679 record from Grisedale, barely 8 km from Riggindale, related by

93

H A MacPherson in which the bird was taken with a blow from a fell-staff, and this bird must have been approaching that stage. In such a long feed it was conceivable that more than half of its body weight might have been consumed, and at the end of its feast, the crop bulged grotesquely from its breast, separating the dark feathers to reveal the whiter under-plumage and down beneath that. It could still fly, though, and, heavily, glided down to what had been one of its favourite perches earlier in the season. The male glowered down at it but made no move, and both birds were still in place when I left three hours later. The juvenile had gone by the time I returned, shortly after dawn the next day, and it was another two weeks before I saw it again, speeding straight through the valley without stopping.

The juveniles attained their full independence during the second half of October, and whenever they appeared in the adults' presence after that they were always approached as intruders. They were about 80 days off the nest by then and obviously roaming far in search of food and exploring for a new home that would sustain them throughout the first winter of their lives. There was often flight display to be seen when they returned, but the young bird was by then an intruder in the natal range and would be, with some reluctance, treated as such. When the 1983 juvenile returned in November that year the male took flight to follow it, and the female got up to circle and watch. Even though the female had little involvement with it, the juvenile approached her and made four half flight-rolls, to which the female reacted but didn't initiate, the passive response again showing that the youngster was being tolerated rather than driven from the area. To further demonstrate that, the adults landed together on a high perch and simply watched as the juvenile flew out of the valley and out of the home range.

Another sign of the juveniles' independence was the adults' resurgence of nesting behaviour. While most of this took place during February and March, and items were added to the nests in most months, the juvenile's independence resulted in a brief up-surge of activity that often saw new nests begun as well as the titivation of established sites. The onset of winter weather and shorter days soon saw the adults revert to concentrating on food, however, but for me, after watching 36 weeks of nest-building, eggs, chicks and juveniles, the ensuing calm left an emptiness that was only assuaged by thoughts of the next breeding season.

That wasn't always the last of the juveniles, though, and the 1984 bird spent the first part of the winter roosting close to the grouse moors, though outside the adults' home range. That meant there were later sightings about the nesting area, and on 26 November that year, the juvenile appeared in Riggindale when the adults were absent. At that time, 121 days after leaving the nest, I was only certain of it being a Lakeland bird and not a visitor from Scotland by the amount of time it spent flying and perching about the valley before leaving again. A visitor wouldn't have known the perches.

What became of the juveniles after that is a mystery. The winters soon set in during these years, and there was often snow on the fells by late November. It would be a hard time for young eagles, and the sad reality, after all the pleasure they'd given me, was that perhaps none of these birds would survive into adulthood.

CHAPTER 10

Differences of opinion

My work on the post-fledging periods continued into the ensuing winters. The juveniles' learning experience rolled over into their independence, and the searches that enabled me to confirm that one had spent the first part of its winter on the edge of the adults' range developed into me following the old birds to discover more about the extent of the range and their winter activities. This led to my identifying that only about 12 sq km of the range, the core area, was by far the most important part of the land they covered – it held the nests, the main roosts and the most reliable food sources. So engrossed did I become with my studies that between March 1983 and April 1988 I was with the eagles in every single week whether they were in the nesting valley or many kilometres away. Locating them necessitated hours of hillwalking on bright winter mornings that turned to heavy and persistent rain or days that saw me set out in search of them before dawn in falling snow.

The red deer rut was a magical time – I once witnessed so brutal a stag fight that one beast's antler snapped in half, making a sound like a rifle shot that echoed through the valley. These were some of my best days. I had the freedom to roam into areas that even the stalkers and shepherds seldom visited at that time of year, and I had the hills and the wildlife to myself. On sunny days I watched ravens sledging in the snow near the lip of steep ridges, and blizzards of snow buntings swept in and away as I sheltered from the icy winds in the lee of peat hags to watch the red deer scratching their living where the gales had exposed some vegetation. I found the eagles hunting grouse about 10 km from the nesting valley on 2 January 1985, but they were foraging more widely than that, and I found them in 10 different valleys that month. That gave me a better idea of the extent of their home range and of how widely they needed to travel in search of food when the days were short and the weather wild.

The deer also struggled to survive, and one incident highlighted the perils faced by human and beast on the high ground in that season. The eagles arrived in the nesting valley shortly after me on 26 January and landed close to the middle nest, which I thought might have been an indication of their nest choice for the year as the top nest had fallen from its ledge on 5 October 1984. It was also close to the onset of nest refurbishment, a task that usually began during the first week of February. The male eagle flew almost at once and flapped hard in front of a tree, and watching through binoculars, I assumed him to be trying to gather nest material, but when I switched to the telescope I saw the truth. He was trying to gain a purchase on the carcass of a deer that had died a terrible death: it must have slipped from an icy place on the crag and was now hanging upside down from one foot wedged in the fork of a branch. How long it had taken to die after its fall didn't bear thinking about. The male persisted for a couple of minutes but couldn't get a grip, and after twice sliding off the body, it relented and flew to a favourite perch, his mate in attendance. They'd have to wait for the deer's leg to rot through and the carcass to fall to the ground before they could taste venison again.

I checked the nests on 3 February and found no fresh material, but on the 5th I saw five sticks carried to the site of the top nest and on the 6th watched the pair spend three hours rebuilding its foundation. The choice had been made, and instead of following the pattern of the previous few years and changing to a nest that was still in good condition, the eagles had chosen to reuse the site they'd used the year before. Nest-building continued apace after that, but they were still roaming in search of food, so on 6 March I decided to make a speculative visit to the nearest heather moorland. It turned out to be an odd sort of day: I'd chosen to visit the wrong area, I didn't see any grouse and, although I saw them, the eagles weren't where I was. They didn't even approach to within 3 km of me, and yet I watched an hour of continuous flying that only ended when the birds dropped into their nesting valley, at a point almost 8 km from where I sat.

As the days passed, I saw the eagles mating, saw many pieces of material being collected and delivered to the nest and, on the 21st, saw some spectacular flight-play between the adults. The male delivered some woodrush to the nest, but instead of staying to arrange it, the female flew from the nest, and the male followed. He swung in behind his mate, and they began a fast, contour-hugging and twisting pursuit along the ridgeside. The male closed in, and the female twice rolled over to present talons and touch her mate's before they suddenly decelerated to glide side by side and then separate, the male to find a perch and the female to collect more nest material. Flight-play of this kind was a common feature before the eggs were laid.

I missed the onset of incubation that year because I'd already instigated the RSPB protection scheme and didn't arrive on watch until that afternoon. The male was sitting when I arrived but was soon relieved by his mate, so there was no doubt that an egg had been laid. It's probably impossible to determine when the second egg is laid by distant observation, but the male appeared very uncomfortable when the low cloud lifted above the nest at 5 a.m. on the 25th. He settled and resettled, readjusted his position with his head down in the cup four times, and when he was eventually replaced, he sky-danced across the valley. It seemed likely that the female had only very recently laid the second egg and that he just couldn't get comfortable on it.

The season soon began to go wrong, however, and I found myself isolated in a job I loved and had held for the previous six years. I felt that my position had become untenable when, by 4 April, I'd been on duty on each of the previous 16 days and had taken most of the overnight stints. In normal circumstances, I wouldn't have been too fussed about this, but I could see the protection scheme collapsing, and in spite of my experience, I wasn't permitted any input and suspected that, as senior warden, I'd still be held responsible if there were problems. I tried to reason with the RSPB officers when the situation worsened but was brushed aside and told not to cause trouble for the new re-gime. The easiest way not to cause trouble was for me not to be involved, and I resigned shortly afterwards, citing the favouritism shown towards the friends of senior employ-ees at my expense. It was a difficult decision to take, but the successes I'd overseen had blinded the RSPB to the difficulties of the job.

It came as little surprise when, within two days of my departure, both the national press and television arrived to feature the eagles, visits that had obviously been arranged during my employment but without my knowledge. When I saw the results, I could tell that the filming and photography hadn't been properly controlled, and one photograph seemed to show the male flying away from the nest that held the eggs without his mate being there. I was concerned because there was no immediate way of knowing what damage might have been caused to the breeding attempt.

I avoided the hide after my resignation and, of course, suddenly found myself free from the restrictions of the RSPB. I no longer had to watch the birds from the floor of the valley or contend with visitors arriving in torrential rain or with psychotic dogs that had never chased sheep until the day they visited Riggindale. I was suddenly free to follow the birds as I'd been doing after the fledge, and for the first time other than for occasional days, I was free to follow the breeding cycle in a way that suited me. I could follow the birds' foraging trips away to confirm their ranging behaviour during the incubation period and make observations that hadn't previously been made with wild eagles. Their using the top nest couldn't have provided a better opportunity to simulta-neously watch activity at, and away from, the nest. With my knowledge of the terrain and the approaches to the nest, and the help of a decent telescope, I knew I could make these observations without a hide and without causing any disturbance to the birds or alarm to the RSPB wardens.

The prospective hatch date was 4 May, so I was on the ridge and in position by 4.30 that morning, quietly secreted among the boulders and outcrops that provided a cryptic background into which my camouflaged form would blend perfectly. There was no sign of life at the hide, and the female eagle was fast asleep on the nest when I arrived. She was still there and hadn't left the nest, when I creaked and crawled my way back over the ridgetop 11 hours later without a single ray of sunlight having reached me. My knees were stiff and frozen and my back was curled into a hunch that wouldn't release until almost an hour later.

It was a similar story on the 5th, with the female sitting tight. There should have been some evidence of the hatch by then but there was none, and when the female repo-sitioned herself on the nest I could clearly see the two eggs I'd seen earlier in the year. Even if they had failed to hatch, I at least knew that, unless they were very good fakes, the bird was still sitting on two eagle eggs. There was still the possibility of the second egg hatching instead of the first, though, and, because I couldn't be certain as to when the second had been laid, I was back in my niche before first light the next morning. As expected, the female was still asleep when she first became visible to me through the gloom, but she had her head up later when the male passed by, perhaps expecting him to visit, but it was another hour before he finally arrived. The female stood slowly and as stiffly, as I had done, following her 16 hours on the nest, but the two great birds at first contrived to hide the nest cup from me. The female eventually stepped around the nest and flew off, and having watched her go, the male then at last stepped over the cup to give me another look at the contents of the nest – there was still one white egg and one suffused with a dull brick-red colour. I obtained another good look at the eggs when the female returned 23 minutes later.

The situation didn't look good, and I thought I was clutching at straws in hoping for the second egg to hatch when the first one hadn't. I didn't spend so much time on the ridge that day and felt pretty disconsolate when I returned home. But I learnt with astonishment that evening, on watching the television news, that the eagles had hatched an egg! It was ridiculous timing, never before had the announcement been made so soon after the hatch, for one thing you couldn't be absolutely certain of there being a chick when watching from the valley floor, and none of the RSPB's wardens had been on the ridgetop to look. I was frustrated because I couldn't visit the valley the next day and instead had to face a gloating Ken telling me that food had been taken to the nest. I told him that I'd seen the eggs, but he wasn't interested, he told me that food had also been delivered that day and he'd personally seen the female feeding the chick.

I found his story too incredible to believe, so I was back on the ridgetop by first light the next day, 8 May. I was in low cloud this time, a dank and clinging mist that soaked the clothes and crept into the lungs. I don't know if it was lost, but on the walk to the ridge I flushed a rabbit at about 500 metres, by far the highest I'd seen in this area. If I was to see or hear a chick, this suggested that there might be fresh food for it close at hand and that was always good news. The cloud began to lift at 8.30 a.m., and I recognised the male on nest duties. That implied that there'd been at least one changeover in the mist and also that the next one shouldn't be too far away. Incredibly after the morning mist, the male was soon panting heavily as he sat sheltered from the wind on the nest and in the full glare of the fierce morning sun. He had to bake for a little while longer as it was three hours before his mate returned. She stepped about, looked in and out, but her mate seemed reluctant to stand. As before, I didn't get a view of the nest's contents until after the bird had left and the other stepped to the back of the nest, but when that happened I saw that it still held two eggs! They were perfectly whole and intact, there wasn't a chick and that didn't come as any surprise.

I later phoned Geoff Horne to give him advance warning that he'd be needed to remove the eggs, but he was uncertain; he'd seen the television announcement as well and was of the opinion that the RSPB couldn't be so wrong as to make that statement without checking the facts. I insisted that I was correct; I had nothing to gain by saying that there wasn't a chick when there was one, but there was still a reluctance to accept what I said. I told the wardens that I'd seen the eggs, but they simply informed me that food had gone to the nest again, and they'd all seen the female feeding the chick. Dawn on 9 May again found me staring at an eagle nest that contained two unhatched eggs. I phoned the RSPB office this time, but I could tell that they just thought I was trying to cause trouble. It was pointless continuing; in spite of the mutual ill feeling between myself and the RSPB at that time, I'd done the wardens' job for them and checked the nest, I'd informed them of what I'd seen and I hadn't gone running to the press to tell tales.

It was 10 days after the first egg should have hatched that the RSPB finally realised that a mistake had been made, and they admitted to the failure on 15 May. I spoke to Ken, and despite everything he'd told me during the previous few days, he now said that he'd never seen food going to the nest and that Stefan was the only person to have made that claim. Without realising, he told me that the announcement of the hatch was on the word of a visitor who had no official involvement with the site. Again, and in spite of my having kept him and the RSPB fully aware of events at Haweswater, I wasn't informed of the arrangements Geoff made to remove the eggs for analysis. As it was, I just happened to be looking out through the front window of my house when Geoff drove past. If he'd been in his car, or had the RSPB conveyed him in their vehicle, I wouldn't have known, but Geoff was in his pick-up and that could only mean he was going for the eggs.

I wasn't prepared for this, and by the time I'd changed into my field gear and set off, they had a 20-minute start on me. They were just entering the valley when I arrived at the car park, but I was soon on the trail; making up ground with every step I passed the team with a cursory nod and reached the hide about 10 minutes ahead of them. I quickly confirmed that the male was still on the nest and found the female perched in the valley head. I showed the birds to Geoff when he arrived, and he asked what had happened that morning. He'd just seen me pass him, so he knew that I couldn't answer the question, and the wardens were still struggling up the valley, so they couldn't either. No one had been on watch since the previous afternoon, even though the eggs were still in the nest. In spite of my advance warning that he'd be needed, Geoff had come alone and needed a rope man on the crag. The wardens were incapable of getting to the crag never mind getting above the nest and looking after the rope, so Geoff and I set off together. If I hadn't seen him pass my house that morning he would have had to abseil into the nest alone and climb back up the rope.

Throughout the walk to the crag, Geoff kept asking if I was certain that the nest contained eggs, and I kept reassuring him that it did. It was, by then, 55 days after the lay, and the eggs would have hatched by then if they were going to. He asked me again when we were almost on the crag and could see the male sitting glaring at us from the nest. We scrambled up through the screes towards the edge of the crag, always keeping an eye on the male, and it was marvellous to see his determination not to desert the eggs. Just as I'd seen with the shepherd in 1982, the male was the last line of defence, and he wasn't willingly going to discharge his responsibilities. He at first sat with his head held high to watch our approach but then lowered it and pressed his body into the nest as we drew closer, his eyes barely peeking out over the nest rim, but as we neared he became unsettled, and when he finally deserted the eggs the male did so with great dignity. With Geoff and I only about 70 metres from the nest, the eagle stood slowly, stepped to the front edge of the nest, took one last look at us and then launched himself into a glide that took him across the valley in seconds to look on from a safe distance while his mate perched disinterested where she'd been when we arrived at the hide.

Geoff and I reached the crag top, and in no time at all he'd abseiled to the nest, removed the eggs and was waiting for me at the foot of the crag. We examined the eggs and returned to the hide to show the wardens that they hadn't been watching a chick being fed and then walked away together. Geoff later had the eggs analysed, and my greatest fears proved to be correct. He told me that both eggs had been fertile, had shown some development and had died about two weeks into the season, coinciding with the period that had seen all the media interest. It was difficult to believe that the wardening scheme could become so shambolic so quickly, but it was a sign of how attitudes would change even to a bird as rare in England as the golden eagle.

Other than 1981, when I was too ill to spend much time with the birds, 1985 was my first opportunity to watch the eagles during a failed breeding season, but as could be expected, there was little of note to record. The birds went about their daily life without a purpose to their actions. The weather was fine, the days were long, and the eagles had time to kill. I saw them playing with large lambs, taking it in turn to catch and drag a helpless creature before they grew bored and left it alone, largely unharmed but by then some distance from the ewe, which would charge down the slope to where it stood, fearful of the next attack. The birds made a series of nest visits culminating on 10 August when they both visited the acacia nest (an old and unused location that the juveniles liked to use as a perch) before the female flew to the top nest, and after flying together again, the male visited the middle nest. This was all in the space of eight minutes, and I wondered if it was part of the nest selection process or if they were just bored. They didn't carry material, however, and none was gathered until 3 September when the top nest proved attractive again.

The eagles continued to defend their valley from all-comers throughout the year and were particularly active on 20 September. At 12.20 p.m. they began a long series of perch-hopping, making short flights about the valley and landing at regular intervals, finding 14 different perches in the space of 50 minutes. After a short rest, they were in the air again and this time circled and sailed beside various crags, the male above the female. They moved down-valley and, most unusually, began to gain height above its mouth. They soon appeared too high to be simply preparing to move to a more distant part of the range. It looked like disturbance behaviour, but there was no one to be seen, and there certainly wasn't anyone close to the nests.

I had one of those inklings that impel you to turn your attention elsewhere and make you scan a wider field. Sweeping the distant vista, a speck crossed my eye line, so I switched to the telescope and saw the unmistakable silhouette of one and then two golden eagles. The resident birds were still circling high above my head, so now, for the first time ever in the Lake District, I had four golden eagles in view simultaneously. I knew the old male from my first site was still alive, but why would he be here and where had the fourth bird come from? Both pairs circled on just as you see neighbouring pairs displaying their presence and their territories during the winter in Scotland. The others were too far away for me to age them, but they couldn't have been establishing a territory as where they circled was wholly unsuitable for breeding eagles and they were closer to my home than they were to me.

At 1.31 p.m., the residents changed their circling to a sweeping pendulum flight that resembled the sky-dance but with much broader and shallower dips; the birds also kept their wings outstretched unlike the sky-dance when they're folded back to give the eagle a heart-shaped profile. The residents performed this swinging flight for 12 minutes, but the other eagles simply continued to circle, apparently without gaining height and apparently unimpressed by the residents. Even though all four birds were inside the Haweswater range, the residents didn't move towards the others, but when the latter turned to move away the resident birds began a directional glide that would intercept them as they neared the grouse moors.

I had to follow them but 3 km and a stiff 400-m climb lay between where I was and from where I could see their destination, so I made a dash for the car. I knew it would probably take the best part of an hour for me to get to the moors, but I'd be closer if I went there and would still have the option to follow on foot if I could relocate any of the eagles. I checked the nests out of habit before turning out of the valley and, to my surprise, saw two ravens poking about on the top site. It was an indication of just how quickly these corvids would usurp the valley if the eagles were to go, just as would happen at the other Lakeland site.

I sped round to the moors and trekked through the heather to one of my regular observation posts as quickly as I could and was almost immediately rewarded by the male circling into view. The female soon followed, but to my dismay, they then turned and flew back towards the nesting valley, flying out of my sight low over the point in the ridge I would have reached had I walked to view from a distance instead of driving to take a closer look. I stayed on watch for another hour, but the residents didn't return and the other birds didn't show themselves. I spent many days searching potential territory areas in the Lakes after that, and revisiting the other site, but could find no signs of their use by eagles. The only logical conclusion was that the visitors were immature birds wandering through in search of a home, and the absence of a live food source in the Lakes probably dissuaded them from staying.

There was another visitor to the area that year. On the evening of 11 October I received a phone call from Nick, a volunteer from that year's RSPB protection scheme. Nick had offered to show the Haweswater site to Mike Tomkies, but his car had broken down, and he was now asking me to advise Mike of this. I drove along the lakeside road and found Mike encamped in an old quarry. We were both wary of the other; I wasn't the person Mike was expecting to meet, and I was still a little taken aback by Nick's presumption and wondered what Mike might be planning. We sat in his van, and once the confusion over just whom I was had been settled (Mike was under the impression that Nick was the warden), we relaxed and began to talk about eagles and drink some wine and whisky. We found ourselves talking through the night, and by the time I left I was in no fit state to be out alone. We arranged to meet the next morning, which proved to be a beautiful day, but I was still the worse for wear and couldn't even face the plod up the hill to see the eagles. I directed Mike to the right valley, without telling him where the nests were, and struggled home to recover.

Nick arrived that evening, and Mike told us what he'd seen as we all walked up the valley the next day. I was impressed that he'd found the nests without any help but more so that he'd identified the locations of nests that no longer existed. He even found the acacia nest, a site that the wardens wouldn't even accept when I fixed the telescope on it or when I showed them a close-up photograph. But Mike knew the signs and had even picked out the ledge that had held the 1969 nest, a site to which the eagles hadn't added material since that time, 16 years earlier.

We only spent about six hours in the valley and only saw about eight minutes of flying, but the talk was good, and the bird arrived at the time Mike had predicted and had entered the valley over the spot that I predicted, so we enjoyed ourselves and the time we spent together. I'd found a kindred spirit in Mike. Like me he'd started his eagle work with little prior knowledge of the species, had taken the published work as a guide rather than as the gospel and had set out to discover new facts and follow the birds throughout the year. Also like me, he'd fallen foul of the experts and suffered because his work wasn't deemed to be 'scientific'. This was a biased view, Seton Gordon wrote popular books, but they're still considered to be among the best eagle books ever written. Mike and I have remained firm friends since that day even though we disagree about many aspects of the eagle's life; my experiences contradict some of his and vice versa, and we have differences of opinion over interpretations and the significance of the records we have in common. But that's one of the joys of fieldwork; no one's an expert, no one's seen it all, and that's why we go out and watch eagles.

Noting new behaviour

The winter of 1985/86 began uneventfully – there were some frosts and heavy snow-falls but also some bright sparkling days, and it was a joy to walk to the valley at such times. Sometimes I saw the eagles there and sometimes I didn't. If I didn't see them there I only had to visit the grouse moors to fill in the blanks or have a day out on the high tops. I saw the eagles killing grouse and being mobbed by peregrines and ravens on the moors, but they were still roosting in Riggindale. Even so, a two-week absence after 16 January didn't come as any surprise. The weather had turned, and the overnight temperature dropped to –20ºC; even the Haweswater lake froze over, and early morning walks revealed fox tracks leading from one side to the other in the freshly fallen snow.

An unbroken white blanket lay across the hills, and more than just the odd patch of snow would lie in the nesting valley from 21 December 1985 to 4 May 1986. It was the hardest winter of my study, but it was a magnificent time to be out on the hills and following the eagles. There were no sheep or deer carcasses available to the birds – any animals that had died before the worst of the falls now lay buried, and the living had retreated to the lower ground where the eagles wouldn't venture. Red deer sheltered in the woods around my home, and predawn walks found many scuffing about in the vegetation on the edge of the village as they eked out their survival. I walked into small groups of deer along the lakeside path that neither bolted away nor stood their ground, they milled around uncertainly, not wanting to move too far from the protection of the woods but knowing that they should be on the hills and wary of humans.

The eagles were absent from their valley, but they had the means to cover vast distances quickly and could seek out better feeding opportunities without even beating their wings. I knew them to be using the moors because the grouse were always there, although the population closest to the nesting valley died out during this winter, as did the grouse in the nesting valley of the other pair of eagles. The heather moor was snow-bound as well, but the grouse dug holes to access their food plants, and the more windswept nature of the moors meant that some parts were only under a light covering. The grouse holes were a surprise for me; I'd assumed that during severe conditions the birds would move to lower ground, even onto farmland. I hadn't guessed that they'd roost among the heather stalks below the snow and dig themselves out during the day. That must be a regular habit of the grouse's close relative, the ptarmigan, in the Scottish Highlands, and one that protects them against snow and predators. I also wondered if the eagles would move to the adjacent farmland edge, but I didn't see them there, only on the heather. When I checked the nests on 30 January they were snowbound and untouched by the eagles. I'd never seen material added during January, but a late check every year helped to reconfirm this record and helped to narrow down the time when refurbishment did begin. The roosts weren't in use either, and I'd discover that the eagles would roost away from the nesting valley for six weeks, taking them close to the laying date. Despite the adverse conditions that winter, the eagles still seemed to survive with no real problems.

Although the eagles were roosting on the moors, sometimes using a pine tree that had been used by the 1984 juvenile, they did still visit the nesting valley, so I did likewise. In early February I walked to the site and found both birds in their second valley, sailing at the cloud base and occasionally drifting up into it where the lack of visibility didn't appear to hamper them. I kept walking as nest-building should have begun, and I was confident that the birds would visit their valley at some point that day. As I reached the last viewing point, the eagles turned towards the valley, and I made a quick dash to follow them. Arriving only five minutes behind them I saw the male hanging on the wind beside the middle nest, but he almost immediately began a long stoop towards the valley mouth. I thought he was about to land in the only big pine tree at that location, but he pulled out to hang above it before dropping quickly into the canopy. I saw a brief scuffle before he settled, and when I switched to the telescope I saw that he held a red squirrel in the talons of his left foot. He stepped out of a clear view, but I could tell that he ate for nine minutes before defecating and flying back up the valley.

It was another example of the incredible eyesight of the golden eagle. The male hadn't just been passing the tree, he'd made a deliberate flight towards it, so he must have seen the squirrel in the tree from a distance of more than a kilometre. Coincidentally, my habit of collecting the pellets of undigested food from below the roosts produced the pellet that contained the squirrel remains, some red fur, a jaw and a few bones. Interestingly, the only other record I've had of squirrel as prey came from a pellet I found three years later under that same roost.

The first refurbishment that year started with the nests still coated in a heavy burden of snow. The eagles chose the middle site for 1986 and proceeded to reconstruct the nest platform on a layer of snow that would eventually melt and, I thought, possibly make the nest unstable. After a period of thaw the nest base became visible, above this was a layer of snow, and this was topped with the fresh nest material. While I was concerned that the structure might collapse, the eagles continued to add material, so they must have been happy with their choice, and I saw them mating on five occasions during February. On the 12th, I watched them couple twice in the same place, an interval of exactly one hour separating the two events during which the female didn't move, but the male had taken material to the nest before returning to his partner. This year was also the first time I'd seen the eagles mating in a tree; most coupling occurred on the ground or on a ledge. My hopes were high for a breeding success, and I was pleased that their nest choice would make it more difficult for the birds to be disturbed by human activity.

The intensity of the nest-building declined after 12 March, but the eagles were always in the valley when I visited them after that, and incubation had begun when I arrived on the 23rd. The RSPB were back on watch, so my wanderings were curtailed, and I wasn't allowed to collect pellets once the team was on site. The wardening team was essentially the same as 1985, in spite of the mistakes they'd made, but they were now officially assisted by Stefan, and as the third warden they had Dave, who'd started under me as a volunteer in 1984. Unfortunately for the long-term monitoring effort and the completeness of the records, none of the team was keen on keeping the behavioural log, and a record form was devised to record the most important points, as selected by the wardens, so, while they recorded any nest-relief they noticed, they excluded the general behaviour and hunting flights and seemed more interested in recording the number of human visitors they received.

The snow had melted from the lower ground by then, but just when the weather appeared to be improving yet more snow fell, and the next morning I was reminded of the dismal days I'd had at the other pair. The snow was heavy and wet, just as it had been in 1980, and it soaked and slowed everything. Even so, there was only a slight frost that morning, and I was surprised to notice that the wardens were all in the village. They said the weather had been too bad for them to stay in the valley even though they had a hide in which to shelter. 25 March dawned clear and bright, but it was warmer and the snow had been melting from before dawn. When the wardens eventually returned to the valley they found that the nest had been deserted and the birds were flying together. Stefan saw the eagles mating later that day, but neither bird flew to the nest. With the nest now deserted, the RSPB decided to commence their 24-hour watches and guard duties. I only discovered these facts because Ken and I had both been called to give evidence at a nest-disturbance trial in Northumberland; a waste of time that prevented me from witnessing the events in Riggindale for myself.

The wardens were very reluctant to talk about the events as we drove across country together, but they did eventually. Ken Shaw met us in Bellingham, so I left the two Kens to talk in private, and after he'd spoken to the other witnesses I went to express my disappointment over the eagle news to him. He was taken aback by what I said, and I had to explain what had happened. Even though they'd talked for about 20 minutes Ken, the eagle warden, hadn't bothered to tell his boss what had happened. But when George drove us back to Haweswater later that day he had better news – the eagles were sitting again. It was assumed that the second egg had been laid, but there were too many things going wrong for my liking, and the accuracy and reliability of my records were being affected because there was no evidence to support anything these wardens reported.

I thought long and hard about my next actions; was there any point in looking into the nest? I knew I would never get permission to do that, but there was little risk of me being seen by the wardens if I did decide to do it. While they checked the nest, they paid virtually no attention to the crags, and I knew I could get close to the nest without being seen. It would be a risk, but could it be justified? All I'd be able to confirm was the number of eggs, and in normal circumstances, I frowned upon disturbance for that purpose. But I knew that one had been laid, and if the nest still only held one egg I'd know that the first had been stolen. I eventually convinced myself that it needed to be done; I had to view the nest contents as soon as possible.

I'd been there on many previous occasions, of course, so I knew the approaches from all directions, and I knew at which points the nest came into view and from where the risk of causing disturbance became too great. I therefore knew which route to follow for the safest access of least disturbance, the point I needed to reach to see the nest clearly, and I knew that to get there I would, at one point, be in full view of the RSPB hide. My only concern was not to disturb the birds, however, and while I had full confidence in my fieldcraft I knew that a kicked loose stone could easily draw the sitting bird's attention and drive her off the nest.

The chosen day, 28 March, dawned with broken skies giving occasional hail and rain showers. These were almost ideal conditions for me: the greyness would extend the twilight and the showers would keep the eagle settled, although this also made it less likely for me to see a changeover or the sitting bird stand to turn the eggs as soon as I arrived. I reached the ridgetop as the skies were beginning to lighten, but all was quiet in the valley. I felt like an egg collector. My eyes used to the greyness, I could see that there was no activity at the hide. The fear of disturbing the eagle was now uppermost in my mind. I questioned the sense of my actions, but I was there by then, the ground conditions were in my favour, and I needed to know if there were one or two eggs in the nest. The ground cover was a mixture of rocky outcrops, heather and snow patches, the best possible cover to conceal a slow-moving camouflaged figure in the uplands. I'd always described the middle nest as a cryptic one and had realised that the juveniles which fledged from here stayed nearby during their first days off the nest because of the concealment and protection it provided; I could now use that to my advantage.

The female was incubating when I got into position, casually looking about the valley at first as the day brightened but also taking short naps. As I'd expected, the wardens weren't so alert and I'd been on the ridge for more than two hours before there was any sign of life at the hide, but at about 7 a.m. one of them stepped outside, stretched and yawned and went for a wander without once looking towards the nest he was guarding. I was incensed that people like this had replaced me, when I thought of the time and effort I'd put into protecting the eagles during my six years; there could have been teams of collectors fighting over the eggs for all he knew.

The male eagle came winging into the nest about half an hour later and stood proudly beside his mate. If the eagles knew of my presence, 40 metres away, it clearly wasn't causing any disturbance. The eagles looked at each other and then out over the valley, not once did they look towards me. The female stood after a minute, stiffly and cramped after a long cold night on the nest, and stepped across the nest cup. As she stood beside her mate I could see what lay beside them, there was one white egg and one rusty brown egg, near-perfect copies of the 1985 clutch, and proof that they hadn't been robbed. The male settled over the eggs before the female left the nest and sat looking down the valley towards the RSPB hide, from which no one looked back.

Once the male was settled I crawled back up and over the ridgetop. It was needlessly discreet, but I wanted to guarantee that no one saw me on the hill. I walked the full length of the ridge and then back up the valley floor to the hide. As I did so the female flew in to relieve her mate, and I watched the male fly off to perch on the *camouflage man*. The warden informed me that nothing had happened that morning, so I pointed out the male and then, with the cloud base dropping, turned and headed for home. I don't know if he ever wondered why I made such a short visit to the hide that day.

Had the first egg still been viable it should have hatched on 4 May, but there was no sign of that happening. If it had been laid as soon as incubation recommenced in March, the second egg should have hatched on the 7th, and much to my surprise, the wardens reported food going to the nest at 10.50 a.m. that day. The events of 1985 made me wary of accepting this information, but I saw food being delivered the next day and also saw a squirt of faeces ejected from the nest, a sure sign that an egg had hatched. I still decided to take another close look at the nest, though. There was an interesting question to be answered: was it the first or second egg that had hatched?

We'd only ever used dates to decide this question in the past, but there was the possibility of the chick being from the first egg. The female might have been covering rather than incubating before the snow or the first egg's development might not have started before the eagles returned. It was probably the only opportunity I'd ever have to answer this question, and it was an opportunity I didn't want to miss, so I went again. I confirmed that it was the second-laid egg that had hatched and then made my circuitous way to call on the wardens. The duty man had seen the male flying that morning, but he hadn't seen the female fly off the nest and return as I had.

The hatch meant that I'd have another juvenile to follow after the fledge, so I kept my visits to the valley to a minimum and instead began to concentrate on a study area in the west of Scotland where I wanted to investigate how eagles behaved within a population, when they had neighbours to interfere with their habits and limit their movements. My visits to Riggindale were still as regular as clockwork, though, because I needed to know that nothing untoward happened that might affect the bird after it left the nest. Everything appeared to be as expected; I accompanied Geoff when he ringed the eaglet, and we confirmed that it was physically sound although it did suffer some food shortage during June.

Food shortages at this time were clearly a regular feature of the eagle's year and may be why large chicks are known to die at six to eight weeks of age in Scotland. June may coincide with the young of many species becoming available, but they are quickly active, healthy and able to defend themselves (in 1992 I'd see a June red deer calf successfully defend itself against two adult eagles in Scotland), and the vegetation is lush, providing cover for the smaller mammals and ground birds such as grouse and waders. Ravens and crows with young also tend to keep their distance and, of course, there is least carrion at this time. It's easy to assume that the winter is the hardest time, but I think the eagles suffered more in June than they did in January. The 1986 food shortage wasn't as severe as the one I'd witnessed in 1983, but seeing the male return to the valley with a red grouse for the nest was a clear sign of hardship. The grouse would still have small flightless young in June, so the eagle must have worked hard for his prize, even before the long flight back to the valley.

There was a supposed shortage of manpower on the wardening scheme during July, so I persuaded the team to allow me to help out with some overnight stints. This gave me the opportunity to know exactly when the bird left the nest, even if I didn't actually see the first flight for myself. These watches proved the 1986 chick to be the most active of all those I'd watched. It spent hours dashing from one side of the nest to the other, jumping onto the ledge and then jumping, hopping and bouncing back across to the stick platform before returning and repeating the whole process. I was certain that, as in 1979, this bird would have walked had it the opportunity to do so. My first 24-hour watch was also unusual in that throughout that period an adult, the female, was only on the nest for a total of eight minutes. The female went to roost on *the swing* three hours before darkness fell, and the male was even less active. He spent almost 10 unbroken hours perched in *the cleft tree*.

I only had 24 hours between my shifts, and when I arrived at the hide the next day I was informed that the nestling had flown. A telescope was fixed on the spot where it had landed, a heathery bank a few metres below and up-valley from the nest, but I couldn't see it at all. As I'd thought it might be a walker, I started to painstakingly scan the ground in case it had moved. My scope soon found its way back up towards the nest and there, poking out from the vegetation on the ledge next to the nest, was the chick's beak. It hadn't flown, as it simply wouldn't have been capable of getting to where it was from where it was supposed to be. This was now 78 days after the hatch, and the female, perhaps realising this, spent the first 90 minutes of my watch perched on the observation tree above the nest, as if waiting for something to happen. The male was still busy, possibly preparing for the long weeks ahead when he'd have sole charge of the juvenile, and later delivered a stoat to the nest that I'd seen him catch in the valley head. The nestling tucked in and then stomped onto the ledge where it settled down to sleep.

The youngster awoke at 10.22 a.m., opened and closed its wings and then hopped down to the nest. It stood looking out over the void, and then in a repetition of what I'd seen in 1984, it nodded its head and launched into its first flight. Immediately swinging up-valley, it hugged the slope in a fairly expert glide, but with a bulging outcrop approaching fast, it flapped its wings and landed heavily close to *the acacia tree*. It had flown about 60 metres, so as the years went by, what I saw was increasingly closer to the long flights suggested in other literature, but even this bird hadn't really left the nest as a master of the winds. It turned to face out from the ridge as if about to fly again but decided to stay where it was and consider its next move. The weather deteriorated after 5 p.m., and it roosted where it stood, on the ground, prone to attack by fox or badger, and apparently unprotected by either adult.

I shifted into 'juvenile mode', and with the RSPB hide dismantled and the wardens gone, I looked forward to another season of long treks and watching the bird develop its skills towards independence. There were to be problems in this year. The change in the weather that began on the fledging day continued, and during the first 30 days after that there were only six that weren't affected by rain or low cloud. The male knew he should be providing for the juvenile, but these conditions hampered his ability to hunt, and the problem was compounded by other factors. The nearest grouse population had become extinct the previous winter, and the felling of the two rookeries closest to the eagles in 1985 had totally removed an enormous source of readily available good-sized prey from the home range, birds on which the male had regularly preyed in previous years. The male caught more stoats for the youngster, but the corvids and grouse of earlier years were absent from the juvenile's diet.

As may have been proven by the first flight, this was an advanced juvenile, which was making open flights at an earlier age and using different perches to those used by the previous juveniles. In fact, this bird used none of the three perches favoured by the previous birds once they'd learnt to fly properly. What I was seeing was very different from those other years, and the youngster was perched in *the cross tree* when I arrived on the 16th. The male was perched close by at first light but soon moved to *the ledge*, and the juvenile followed him there 15 minutes later; it was by far the earliest I'd seen a juvenile on one of the adults' high perches. The male appeared unsettled by this intrusion and walked about on the ledge as if claiming it as his own, but when he finally settled the juvenile began begging for food and pecking at the adult's talons, knowing them to be the usual source of food. The male didn't like this and suddenly snapped his beak at the youngster, causing it to jump back in alarm. It was a surprise to me as well – the first time I'd seen the beak used in anger.

When it saw the female, the juvenile flew to try to coax her into providing food, but she didn't want to know and dropped to land on a rock. The juvenile was highly frustrated now, and probably very hungry, and it flashed its talons at her as it flew by to flash at a sheep and trail its hangings legs through some bracken before landing on a rock in the big screes. The juvenile then jumped onto an old sheep carcass and fed on the desiccated flesh for six minutes before moving on. It was the first time I'd seen a juvenile choose to feed on carrion at this stage, but it would be by no means the last. Once it had found a fresh carcass and was happy to feed there, the male stopped even trying to find fresh prey for the youngster.

A new pattern of behaviour was set, but the juvenile was, at least, still in the valley. I didn't see any of the development that resulted in the food pass after 1984, and this bird, in 1986, soon began its adventures. Arriving in the valley before first light a week later, the adults were immediately active and, at 5.25 a.m., turned over the ridge and flew into the next valley. The male reappeared over the extreme eastern end of the ridge, over ground the adults generally seldom visited because of the amount of human activity in that area, and circled on. Although it was often difficult to locate the juveniles at first light if they weren't calling, for some reason I just knew that this bird had left the valley. I began to climb over the ridge, and when I reached the top I could hear the juvenile calling from the far side of the corrie. It had left the valley 12 days before any of the previous birds and had gone in the opposite direction. When I relocated the male, I sensed that he was uneasy about this early departure, even though the juvenile did little more than perch and call before returning to the valley an hour after I'd found it.

As with the other juveniles, once the 1986 bird had left the valley for the first time it was out of it every day, spending up to six hours away on each excursion at first and feeding while it was elsewhere. I climbed to the ridgetops in search of the bird three days later and followed the lip of eight valleys before eventually seeing the juvenile circling to gain height over a distant valley before it turned and flew back to Riggindale and the adults. Instead of accompanying the juvenile, the male had already deserted it, a sure sign that it was already leaving the home range. The juvenile had, in effect, missed four weeks of the development I'd seen previously. If this pattern was to continue I knew I'd lose track of it inside three weeks, and the pattern did continue.

Even though I knew the juvenile to be roosting in Riggindale most of the time, it soon left on its adventures and left me with the adults in the valley. Finding the bird became a thankless task. I tried to get up high for first light to at least watch its flights, but I'd lose it if it dropped into the first valley and it was seldom there by the time I arrived, and if it was still there it usually flew straight out. I cold-searched but had little luck, it wasn't using the grouse moors, and carrion was scattered far and wide, usually in the bottom of the valleys. I walked the ridges, staring down and listening into each of the valleys, but the bird was away, and more often than not, I couldn't find it. On the one occasion I could pursue it on a long flight, the juvenile led me to some derelict moor 18 km in a straight line from my home. The eagle only had 9 km to return home as it could fly in a straight line, but for me the return distance was probably doubled by following the ridgetops. Even so, there were still some similarities between this and the earlier birds, and on the very next day I watched the juvenile fly to the nest from which it had fledged and stay there for three hours. It was there again the next day and again four days later. The juvenile seemed to be as confused as the adults; by the time the other youngsters were venturing that far afield they'd stopped visiting the valley with any regularity and were ignoring the nests when they did appear.

The juvenile was again in the valley when I arrived at 5.30 a.m. on 10 September, and soon found its way to a sheep carcass. It was constantly harried by six crows but had a good feed of 80 minutes. The length of the feed suggested that the juvenile was still struggling to find food, and this was confirmed the next day when it fed from the same carcass for an hour. Perhaps in revenge or perhaps in the knowledge that food was in short supply, the eagle defended the carcass for 30 minutes after the first feed and did so for 45 after the second. It was defensive during the feeds as well, turning to call and hiss at any crow that approached too closely, and especially at the ones that ran in to tweak the eagle's tail, giving the young feathers what was probably a painful tug before the eagle could swing around and glower at the crow. These were frosty mornings at a time when I expected the juvenile to be feeding from carrion, so I wasn't at all surprised to find it on the same carcass for the third day in succession. The crows appeared to have the upper hand on this occasion; the eagle was clearly unsettled by their antics, and its

79-minute feed was liberally interspersed with bouts of tail-pulling by the crows and retaliatory chases by the eagle, the latter loping across the ground in hops and skips at one crow before dashing back to chase another from the food. It continued this for 22 minutes after the feed, running and flapping to scatter the crows, and, in a surprising reversal of roles, continued to chase the crows while the adult male ate his fill. I think we were all confused by this point.

It was another two days before I noted more feeding, and just to continue the mix-up, I saw the juvenile feeding from a crow kill the male brought into the valley. The male had eaten for 15 minutes before leaving the carcass for the juvenile, but the latter didn't seem too interested at first and picked and played with it before finally eating it. I had the juvenile in view for nine hours that day, and when I left all three birds were perched together in *the acacia tree*. The juvenile was even still there when I returned 18 hours later, but it must surely have moved during that time. All three eagles were in the valley together again on the 19th, and it seemed as though they'd settled back into a similar pattern to previous years, though at what point in the pattern I wasn't certain. What I also didn't know at the time was that when the juvenile flew to land behind a bush that day it would be the last time I saw it.

I only saw the female on the 22nd and then saw no eagles until the 29th, in spite of yet more cold-searching and dawn and dusk roost watches. During that week I watched ravens visit both of the main eagle nests, and I even saw a crow on the middle site. It was as if the eagles had gone for ever, but then, on the 29th, I saw the adults flight-rolling and performing their parallel glide. I knew then that the juvenile had gone, and their absence had been due to the adults re-establishing their home range, just as I'd seen in other years. The juvenile had probably reached independence after 63 days, some 17 days earlier than the average for the previous three.

I was convinced that the differences I'd noted between the three juveniles, which had followed a pattern of behaviour that varied by only a day or two, and the 1986 bird, which failed to follow any pattern, was due to the change in food supply. The loss of the grouse and the corvids (the absence of rooks also kept the jackdaws off the fells) prevented the male from supplying fresh prey for the juvenile, so it had to turn to carrion to survive. With carrion carcasses usually being few and far between at that time of year, the juvenile also had to travel further in search of food, and the adult male, perhaps set in his ways, abandoned the juvenile before he should have. The situation wasn't to improve; the grouse couldn't re-establish their populations over night (the extinct population clearly couldn't return), and the mature beech and oak trees that had held the rookeries were replaced by saplings that wouldn't even hold a chaffinch nest. While it failed to match the behaviour of the earlier birds, the 1986 juvenile set a precedent that was followed by all of the subsequent chicks reared at Haweswater. I was able to separate the 1982 to 1984 juveniles as being from the live-prey years with the remainder being from the carrion years. The distinction was that obvious.

As I was creeping about above the middle nest on 5 August, the juvenile swung in to land at 5.43 a.m., so I stalked the bird and was able to take a couple of reasonable photographs of it on the ground, even though I didn't use more than a 200 mm lens. With this in mind and the juvenile apparently gone from the area, I thought it might be nice to have a photograph of the adults, so I set my mind to that task. There was no chance that I'd be allowed to photograph at the nest, and I didn't want to do that in any case, it was too easy, so I had to try at a carcass, and September was as good a time as any to put the plan in action. I felt there was little chance of success given all the options at the eagles' disposal but decided that a good place to try would be below one of the flight-lines along which the eagles habitually flew at low elevation, giving them every chance of seeing the carcass, if not the hide I'd have to build.

I selected a likely location from the valley floor and soon found a large boulder close to a piece of level ground on which I could lay the bait. I set to work scooping out rocks from the uphill side of the boulder and banked them up to form a wall that flowed into the natural angle of scree slope so as not to leave any sharp angles or obviously man-made shapes. The front, with the camera slot, was more difficult to disguise but I banked it up with vegetation and moss-covered rocks and on the inside even placed a flat rock on which to sit and a shelf for my notebook and cup. I found some old fence posts and collected some planks from the RSPB hide destroyed in 1982 for the roof and covered these with netting to hold a covering of moss, grasses and bracken. As a final touch, I balanced a few rocks on top of the posts to break up the sloping flat surface of the roof. Now all I needed was a carcass and for the eagles to accept it.

There were no dead sheep or deer in the valley at the time, but I found a freshly killed badger on the road close to my home a couple of days later, and knowing that to be part of the eagles' natural diet, I thought I'd take a chance. Laden with the badger in my sack, the tripod, camera and lenses, spare clothing, bait-box, a pocket stove, pan, tea and water, I set off up the valley on 29 September. Both eagles were in the air as I walked, and they performed a flight-roll at 6 a.m. before separating. When I reached the RSPB's observation post the male eagle was on *the ledge*. There was no one to walk me into the hide, but that wasn't going to stop me. Even if I spent eight hours in the hide and saw absolutely nothing I hadn't carried a dead badger all that distance just to turn round and walk away again. The eagle was still perched when I laid out the carcass and settled into the hide, but he'd gone by 7.10 a.m. The session turned into a long wait. Even though I'd left viewing holes in the front wall of the hide I was frustrated at not being able to check all the perches or see the birds. Meadow pipits flitted about the hide, and I heard the distinctive stiff beat of a raven's wings as it passed high overhead. There was no urgency in its flight, and I wondered if the eagles had left the valley, possibly because of my presence.

Some crows called, and through a gap in the roof, I could see the male eagle perched on the crags above the hide, but he flew after a minute, and it was all quiet again with not even the pipits bothering to keep me company. More crows called, and suddenly with a swoosh of air, the male landed on the rock beside the carcass. I fired off some photographs, and he didn't seem to hear the camera. He stood craning his neck to see if the badger was dead, even though I'd deliberately laid it on its back with its legs outstretched and the pale belly hair on display, before walking across to pluck and feed from the carcass. He only stayed for three minutes, but I couldn't believe my luck. I'd read many tales of photographers clambering into hides at the dead of night to avoid being seen by eagles and of two people approaching a hide in daylight so that one could walk away as a decoy to deceive the eagles into thinking that the humans had gone, but for me it was simple: I set out the carcass in full view of the eagle, climbed into the hide, and the bird was down and feeding less than three hours later.

Neither bird came down after that, but buoyed by the experience I was back in the hide at 6.15 the next morning, and the eagle came to the carcass at 6.58 a.m. He ate for 25 minutes this time, and wanting to save some shots in case the female appeared, I lay back to enjoy every second of being so close to the great bird. His feed completed, the male hopped away, wiped his beak and flew out of my sight. With another whoosh of air the female arrived at 9.19 a.m., and she too ate her fill. A few photographs later, I carefully slid the camera from its slot and sat and marvelled as she tore at the meat. What I'd expected to be the most difficult of the tasks I set myself luckily proved to be the easiest of them all.

As in the earlier years, there was a slackening off of activity with the departure of the juvenile, and it was 20 November before I noted anything else of particular interest. On that day both the adult eagles took long feeds and both visited the middle nest, suggesting that it would again be in use the next year. I called in on Geoff Horne a few days later, and the telephone rang just as I stepped into the house. When he joined me, Geoff had bad news. It had been the RSPB on the phone, calling to tell him that the juvenile was dead.

Ten days after I'd last seen the juvenile a young eagle was being seen in North Yorkshire. It settled into a relatively small area and was seen killing rabbits, but it was found dead beneath power cables on 21 November, its ring identifying it as the Haweswater bird. There'd been atrocious snow storms at that time, and the bird had been electrocuted, possibly blown into the cables during a blinded flight or blown from a perch, as it was found close to a pole that held the cables. It had only lived for 121 days as a free-flying eagle and had flown to die about 76 km from the nest. It is the only juvenile whose fate we know for certain.

CHAPTER 12

Mixed fortunes

Snow lay deep in the valley during January 1987, and the eagles were absent again for long periods. Nest refurbishment began on 4 February, and a good solid and compact layer about 30 cm thick was added during the next 10 days. My roost checks produced pellets containing sheep wool and rabbit fur and bones, but I didn't actually see the eagles feeding until 22 March. That was one of the earlier laying dates, but it came and went in 1987 without anything happening. The female didn't lay on the 23rd either, but I had high hopes on the 24th when she visited the nest shortly after I arrived. She left 16 minutes later, and the male flew in to replace her. I was used to the male taking the first stint of incubation, but he appeared unsettled on this occasion and called as three crows flew by; he didn't fly off in pursuit or leave when his mate was dealing with a peregrine, but he didn't sit on the nest either and left after 15 minutes. That was an unusually long visit for the male at that time of year without there being eggs in the nest, but the female didn't replace him and, in fact, the male delivered material to the nest before the female next landed there. The eagles' activity declined after this, and during eight-hour watches on consecutive days I didn't once see the female visit the nest. It was a similar picture during the next three days, and it looked as though we weren't going to see eggs in 1987.

The Haweswater eagles hadn't failed to lay eggs since 1968, regardless of the pressures of harsh winters, but that now looked to be a real possibility. When I arrived in the valley at 6.30 a.m. on the 29th I could find neither the eagles nor the wardens. I wasn't able to spend all the daylight hours in the valley, and with the wardens only being on duty during office hours, there was a real possibility that something could already have been missed. I stayed at the hide for an hour but saw nothing. If a breeding attempt was about to be made I'd have expected the birds to be on show, but if they'd already failed or been robbed they'd have no reason to stay.

There was no one else in the valley, and little prospect of the wardens arriving for a couple of hours, so I decided to check the nest. The eagles weren't, apparently, on the verge of laying eggs, so I felt that a quick visit by someone who knew what he was doing wouldn't have any adverse effects. I wanted to give the eagles every chance to reveal themselves before I did anything that might cause disturbance, so I started by walking along the valley floor to see if I generated any response and planned to reach the ridgeline via a view of the top nest. I hadn't seen the eagles adding to that nest in 1987, but it was there so it may as well be checked. I'd then double back along the ridge-top before dropping to view the middle nest from above, as in 1986.

Typically, the female and then the male circled up from behind the top-nest crag within 10 minutes of me leaving the hide. They crossed the valley and settled on the rocks opposite the middle nest. It was poor timing; they'd caught me in no-man's land, halfway between the two nests, with the one I expected them to use between the RSPB's hide and me. I walked on more quickly and regularly checked to ensure that the birds were still perched. At top speed I angled up towards the *bilberry peaks* and from there could see that the top nest was unchanged from when I'd checked it two months earlier. The eagles were still perched, so I scrambled up to the ridge-top and sped along towards the point from which I'd descended a year and a day earlier.

I climbed down towards the nest. There was no need for discretion on this occasion; in fact, with the eagles perched opposite me, it was best for my actions to be as open as possible, to allow them to see what I was doing. It was risking eliciting some disturbance behaviour, but it was better for that to happen than it was for the eagles to be uncertain of my whereabouts. I went beyond my secluded viewpoint of the previous year and dropped to a lower ledge. From there I had a clear view into the nest. The eagles still hadn't moved, which wasn't a good sign, and it was made worse by what I saw. The nest was in a very poor state of repair, there was very little fresh soft lining material, such as woodrush, and no cup had been formed. There was also snow on the nest, and single streak of faeces ran down the outside of the front wall. These weren't good signs, but it confirmed that no eggs had been laid.

I followed an even more obvious route away from the ledge, and the eagles stayed where they were, unconcerned by my actions. Back on the ridgetop I noticed that the wardens had arrived, so I dropped back down to meet them. I made no secret of what I'd done, and I think they were pleased to have it confirmed from a reliable source that nothing untoward had happened at the nest. I directed their attention to the eagles, and we watched them mating almost immediately. I stayed for a couple more hours but only short flights followed, so I left the wardens in peace and returned home. That evening, to my astonishment, I was informed that the female had gone to the nest at about 2 p.m. and that incubation had begun, in the middle nest, at about 4.40 p.m.

The incubation period appeared to progress without a hitch after that, but I wasn't too surprised when the prospective hatching date arrived and passed without any news. During the next couple of days there was no burst of activity, the male didn't carry food, and the female didn't sit any tighter. I was in the valley by 5.30 a.m. on 15 May, but the first changeover wasn't until two hours later. The male didn't have time to sit before the female returned, but before she could sit the male did so, and she flew off again. The female landed on a rock to preen, and I was surprised to see a crow dash in and grab a discarded secondary flight feather the eagle had just pulled from her wing. Satisfied with the condition of her plumage, the female then made three nest visits, twice with material. The male stood with each arrival but was beaten into flight each time until the third when he dashed off and made three display dips as if pleased to have escaped. I tracked him to a perch but missed him leaving it half an hour later, so I wasn't sure what he'd carried to the nest three minutes after that, but I then kept a closer watch on him. During the next 18 minutes I saw him catch, pluck and deliver two ring ouzels to the nest. This confirmed that an eagle egg had hatched, and being 47 days after incubation began, it also told me that it was the second egg that had hatched, just as in 1986.

Happy with events in Riggindale I travelled north, but when I returned from my Scottish study area on the 26th it was to learn that the eagles had failed. I was amazed, small chicks certainly do die in the nest but there was no apparent reason for it. There was no way of knowing what had happened at the nest, and I struggled to learn what the wardens had seen. All I could glean was that the adults had lost interest in the nest, and it only contained the unhatched egg when the wardens checked it a few days later.

It was also natural for the eagles' behaviour to fall into a slumber after a breeding failure, and this year proved to be no exception. The resultant lack of any wardening interest gave me the times of day I wanted for my activities, the first and last few hours of daylight when the wardens weren't in the valley. I collected pellets on the 27th, one of the few occasions I was able to do so during the summer months and found 26 from the nests and 42 perches I checked. Most contained only sheep's wool, but the others showed the diversity of the eagle diet: the species represented included fox, badger, stoat and rabbit, kestrel, pigeon, crow and meadow pipit. There were no ouzel or vole remains, even though I knew those to have been eaten, and no evidence of red deer in the diet at that time of year.

As could also be expected, the little activity the eagles did perform included a bout of nest-building. I saw both birds on the top nest on the 31st and, a week later, saw them delivering soft material to the same nest. The male also visited the *acacia* nest that day, and two days after that I saw the eagles nest-building on an old roost ledge that the male had used until 1984. A visit there on 9 June found 10 sticks, some heather and a few eagle feathers. There were fresh sticks on another ledge on 7 July, and the female spent 34 minutes on the *acacia* nest two days after that. On the 21st I found more fresh material on the 9 June nest, and that the centre of attention had moved along the ledge, and on the 30th there was fresh greenery on the top nest. While all this activity was of interest, there was probably little point to it, I'd seen it all before, with new nests started and old ones refurbished, but the eagles had only ever laid eggs in two nests since 1975 and I didn't expect that situation to change.

The contrast between these last three years and the three previous ones had been stark to say the least, from three chicks fledged to one that had died, so I hoped for better news in 1988. There were other changes afoot, though. There'd long been talk of the area becoming an RSPB reserve and that eventually came to fruition during 1988 via an access agreement with the landowners, North West Water. I was confident that the eagles would be better managed after that and that the poor decision-making of recent years would become a thing of the past. There was another change as well – I found myself working for the RSPB again! I'd be based in Hawick that summer and on Mull in 1989, so I'd miss the breeding seasons but I wasn't too concerned by that. I'd seen most of what I expected to see at that time of year and would still have the winters and the post-fledging periods should there be another juvenile.

After two years in the middle nest, I was certain the eagles would return to the top nest for the 1988 season, and seeing both birds there on 25 January seemed to confirm that belief. Neither bird carried material until 3 February in 1988, but on 28 January 1989 I saw nest building in January for the very first time when the male delivered two 2m-long sticks to the top nest. The first soft material reached the nest on 4 March in 1988, but after that both eagles left the valley, the male east towards the grouse moors and the female to the north. This suggested food shortages, and the lack of sheep carrion that year was further evidence of an increasing problem. And this came into stark relief when I witnessed what was at the time a unique event during my years with the eagles.

I reached the valley at 6.30 a.m. on 10 March 1988, and the male delivered a stick to the nest an hour later. It was a cold day; an incomplete layer of snow covered the valley from ridgetop to floor, and a bitter wind was blowing. I was settled on the north ridge-side having checked some roosts when the female called at 8.20 a.m., and I assumed it heralded the male's return. I waited as the female flew to her favourite perch, but it was seven minutes before her mate eventually entered the valley. To my utter amazement, he was carrying the hind leg of a red deer. It was the first time I'd seen an eagle carrying food for any distance outside the breeding period, and he'd brought this in from outside the valley! He swung low through the mouth of the valley and kept close to the ridge, flapping his wings to maintain his momentum as he passed my position. Even though he'd struggled to carry the leg for more than 5 km, he didn't land immediately but circled for three minutes below the perched female in the valley head before landing next to the big screes.

As he landed the female began to call and continued to call for six minutes and only stopped when the male flew from the food. Eagles weren't supposed to provision the nest during incubation (which I'd seen at both sites), and males certainly weren't supposed to supply food for their mates during the winter. Yet again I was witnessing something the experts said didn't happen. The male didn't eat during his time beside the food and when he flew he made two display dips, but the female stayed on her perch. He circled below his mate and made eight more dips, but still she didn't fly. He performed another nine dips and circled again before making five more dips. After the last one he swung across the valley and flew straight to the top nest, stayed for a minute and then flew to settle less than a metre from his mate. This was very intriguing: if it was provisioning, I couldn't understand why the female hadn't claimed the food and if it wasn't, I couldn't understand why the male had carried the food so far and then displayed so actively without feeding.

The eagles perched together for half an hour before the male returned to the food, and he called four times before immediately taking flight again. It was as if he was trying to entice his mate down to the food, and had it not been for the calling, it would have been very similar to his provisioning of the juveniles. The male returned to the nest at 9.35 a.m. and flew off five minutes later to mate with the female and then return to spend 22 minutes on the nest; he even sat in the cup for 15 minutes, and I was at a complete loss to explain what was happening. When he flew he returned to *the ledge* and stayed there with the female perched above him in *the hole*. It seemed as though the food had been forgotten about (it was by then more than two hours since the male had arrived with it), but there was more to come.

The male was flying again after half an hour, and he performed three display dips as the female watched and called. After these he dropped to the food and ate for 16 minutes. Satisfied, he flew again, but this time he carried the leg with him. He circled for four minutes and then landed to catch his breath by panting hard after the efforts he'd made. On the wing again after a minute he carried the food to a higher ledge, and the female was now in flight as well. She circled over the male, and once he'd returned to *the ledge*, she dropped down, called and began to eat. It was a long and convoluted affair, but it was food provisioning. Given the uncertainty, the apparent confusion and the delays, it seems likely that what I'd seen was the first-ever example of non-breeding season food provisioning of the female by the male, and it was possibly the first record from any British eagle site. I would go on to see provisioning every breeding year after that, and yet, intriguingly, I'd never seen it before that day.

My concerns about the eagles' future weren't at an end, however. With the area now a nature reserve rather than a species protection site, a decision was made to keep the hide in place for the middle nest regardless of where the eagles chose to lay their eggs. I had grave concerns about this. While I'd thought the permanent RSPB presence would improve life for the eagles, this seemed to be a step backwards. Geoff and I had shown that the top nest was only just within reach if a potential egg collector made an obvious approach, but there was no chance of preventing a robbery when starting from the middle hide. The decision was taken to restrict public access to the site as the warden wanted to control the expected increase in visitor numbers once the reserve agreement had been announced, but it made it impossible to view the floor in the valley head and increased the likelihood of the eagles being disturbed.

When the birds successfully reared a chick that year, and did so again from the top nest in 1989, it was deemed to have been a good decision, and the hide was moved even further away from the nest after that and put lower in the valley with an even more restricted view. When I visited the ridgetop during the season not only did I find an arrow made from stones pointing towards the nest crag and groups of people sitting watching the birds, I was even told to keep back from the edge in case the wardens saw me!

I saw the male take the first stint of incubation in 1988, on 22 March, but then left for Hawick and missed most of the incubation period. The egg hatched as expected after 43 days, and I arranged to be in the valley when Geoff arrived to ring it. With the top nest in use, Geoff needed a rope man so when he asked for assistance I volunteered again and off we went. The wardens remained at the hide while we ringed the chick. I was later told that the head warden wasn't happy with me even being in the valley never mind on the crag, but what did he expect? Geoff needed someone he could trust, and

I'd been with him on many occasions and had held on to slipping belays while he was on the rope. In 1989, when I was on Mull, Geoff received no help and had to abseil to the nest, ring the chick, abseil to the foot of the crag, scramble all the way back up, collect the rope and then clamber back down again to return to the hide, while the warden sat on top of the crag, out of site of the nest and unaware of what Geoff was doing. When I was there it was to help Geoff as he was ringing the eagles and peregrines for our benefit but at his expense. Now it was just something the wardens felt obliged to be involved with.

The 1988 juvenile proved to be a slow developer and didn't leave the nest until 83 days after the hatch, so I hadn't missed much of the post-fledging period before I returned from Hawick. This bird was a jumper and had only just reached its safe perch on *the dome* when I arrived to see it for the first time off the nest on 30 July. There was little activity during the seven hours I was on watch, and as the wardening team couldn't tell me anything about the food situation, I was interested to see how this juvenile would fare. By being on a safe perch it was already behaving more like the live prey birds than that of 1986, but during my first four visits I neither saw the juvenile feeding nor the male hunting. I located the juvenile in *the cross tree* on 5 August, and it was there for at least nine hours, three days later it was in the same place for at least 12 hours. As I still hadn't seen it feeding, I decided to check its perches when I next entered the valley.

I walked to the site to arrive at 4.45 a.m. on the 10th fully expecting the bird to be in *the cross tree* again. I knew my actions would probably disturb it, but at two weeks off the nest, its flight feathers would be fully grown and I knew it was a strong flyer. This was, of course, the first day on which I didn't find the juvenile on that perch, but that was good news, I wouldn't disturb it after all. It was actually back on the nest and stayed there for two and a half hours as I scoured the valley. There was plenty of evidence of the juvenile being fed, and it was just like in the earlier years. There were pigeon pluckings on Short Stile, but as could be expected, most of the remains were by *the cross tree*. As well as down and splash from the juvenile, there were the remains of two more pigeons, at least four corvids and some rabbit fur. There was more of the same below a nearby tree and even more on *the dome*. Elsewhere I picked up signs of at least five more crows, two rabbits and three foxes. The latter were on the *bilberry peaks*, and so had been fed to the juvenile while it was still on the nest. I suspected that many of the other pluckings related to nestling food, but unlike in other years when the top nest was used, there were no deer calf remains on the *peaks*. It wasn't until the 16th that I eventually saw the male delivering a crow to the juvenile, but I saw it feed from carrion on the 21st and so knew that there was still a problem with the food supply.

In 1989 I didn't return to the valley until 17 August, but I saw the juvenile visit the top nest that day before it winged its way across to the big screes and settled on a boulder. Its approach appeared to be casual, but through the scope I could see a fox's head peering out from beneath the rock. The eagle stayed there for two hours with the fox moving from one end of the rock to the other again and again, but it didn't dare make a dash for safety. It knew the eagle was there and wasn't going to run until the bird moved. And when it did move it sprinted across the ground and dived into another bolthole before the eagle could attack.

These two juveniles behaved very much alike, but there were differences between them and the previous four. Their behaviour seemed to be an intermediary stage between the live prey and the carrion birds. The male was able to catch live prey in 1988 and 1989, but the juveniles were feeding readily on carrion before they left the valley. These two also took almost as long as the 1982–84 birds to make that first flight, but once they were out of the valley they were roamers in the vein of the 1986 bird. Both of them found food easier to locate in the valley nearest my home than in Riggindale, which made it easier for me, and I found juvenile roosts there in both years. They played the games the others had played, riding sheep and deer and tearing at the ground as if it was food, but the adults didn't teach any lessons. The greatest interactions with other species were when gulls joined the crows to mob the eagles as they moved along the lakeside. The food source in that valley was soon exhausted, and I followed them as best I could, but as in 1986, they were distant wanderers.

I saw the juvenile on 28 September in both years, but again in both years, there were long gaps without sightings after that. The 1988 bird was present on 10 October, but it was independent by then, and the 1989 bird was gone even before that. The adults' resurgence of nest-building activity was always a good sign of the juvenile's departure, and in 1989 they began to build a new nest at the beginning of October. It would never be used, but it would become full sized, which was more than could be said for most of these efforts. It was on a new ledge on the top nest crag, and the birds spent 45 minutes of active building on this the first day of effort. When I checked the nest two days later it was already more than a metre across and half that deep, but they soon lost interest, and although a few more sticks and pieces of heather were added after that, I didn't see any more material taken in until 15 November 1989. The birds were back in winter mode by then. The eagles added to the top nest that year, and if it were to be used in 1990 it would be the first time they'd used the same nest in three consecutive years, but as it was, they weren't allowed to make a choice.

After a largely fruitless series of cold searching in the surrounding hills, I was back in Riggindale on 22 December. I saw the male arrive at his usual winter roost, circling above it to check the site security and then, once happy, whiffling down and onto the branch. He always almost froze on arrival, becoming suddenly stiff and deliberate in his movements before he readjusted his feet, ruffled his feathers and settled down for the night. By 4.05 p.m. it was too dark to search for the female, which usually roosted with the male, and I realised that I hadn't seen her for almost a month. It was the longest gap I'd had when I was available to look, but I wasn't too concerned. I hadn't attempted any roost watches for some time before that and knew from the signs on her favourite perches that she was still about and was probably roosting further up the valley than the male.

I couldn't return to the valley for six days, but 28 December dawned clear and frosty, and I was encouraged to walk rather than drive to the site. As always I checked the six main perches on entering the valley but, failing to find an eagle, then turned my attention to the nests. The top site was empty but the nest looked in good condition, but the middle nest wasn't there! There'd been no storms or heavy snowfalls during the previous six days, and yet there didn't seem to be a single stick on the ledge. I decided to take a closer look and dropped down to the valley floor, crossed the beck and scrambled up through the screes. I'd planned to go directly to the nest, but I could see the nest pile at the foot of the crag and thought I'd get a better photograph from above, and so diverted along the foot of the crags to scramble up a gully and then down to the ledge I'd visited in 1986.

All that remained on the nest ledge was a rotten heap of compressed and mouldered material. I took a few photographs and turned to climb a gravelly runnel that would lead me to the ridgetop, but after a few steps I noticed a scuffing that made me suspicious. The possibility of the nest being deliberately destroyed entered my head, so I decided to climb down and take a closer look. As soon as I turned, I saw a man in the valley below me. He was beyond the hide site, but there was no harm in that at this time of year. However, I ducked down among the rocks to keep watch. It was a good idea; the man skirted the screes above the usual footpath and then stopped to look directly at the nest through binoculars. He spent about five minutes scouring the site before moving off up-valley. As soon as I knew it was safe to do so, I scrambled up to the ridgetop and followed from above. By 11.40 a.m. he'd reached the foot of the top nest crag, and I saw him pick up a stick and hold it at arm's length as if to judge the height of the nest. He then deliberately pushed the stick in the ground vertically below the nest, scanned the crag again and began to climb higher. I waited and watched, but he turned higher up the ridge and disappeared into the low cloud. There was no point in my following him; I wouldn't know how quickly he'd be walking and I wouldn't be able to dally if I caught up as the pursuit would have become too obvious. Also, the distance I'd have to keep behind would mean that, in the mist, I wouldn't know which way he turned when the nest ridge joined High Street, the main ridge.

I looked around and was relieved to see Stefan at the hide site, so having walked 8 km, climbed 300 metres up the ridge, dropped half way back down to check the nest and then back up and along the top, I dropped the 300 metres back to the valley bottom to talk to Stefan. I told him what I'd seen and borrowed his car keys. The man I'd watched must have had a car parked at the lake head, so I trooped down to that and sat in Stefan's car to wait.

I was still waiting when Stefan returned, and it was 2.30 p.m. before the man reappeared. He walked straight through the car park and around the first bend in the road. He must have parked further down the road, which, I thought, was a little strange in itself. I'd intended to play it cool, to give the man time to reach his car, stow his gear, take a breather and then move off, a couple of minutes at least, but Stefan had other ideas. As soon as the man was out of sight Stefan started the engine, revved up and was off in hot pursuit. We sped past the man after about 100 metres, so I stopped Stefan and we had to pretend to be looking at ducks while the man walked past us again. We now had all the parked cars in view, but as I was in the process of saying that we should wait Stefan was off again, foot to the floor. There were 25 geese for us to look at this time, but we were running out of things to count, so I stopped him again and insisted that we wait for the man to reach his car. I was concerned that we'd already made him suspicious, but my own suspicions were raised when he finally did stop at a car. Even though the car park was half empty and there were other parking points between us and it, the man stopped at a car that was simply pulled halfway onto the verge. Armed with his vehicle details Stefan and I returned to the village to inform the warden of the events I'd seen. He wasn't convinced that the nest had been deliberately destroyed and tried to tell me that it must have fallen out naturally, but when he announced that he and Stefan would be working on his holiday cottage the next day, I decided to do what he was being paid to do and prepared to visit the nest again.

29 December dawned dry with increasing cloud and the promise of rain that could destroy any evidence. I didn't want to waste any time, and so cut straight through the screes towards the crag. There was only one route to the nest without using ropes and on the very first foothold I found a boot print. I climbed up for a closer look at the nest ledge itself. There wasn't a single stick left in place. All that remained were the rotten remnants, a compost of sticks that had probably been collected by the eagles more than 20 years previously. And right in the middle was a boot print, size nine. I told the warden that the destruction was definitely deliberate, and he and the team puzzled over the motives for such an act. They theorised about it being a farmer worried about the threat to his lambs (even though the local farmers were sympathetic towards the eagles) and almost convinced themselves that it was the work of someone who held a grudge against the warden himself! I suggested that it was the work of an egg collector who'd be raiding the site in 1990.

It was obvious to me: if the eagles had two nests the best way to guarantee the use of one was by destroying the other, the one closest to the RSPB hide. The hides had been moved further from the top nest, the wardens weren't capable of reaching it in time to prevent a raid, and the eggers must have been aware of these things. They'd obviously visited the site during the 1989 season and realised the ease with which they could take the eggs. They'd be able to take them during daylight if they had the nerve!

CHAPTER 13

A difficult year

I was determined to counter the nest destruction and vowed to rebuild the nest myself, believing that fresh material on the ledge might encourage the eagles to complete the job themselves and foil the eggers' plans. Unfortunately, the warden wanted to join in, and so I sat in my vehicle in the Haweswater car park on 2 January 1990 and waited for him to arrive. I was fully equipped with twine to tie bundles of sticks, a rope to hoist them to the nest and another to secure my own place on the ledge added to my usual daypack. I waited. The appointed time came and went, and an hour later I decided that he wasn't coming so I set off alone. I'd wasted so much time in waiting that I wouldn't be able to rebuild the nest that day. I didn't want to be on the crag when there might be visitors about, but knew I still had time to collect and bundle sticks ready to be positioned the next day, whether or not I was alone. The eagles left the valley before I'd reached the hide site so I hadn't disturbed them, and I hoped they wouldn't return until after I'd left the crag. I spent a couple of hours collecting loose sticks and heather and left five piles at the foot of the crag before deciding it was time to leave. When I returned to the village I discovered that there was no reason for the warden not to have joined me, he'd just decided to join in with the repair work the next day without bothering to tell me.

To my surprise, he was ready the next morning but insisted that his son should tag along as well. When we reached the crag they saw the sticks I'd collected the previous day and realised that most of the work had been done, but they made a token effort to collect a few more sticks and I thought that the extras would at least help to provide a solid base onto which the eagles could add their own material. It was the first time the warden had been close to this nest, and after one look and hearing about 'the leap' he decided that I should go to the nest alone; it was a decision I'd already made.

I scrambled up to the nest, tied myself to a rotten tree for some psychological protection and lowered the rope down to the others. I called for the larger sticks first, so I could tie them together to form a solid base and then brought up the thinner ones to intertwine and heather to add some bulk to the structure. In an attempt to ensure that the nest didn't slide from the ledge I added some short stakes and buried their tops under clods of earth, and the work seemed to be going quite well. They called up that the last load was attached and, leaving me to deal with that, went to look at the top nest. With the last bundle woven in and secured I stepped back to take a critical look at my handiwork. I clearly wasn't an eagle! I seemed to have made quite an effort for little return but consoled myself with the knowledge that the ledge now had fresh material in place and that the eagles hadn't seen me there. I'd deliberately left the broken ends of any fresh sticks pointing outwards and had laid pale-barked rowan branches on top to contrast with the darker background. As a final touch I added some woodrush, leaving the roots in view to show that it hadn't grown there. I'd have to wait and see if my efforts were in vain, but I was satisfied with what I'd achieved, made the leap and scrambled back down the crag. It was no wonder there didn't seem to be much material on the ledge, the largest pile of sticks I'd collected the previous day still lay at the foot of the crag; the others had gone before the job was completed.

I made my way down to join Stefan at the hide, and the female eagle appeared almost immediately. She swung in close to the crags and circled by the nest I'd just left and was joined by the male. Perhaps they had seen me and had come to inspect my work. Through the telescope I could see that the female was carrying a stick. I tried to will her onto the nest, but when the male turned away the female dropped the stick and followed him across the valley, possibly disturbed by the others who were now returning. My heart was thumping, and I now had the worry of whether my efforts had deterred rather than attracted the birds.

I hadn't seen the eagles for 10 days, so I drove to the valley before first light on the morning of 18 January, arriving in the car park at about 7.15 a.m. to try to see the birds before they headed to the hunting grounds, assuming that they had roosted in the valley. I'd heard a car pass my house shortly before I set off, but farm and works traffic was often moving by then. I became curious, however, when I noticed the glare of the headlights ahead of me as I drove way past the hotel. It would have meant little if this had happened during the summer or at a weekend, but this was a Thursday in January. There were winter hillwalkers, of course, but this was just a grey old Lake District day, ideal for eagle work but not much use for sightseeing.

As I pulled into the car park I took a quick look at the other car and immediately recognised the registration number. Protectionists share the numbers of suspicious cars they see, and this one was top of the list. It belonged to Colin Watson who, at the time, was the most notorious egg collector in Britain and a real thorn in the RSPB's side. The recent events all fell into place, but I derived no satisfaction in knowing that my interpretation had been correct. Colin knew all of the peregrine and raven sites in the area, so he must have been after the eagles. I knew the fallibility of the protection scheme, and the wardens' reluctance to take the interference seriously, so I knew there was a real chance of him succeeding in taking the eggs. To make the situation even more frustrating on a personal level, I'd be working elsewhere for the RSPB only a few days after the first egg was laid and would thereafter have no influence over how the site was protected. These thoughts rushed through my head along with a more pertinent question: why was an egg collector at Haweswater in January?

I couldn't just sit in my car and wait for him to make the first move, so I carried on as normal, put my pack on my back and set off for the valley with my telescope and binoculars on display. I didn't look behind me until I'd reached the bluff from where I'd taken car numbers on many earlier occasions, but while Colin's car was still there I couldn't tell if he was still in it or if he'd left it. I didn't dare swing either the scope or the binoculars to take a look. I put on a spurt once I was around the corner and raced up to the top hide site where I could stand fairly well concealed but in a place I could be expected to use without obviously trying to hide. The situation was the same as in the car park, I had to behave as normally as possible and act as if I was unaware of what might be happening while at the same time looking for men and not eagles and noting everything that didn't seem correct. In fact it was similar to some aspects of the eagle work itself; the egger knew I was there and hiding might affect his behaviour, so I had to do everything as openly as possible.

I'd seen both eagles on the walk to the old hide site (the one whose use had deterred egg collectors in the past but which was now deemed to be too close to the nest) and began to scan. Having checked all the perches and nests the best way to look for eagles from the bottom of a valley is to scan the skyline and that was perfect for me. If the egger crept over the edge to see where I was he'd see me sweeping the ridge and decide on his next move, and at 9.30 a.m. I noticed some movement above *the acacia tree*. My binoculars didn't pause, and the sweep continued through 360°. A quarter of an hour later, I saw two men ensconce themselves among the ridgetop rocks down-valley of the top nest; the accomplice must have come in a separate vehicle.

It was an awkward situation, I wanted to know what they'd planned, but they weren't going to do anything with me watching them. I didn't know how long they'd be willing to wait, but there was no sense in forcing the men to change their plans and return on another occasion, when they might not be seen. I gave the skyline another sweep, packed my sack and set off again. I didn't retrace my steps but crossed the beck and angled up the opposite slope as if on a search route to the next valley. I was certain the men would be watching me, but as was my habit, I stopped every few minutes to scan around as if checking for the eagles before moving on again. I checked on the men every time I stopped and they hadn't moved. I then had a stroke of luck; during one of my pauses the female eagle arrived to circle over the valley head (I assumed that the eggers must have seen her as well) and then turned to head out in the direction I was walking. If she'd gone the other way I'd have been stuck, but she didn't and I had the perfect excuse to speed up and not turn round again.

I turned out of the valley and continued until I was certain to be out of sight and then quickly clambered higher and belly-crawled between the rocks to get into position. I picked out the eggers through the scope, they'd set off as soon as I was out of the valley and were making quick progress towards the crag. Like me, they kept stopping to look back and make sure the coast was clear, but they were soon on the crag. The man I knew to be an egg collector wore a waxed jacket and green Wellington boots while the other wore a dark camouflage jacket, denim jeans and a woolly hat; neither carried a rucksack, so they weren't equipped to destroy the nest. They were on top of the crag by 10.20 a.m. and were on a ledge directly above the nest five minutes later. They went beyond Geoff's abseil point, and with camouflage-man sitting above to act as the lookout, the first one crouched in a corner with his back towards me.

I couldn't see exactly what he was doing, but by his actions I assumed he was trying to drive in a metal spike to act as his belay. Camouflage-man scanned the valley through binoculars, staring down to look for the wardens and along the ridgetop path looking for walkers, but there was no one else about. After 27 minutes, the men swapped roles and camouflage took over for the last five. The job completed, they climbed back up the spur of the nest crag, but like me, they didn't retrace their steps. They climbed more directly and stopped to point, and I guessed they were planning their escape route. They stood again at the lip of the ridge, pointing and talking for five minutes before continuing into the next valley and towards the car park.

Unlike them, when I left the valley I waited a couple of minutes to make sure they'd gone before setting off down and across the nesting valley and up to the bluff at the valley's mouth. I was well used to this routine and settled among the hawthorns to await their arrival. There were only five cars parked at the head of the road; my own, the known egg collector's, one that had just that minute arrived, the RSPB reserve vehicle (parked nose-to-tail with the egger's car!) and the fifth that must have belonged to the accomplice. I noted the registrations and waited. It was three quarters of an hour before the men returned, and when they did they jumped straight into their cars and drove off immediately. There was no need for me to follow them again, so I sauntered over to my car and drove home.

The warden's car wasn't outside his house, so I telephoned the RSPB's investigation unit directly and passed on the information I'd collected. When I later saw a light in the warden's house I called round to tell him what I'd seen. In spite of the reserve car being parked next to the egger's, and my report to The Lodge, he was unaware of the incident and demanded to know why I hadn't told him about it before anyone else. 'You weren't here and I had to get the ball rolling' didn't seem to be a satisfactory answer, and he immediately phoned Dave and told him to check all the peregrine sites. This heightened my fears for the eagles even more. He was panicking, and I had to point out that the egger wouldn't be hanging around peregrine sites in January and nothing could be done about it even if he was, except warn him that the RSPB were aware of his presence.

I learnt the next day that I wouldn't be re-employed by the RSPB's species protection department.

The wardens were clearly worried about how it would reflect on them if they were on duty the first time the English eagles' eggs were stolen. I was energised and confident and pointed out that the RSPB would never have a better opportunity of catching this particular egg collector. All that was needed was an advance hide that was only approached during the hours of darkness, some night-vision binoculars, two-way radios and a listening device. With two months still before the eggs would be laid, there was ample time for a perfect hide to be constructed on the ridgeside in a location that would be invisible to those who didn't know about it and approachable without disturbing the eagles and for the radio equipment to be installed and tested. I even knew the ideal place for it to be built and volunteered to build it, but I was moving too quickly. While I wanted to get everything in place as soon as possible there were delays and disagreements. Health and safety on the hill became an issue, and I could see the confidence ebbing away as the days went by. I pointed out that there was no real risk of the eggs being stolen; the egger would only go equipped to abseil from the spike, so if we removed that he wouldn't be able to get to the nest. I said that with the evidence we had we could get a prosecution without the egger actually going to the nest, all the wardens had to do was stay awake and stay alert. And I asked them to think of the publicity the RSPB could generate by catching this particular egg collector on the nest crag of England's only golden eagles!

It was imperative that we moved quickly to ensure that everything was in place before the wardening effort increased at its usual time in March, and I almost demanded that, if nothing else, the spike had to be removed as soon as possible. To me that meant the next day, but the warden had to be involved again so it couldn't be done the next day. The weather worsened almost immediately, and the area was hit by gales and snowstorms that prevented us from doing anything on the crags. The job could have been done at once, but removing the spike might now require a safety team that would be on the crag during the nest-building period. There was a real possibility that we'd be the ones disturbing the eagles.

There was a break in the weather and a thaw that cleared the worst of the snow, and for once, we acted when the time was right. I borrowed a long rope from Geoff, and for poetic justice, he loaned me one he'd retrieved from the top of a peregrine crag that had been left by the very egger whose spike I was about to remove. The warden and I set off from the car park, but we were still playing games. The warden, who was travelling light, forged on along the path at a brisk pace, whereas I carried a 30-m rope and bits of safety gear. I knew what he was up to, and he wasn't going to beat me to the top of the ridge, no matter how much gear I was carrying. We arrived together, but I would have preferred not to be dripping with sweat.

Refreshed, we set off again to Geoff's unloading spot (where all the gear was assembled and checked prior to his abseil), and I prepared myself. I wouldn't be abseiling, but this would be a risky task on such wet and soggy ground. The first step down to the abseil point was a slither onto a broad ledge, but from there the route was a very narrow muddy path with some heather hand-holds on one side and the sheer face of the crag on the other dropping straight down to the screes. In dry conditions and with Geoff I happily walked along the path without protection, but in these conditions I wanted to know that I was safe.

The warden found it highly amusing as I trussed myself up with the rope and secured it around a car-sized rock, but he wasn't volunteering to remove the spike. Geoff later told me the glee with which the warden recounted this tale and how that glee had diminished when Geoff told him that I'd done the right thing and he would have done exactly the same. I knew not to take risks in these situations. I gave myself enough slack to reach the spike, and not go too far if I slipped, and carefully inched my way along the path. I pointed to where I'd be going, but the warden told me it was the wrong place – strange given that I was the only other person present when the spike was inserted. I said the spike was further round from where Geoff abseiled, but he said that there was nothing further round, even though three more steps took me past Geoff's abseil point and another two took me to the spike!

When I arrived at where I knew the spike to be there was nothing to be seen. The ground was muddy with a dusting of thawing hail that wasn't deep enough to conceal anything. I recognised the corner in which the egger had been active, but all that lay there was a flat stone. I turned it over, and the top of the spike became visible. It was buried to its full length with only a welded loop clear and accessible. The stone it lay under didn't even jiggle when touched; the egger had done a really good job, and I realised this even more when I tried to extract the spike from the partly frozen ground. I first photographed what was visible and then took another with the stone in place, but to shift the spike required a few kicks with my boot to loosen its grip. I wasn't worried about scuffing the ground as it was certain to freeze and thaw again, and the weather was sure to be wet enough to hide any marks I left. With the 40-cm spike removed, I replaced the stone and edged my way back, packed the rope back into my sack and was about to bag the spike when the warden volunteered to carry if off the crag. I've never seen it again.

With time passing, I wanted to know what the plans were for the protection scheme, but in spite of everything I'd seen and done on their behalf, the wardens had clearly been told not to keep me informed. It soon became clear why during a conversation with Ken – it seemed that the wardens had almost convinced themselves that there wasn't going to be an attempt on the eggs and that it was all a ruse to disrupt the 'smooth running' of the scheme. The relevance of the middle nest being destroyed without anyone's knowledge and the egger waiting until I was out of the valley before inserting the spike didn't seem to have crossed their minds until I mentioned it.

Even though it was now safe to assume that the eggs wouldn't be stolen, nothing really changed. A decision not to catch the egger had been taken and, instead, the RSPB chose to increase the wardening presence by having watchers on the ridgetop as well as on the valley floor. In other words, they were going to frighten him off – they may as well have telephoned him to tell him that the spike had been removed! I was furious and told the wardens that as well as not getting the best catch ever achieved by the RSPB all they'd be doing was sending the egger to Scotland where he could confidently steal eagle eggs without fear of being caught.

I left the humans and returned to the eagles. I only noted nest material being delivered on 3, 8, 14, and 20 February, and it all went to the top nest. My attempts at nest-building clearly weren't up to scratch, and the middle nest wasn't to be used. On the 22nd, I watched the eagles mating, the male displaying and the female feeding for 68 minutes, so I could assume she'd be in good condition to produce fertile eggs for the ninth consecutive year. The weather became more unsettled after the 17th, and my good day on the 22nd became a foul one on the 23rd. Storms lashed the area and flattened ancient oak trees around my home, and the heavy rain turned to heavy snow on the 26th and continued to fall until 1 March. When I returned to the valley on the 2nd, I was astonished to find that the nest was now almost fully refurbished; it even had a soft platform and the makings of a cup in the woodrush and grass. A further nine pieces of material were taken on that day, but that was the most activity I'd see that spring; the eagles had rebuilt their nest during weather that had virtually kept me housebound for a week.

I had only brief views of the eagles two days later and failed to see them at all during my next three visits, so I decided to climb up and have a good close look at the nest. I could see that it was now finished but also that, presumably because of the weather, it was a very loose construction. The sticks weren't bound together and never before had the top looked like such a separate feature from the established bulk, not even in 1986 when the eagles built on top of snow. I noted that the cup wasn't in the usual position either; this year it was at the front of the nest where it would be less well protected and more visible to people on the ridge. I mentioned these facts in a passing conversation with the wardens, but such details were of little interest.

I saw the eagles mating on the 17th and 22nd, and the female spent much of the latter day simply perched as if in pre-laying lethargy. No egg was laid, however, and there was still none in the nest when I took a look on the morning of the 26th. I went to the valley with Nick that afternoon, but there was no activity until 5 p.m. when both birds arrived with material. The male left to collect another stick, but although the female had sat low, both birds then flew off again. The female dropped to a carcass at the foot of the nest crag and ate for three minutes before flying about the valley and sweeping back to the nest. She went low with her head down, stood fully and then sat. The egg had been laid during her last visit, at about 5.15 p.m., and the game was on.

The 26th was the second latest date on which the female had laid her first egg of the year, so everything was in place and ready, and the protection scheme began the night of the 28th! It might have seemed logical to wait until the second egg had been laid, but the eagle would still have laid that egg if the first had been removed. The egger could have been planning to make two visits, but that idea was lost on the wardens as well. The head warden and his first assistant took the first 24-hour ridge watch, and Dave and I replaced them at 6 p.m. on the 29th. I couldn't believe my ears when we arrived: we were told that it wasn't worth staying awake overnight because it was too dark. I only just managed to keep my mouth shut. As it happened, the night of the 29th was clear, so I told Dave that we weren't going to sleep. We tucked ourselves into the rocks away from the path and split the night into shifts so we could take turns at dozing in bivi-bags beneath the starry sky. We told our replacements to do the same.

That was my last official watch at Haweswater, and I was glad to be out of it. There'd been problems or something had gone wrong during each of the five breeding seasons since I left the scheme, but the RSPB continued to employ the same people at the site. I had to move away for my next RSPB job, as warden of their Geltsdale reserve, but that was in Cumbria, and I was able to make fairly regular visits to Riggindale to see how the season was progressing. The ridge watch became a shambles as the weather deteriorated again, with the wardens either sleeping or 'unable' to watch, and it was the warden himself who was the first to abandon the ridge during the night. And then suddenly, on 22 April, the eagles stopped incubating and deserted the nest.

The eagles building during the worst of the February weather had resulted in an unstable nest that had 'settled' after completion. The eggs had rolled to the back and become wedged against the rock face where the eagles couldn't cover them. After Geoff had removed the eggs for analysis, he told me that the gap at the back of the nest was large enough for a chick to fall down, so I suggested that we should think about repairing the nest ourselves. It was only talk at the time as we were all too busy with other species to drop everything and turn our attention to one that wouldn't breed again that year. The RSPB wouldn't, of course, allow us near the nest at that time of year anyway. I was hamstrung by a scheme to protect hen harriers at Geltsdale, where adults had been shot in 1990 and nestlings trodden into the ground, as well as all the general reserve work, and could only make brief visits to Haweswater where, not surprisingly, the wardens showed great reluctance to tell me anything about the eagles even though we worked for the same company and it was effectively me who'd prevented the eagle eggs from being stolen.

I couldn't spend any length of time in Riggindale until October that year, but I was able to deduce the events of earlier months from what I found. The middle nest was by then well on its way to being rebuilt on top of my efforts, the acacia nest had been added to, and the roost ledge onto which sticks had been carried in 1987 now held a distinct nest platform. There were also new sticks on ledges in the eagle's second valley, and it was clear that the birds had been greatly frustrated by the outcome of their breeding attempt and were going through the act of testing out the positions of potential new sites. I didn't expect them to use any of the new sites, so the middle nest seemed to be the most likely place to hold the 1991 attempt, especially as, on my first visit to the valley after Geltsdale, I discovered that the top nest had almost all fallen from the crag.

Having helped the eagles to rebuild one of their nests, and seeing my efforts accepted, I thought it a good idea to start the repairs of the top nest. I put the idea to the warden, and without committing himself to it, he suggested the idea to Geoff, and Geoff suggested it to me, so I concluded that it must have been a good idea. Geoff and I started to discuss how best to go about the operation. We knew it would be different to the middle nest as the top one wasn't based on a level ledge. We talked about making a cradle to be bolted to the rock face or tying on the new structure, but we finally agreed that it would be sensible to keep it as natural as possible.

The work had to be carried out during the winter, of course, between spells of bad weather and during the shorter days, but whatever we planned Geoff and I were repeatedly delayed by the warden insisting on his own involvement but then never being available to help. We became weary of his having to control everything, even though he couldn't be physically involved, and decided to pre-empt the situation. Geoff had some work leave due so he booked it, and I told the warden that we'd be repairing the nest on 9 November. He said we couldn't because he wasn't available on that date, so I reminded him, again, that we'd be doing the work for the eagles' benefit not his, that Geoff and

I were working in our own time and at our own expense and that Geoff couldn't just walk away from his job whenever it pleased him. The warden reluctantly agreed, but he insisted that Dave accompany us. I don't know what he thought we'd be doing, but I assumed that an RSPB presence at the time would enable them to say that it was an RSPB project, just as it had been the RSPB that had removed the egger's spike. The warden also insisted that we do the work in the early morning, as if that wasn't what we'd do anyway, which was fine because Dave was a postman and wouldn't be available at that time. As it was I confirmed the visit on the night before, and Stefan and a volunteer plodded their way up the valley some time after Geoff and I had reached the crag.

We made it to the top of the crag, ensured that the belay spike hadn't been replaced, looked for evidence that might suggest that this nest had been deliberately destroyed and then, satisfied that the fall had been natural, set about our task. With Geoff safely on the nest, I scrambled back to the foot of the crag and sent up the material. The fresh sticks and heather the eagles had added to the nest in the spring were sent up again and four sack loads of turf went up to stabilise the structure and plug the last of the gaps between the nest and the rock face, which Geoff compacted by jumping up and down on the spot. This nest would certainly have a solid base. Two more loads of sticks went up followed by two of soft material, Geoff jumped up and down again and I checked the level from the *bilberry peaks* and that was that.

Satisfied that the nest was safe again, we packed up and headed back towards the RSPB hide, thinking of the coffee that Stefan would have ready for our arrival. We neither hurried nor dawdled down the valley but when we walked over the last rise it was to see Stefan and the volunteer walking away from the hide. This proved another one of my theories. Stefan was by far the most observant of the RSPB's eagle team, and yet because you start uphill to leave the nest crag, he'd lost track of us and had assumed we'd gone over the ridge. It confirmed to me beyond all doubt that the RSPB's hide was in the wrong place – if the wardens saw an egg collector they'd be too far away to stop him and they wouldn't know in which direction he'd left.

I continued my eagle work and, as was usual for this time of year, found the birds wandering quite widely and leading me over the hills and valleys as they did when I had a juvenile to watch. The grouse moors were still the favourite place to visit, but the birds also spent time in the valley nearest my home. Searching there on 2 December produced a naked-eye sighting of an eagle, and when it winged by me I was astonished to see the white wing patches and tail base of an immature bird. It flew across the lake, over the ridge and off towards the grouse moors. It's almost impossible to age immature eagles to a specific year, but even though the time was right for it to be a south of Scotland bird, I wondered if it might have been the 1989 youngster returning to exploit the grouse again. On a later date, I also noted a hen harrier that had been wing-tagged as a nestling in Perthshire.

Such records brightened the days, as did reaching the high tops through snowdrifts, spindrift and frozen cornices to walk the unbroken snow back to my home. I did that on the 19th to follow the female eagle, but it was a lot more difficult getting up the partly frozen snow-bound ridge than when it was green and grassy, so I soon lost track of her but the walk produced a couple of snow buntings and a flock of 14 ravens feeding on a dead deer. The weather immediately changed for the worse, and I couldn't reach the valley again until the 29th, but I was pleased to see both nest sites heavily snow bound. I knew that would help compact the new material on both sites to form level and solid foundations for the eagles to use. But the nightmare year still wasn't over.

As I set off for a short walk on the 30th, I met Stefan and he told me there'd been some vandalism in Riggindale. I immediately thought that he meant the nests. Stefan had been sent to take a look, so I grabbed my gear and hitched a lift with him. It wasn't the nests, it was the hide, which the RSPB had stopped dismantling for the winter. All of the windows had been broken, the locks on both doors were smashed, and the worktops and furniture torn apart and strewn on the floor. Cups and plates were scattered among the debris, and the gas stove had been battered with a hammer. The knobs had been broken off and the gas cylinders rolled down the hill. I found a noticeboard and a frying pan about 200 metres away and, retrieving them, found keys that had been thrown away. Mattresses, leaflets and books were soaked through, and the contents of jars and cupboards emptied onto the floor. Virtually the only things that weren't damaged were the photographs on the walls.

No one knew when it had happened as the team hadn't been to the valley for more than two weeks, and I rarely went near it; I'd look at it from a distance and call in if Stefan was there, but it was too far away and poorly positioned for it to be of any value to my fieldwork. No one knew who was responsible for the damage, but the RSPB's osprey hide at Loch Garten was destroyed at about the same time so it was obviously an arranged event. I wondered what would happen in 1991. Would the eggs be stolen, would anyone notice, would anyone care? It was a disappointing end to a disappointing year, and I feared for the eagles' future.

CHAPTER 14

A Scottish sojourn

I was glad to see the end of 1990. While the breeding season could be correctly written off as a natural failure, it didn't feel like that. From the egg collector in January through to the destruction of the RSPB hide in December the year seemed to have been a litany of misadventure. The only saving grace was that the eagles were still alive to make a breeding attempt in 1991, but I had dark feelings that this was the beginning of the end. Having made one serious attempt on the eggs, I was sure the collectors would try again in spite of, or perhaps because of, the RSPB's presence. After five successive years of problems, the loss of the eggs seemed almost inevitable, and I wondered if it wouldn't have been better for me not to have seen the eggers at work. If the eggs had been stolen in 1990, there may have been a regime change that would have rediscovered the importance of the English eagles.

I could only make a few brief visits to Riggindale during the 1991 breeding season, but I was pleased to see that the wardening team was changing, until I realised what was involved. The team was reduced not upgraded, and incredibly given the events of 1990, the site protection was left largely in the hands of inexperienced volunteers. They didn't even consider an overnight ridge watch even though the eagles would use the middle nest that year, a nest that could be reached without climbing equipment. It was sad and maddening to witness the running down of the site: apart from the eagles, the Haweswater area had the densest population of peregrines in the world, with five pairs rearing 17 chicks from a small part of the reserve area in 1984 when I was senior warden (with one successful pair less than a kilometre from the successful eagle nest); those same five sites would rear a combined total of one chick in 1991. The team informed me that they were surprised to see the falcons incubating one day, but when they next looked a week later they weren't. They had no idea what had happened or when the failure had occurred, even though they drove past three of the peregrine sites every day on their way to the eagles.

And the eagles didn't help themselves in the long run; they bred successfully in 1991. A single chick was reared, but I was unable to spend much time with it even after it had left the nest. I made a few visits but it was the first youngster I hadn't followed since 1980, and the wardens weren't interested; they last saw it on 6 September, well before it had left the home range.

I spent 1990 and 1991 wardening at Geltsdale. It felt as though it was time to move on, and 1992 provided me with another opportunity to become more deeply involved with Scottish eagles. I followed the Haweswater birds during the winter of 1991/92 but left in February to work on the second national golden eagle survey. I'd pulled out of Islay and Jura in 1982 because of ill health, but I wasn't going to do so again and would finally get to survey the magnificent island of Jura, and would do so again during the 2003 survey.

In 1992 the RSPB employed me in the north Argyll study area, which I'd been visiting since first working there with Geoff and the team in 1985, so I knew the ground and many of the birds. It was a welcome return to eagle work; I'd only found myself at Geltsdale because having twice been verbally promised work with the sea eagles on Mull for 1990 and twice accepted it I was told in January 1990 that there wouldn't be a job for me on Mull that year. I'd worked the previous season and that had proven to be the most successful to date on that project. There were still only two pairs of sea eagles there at the time, but one pair had laid three eggs, and both pairs had reared two chicks. I'd also managed to find the time to survey the golden eagles better than had been achieved in any year outside the national surveys (I proved that to be their most productive year to date and I even confirmed breeding at sites that were long thought to have been deserted), but that wasn't enough to see me re-employed.

In 1992 I found myself living in a converted garage inside a plantation. It was reminiscent of the 1979 caravan in that it was midge infested and surrounded by spruce trees, but the comparisons stopped there. While I couldn't see a nest from the back door, the cottage was on the boundary between two pairs of eagles, so I could watch territorial disputes and hunting flights while I ate an evening meal on the veranda. The location also enabled me to put some good time in on one of my pet projects. As well as realising in 1979 that little or nothing was known about the post-fledging period, it was also pretty obvious that little was known about home ranges, and this was what I wanted to examine next. I'd studied the fledged juveniles in the Lake District, following them uphill and down dale and during the winters, but I knew that would be dismissed as 'England' and therefore claimed to be irrelevant to Scottish eagles. In 1992, however, I had the chance to make some observations within a population of eagles.

Finding myself living in a Scottish glen surrounded by a study area that held 20 pairs of eagles was a dream come true and an opportunity that couldn't be missed. When monitoring the breeding attempts I didn't simply walk in via the most direct route I approached from a different direction on each occasion to map the birds' locations, record their behaviour in relation to habitat, identify their foraging areas and prey species, follow their flight lines and track them back to the nest. In that way I was able to map eagle territories more accurately than had ever been achieved before, but my work counted for very little.

I had to manage my time very carefully, though. I was employed to monitor breeding performance not track eagles through the hills so I had to ensure that the paid work was completed on schedule, but the two things could be combined. It was easy to walk between ranges, and the straightforward monitoring that was required was very easy and not at all time consuming. It was how the old eagle men worked, and I realised why there was so little detail in their published work. The survey instructions required me to check on territory occupancy at all the sites before the eggs were laid, to check later that the birds were sitting, to check to see if there were chicks in the nests and, finally, to see if the nests held a chick that was large enough for the breeding attempt to be deemed a success. There was nothing else, it was monitoring. The bottom line was that I had about 180 days in which to do 88 days work.

Days were lost to the weather, of course, but once an occupied nest had been identified, it was easy to check two or three a day, and once pairs started to fail and the days grew longer, it was possible to complete my rounds of the active sites in three or four days. I spent the remainder of the time watching the birds behave normally and undisturbed in and around the nest area and also in the more remote parts of their home ranges. I had ample time to compare my English records with the behaviour of 'real' eagles and see that, surprise-surprise, the English eagles were no different from the Scottish ones.

I still had spare time on top of this and made myself available to help out the field-workers who were struggling with their tasks. I visited Jura with Roger Broad of the RSPB, and together, we covered the entire island in about four days. We confirmed breeding where it hadn't previously been recorded and produced evidence to show that some ranges had been divided between two pairs. On one day I found the skeletons of two stags that had died nose to nose during the rut. It must have been a horrible death for one, if not both, of the beasts.

I also found myself looking at 10 eagle sites in Perthshire in 1992, where I made repeated walks of more than 40 km to check three sites in a day. It was worth it even if I had been given unreliable information about those three sites. I was told that all had been deserted but that they had to be checked, so off I went. I could have driven and walked to each in turn, but it was easier to park the car at the mid-point and do a circular walk. I didn't see any eagles at the first site, but I found the old nest being used by a pair of peregrines that would breed successfully that year, and I found eagle signs (feathers and down) at a rabbit warren in the second range. My information was that the third deserted site was in a gorge, and even though I was under the impression that I'd find nothing, I approached cautiously as I always did (it's better to be prepared for the unexpected than it is to blunder in and stumble headlong into a situation you can't easily retrieve), and it was just as well that I did. I found some crow pluckings at the top of the gorge, and as I crept along the edge I found more and more pluckings. I eventually spotted the edge of the nest jutting out from behind a rock and eased myself into position, stealthily creeping along the inner edge of the gorge until I could see the nest properly. On it, less than 20 metres away, sat a healthy eaglet and beside it stood one of the adults, totally oblivious to my presence as it tore at a grouse and fed slivers of meat to the chick.

I'd already taken my camera from my sack, just in case, but knew that I was on the last frame or two and that I didn't have a spare film with me. I was also cursing for not carrying the telephoto lens; I wasn't expecting to find anything and didn't want to be weighed down unnecessarily on the long trek, and so had left it in the car. But, even through the standard 50mm lens, I took a reasonable photograph of the bird on its nest. I wound on the film as carefully as I could but tore the perforations and knew there were no more pictures to be taken – I'd already squeezed 38 out of that film. How I cursed! And when the bird spread its wings to sweep away from me I saw the most unusually plumaged eagle I'd ever seen.

I also found myself back on Mull during 1992 where I had to undertake some supplementary feeding of the sea eagles at around the hatching time. I'd already done some feeding on Mull (and seen some magnificent stoops and dives to 'catch' the food I'd left out for the eagles), but with a new nest in use, I had to be shown to the dump site, so Sean and I set out with a bag of hares that first afternoon. Sean knew the food was being taken, but no one had actually seen the eagles feeding at the dump.

I read the field signs at the food dump and announced that eagles weren't taking the bait. Sean was nonplussed: he'd seen the eagles over the site, the carcasses had been eaten and there were plenty of pluckings to be seen. But that was the evidence I used, the pluckings appeared to be the work of buzzards and ravens. I moved the dump site, so that it was visible from a secluded stretch of road, and changed the feeding times. We almost immediately saw the sea eagles collecting and removing the carcasses, and it was proven that they hadn't been getting to the food beforehand.

It was back to north Argyll after that excursion and that was the place to be as far as I was concerned, even if I did have to play another game of hide-and-seek with the egg collector I'd watched in Riggindale during 1990 as he went in to raid one of the eagle nests I was watching. But I didn't simply enjoy the area because of the eagles: the location within the Argyll mountains was magnificent, the opportunities to escape to the fastnesses of the hills were endless and there was also the other wildlife, such as the ubiquitous red deer that tramped about the hills and in the garden of my cottage. The cottage itself held attractions, and I'd find myself hand-feeding and playing with wild pine marten kits that the mother brought to my doorstep. My searches of the eagle foraging areas saw me on the high tops with the mystical ptarmigan, and the walk-in to one of the eagle sites took me past black-throated divers, a merlin nest in grass rather than heather and across a broad swath of Scottish bog with its populations of curlew, greenshank, golden plover and dunlin, all waders of the wild hills. The dawn chorus on that walk had to be heard to be believed, and there, sitting on its nest at the end of my walk and watching every step of my approach, was the eagle, a bird that once allowed me to stand 3 metres from her as she brooded her eggs.

That year I monitored eagles in about 45 different ranges, worked a great swath of the western Highlands and covered sites on two of the most inspiring of the Scottish islands – it had been a magical time. I dread to think how far I walked and how many thousands of metres of climbs and descents I undertook, but there were few places in north Argyll that didn't feel my boots in 1992. When I returned home at the end of the season I was probably even fitter than after I'd completed my post-fledging project eight years earlier.

The Lakeland hills were a soft option after the west of Scotland, but the Haweswater eagles had bred successfully again, and there was a fledged juvenile waiting for me. Covering the ground around my home in the autumn and winter would see me maintain condition in readiness for the next breeding season. The juvenile behaved like those that came after the failure of the live food supply in 1986, and the winter months saw me watching eagles that had been together as a pair for 10 years. Their routine was set and predictable, but to me there was nothing monotonous about their lives. There was always a thrill in seeing the first piece of nest material being collected, seeing the first flight display of the year or in checking the roosts to remove pellets that might contain the fragments of a prey species other than sheep. There might be the jawbone of a stoat or the feather of a bird of prey, and when looking for pellets, it was always interesting to discover which roosts the eagles had used.

But the biggest thrill at that time of year was to stand in the valley bottom in the fading light on a bitterly cold and snow-swept evening to watch the eagles come down to their roosts. To see them plane along the ridgeside to circle and stall above the roost, looking down to check on its security, before suddenly furling their wings and stretching their legs to tumble to the roost in the long drop with the talons reaching out and the wind being spilled from half-closed wings as the eagle dropped and rocked from side to side through the air until it reached the branch and landed with the delicacy of a swallow on a line. The eagle would pause, refold its wings, look around and often give four or five yelps before turning to face out from the rock face behind the tree, lightly ruffle its feathers and then sink a little on its legs and rub its head into the feathers of its shoulders as it settled down to see out the 16 or 17 hours of freezing-cold winter darkness. While there was great joy to be had working with eagles in Scotland, I could never deny the thrill of seeing such events in England, barely 8 km from my home and with me standing on the open hillside only 300 metres from the eagles.

In March 1993 I travelled to the Outer Hebrides to spend almost all of the next 18 months away from the Lake District. I'd spend the summers on Harris and Lewis and the intervening winter on the Uists. The RSPB employed me as a roving conservation officer with a brief to take part in the national surveys of merlins, and black-throated and red-throated divers. I'd survey corncrakes and waders, and during the winter I'd walk the coastlines of the Sound of Barra and the Sound of Harris to collect data for the proposed Special Protection Areas in those locations, counting sanderlings and knot, godwits and curlews.

In the summer I'd tramp the raised bogs of Lewis to find dunlin nests as I picked my way out to the diver lochs where I was measuring water depth and sampling the invertebrate and fish populations; I'd walk the runways of Stornaway airport at night to listen for crexing corncrakes; and I'd search out and help protect the incredibly rare red-necked phalaropes that were threatened by egg collectors. These tiny birds whizzed about the emergent vegetation in the shallows and nested on the floating mass that divided a loch in two, a mass of plantlife that barely carried my weight above the unknown depth of water of the black-watered lochan.

I went to the Flannan Islands as part of a team to estimate the population of storm and Leach's petrels that nested in the burrows around an old lighthouse, the loss of whose past occupants had formed the libretto of an opera. The diver work saw me walking the shoreline of lochs, which also held wild populations of greylag geese and whooper swans, where the eerie song of the diver echoed across the moors on cool still mornings. The 10-km merlin squares had to be covered meticulously, and while one included the small islands of the Sound of Harris, the other was upland habitat of immense beauty and wildlife importance. In that square I not only found six pairs of breeding merlins but also 12 pairs of greenshank. There were also dunlins, golden plovers, black-throated and red-throated divers, and eagles – there were always the eagles.

In that merlin square I found the occupied nests of four pairs of eagles, three of which bred successfully. There were eagle nests that defied any attempt to ascribe them to a particular home range when they weren't in use and nest locations that furthered the conclusion I'd reached in north Argyll that many eagles must occupy overlapping territories where a change in nest use from year to year would see a change in the location of the range 'boundary'. On an offshore island I found golden eagles that seemed to feed exclusively on fulmars during the summer months, and on that island was also a sea eagle's nest. Those birds failed with their breeding attempts for unknown reasons in both of the years I was there, but the area was well suited for the species, and I'd see immatures born on Mull and Skye as well as the adults that occupied the site.

But it was the golden eagle that attracted me most strongly. There were pairs nesting on sea cliffs and others on big crags in the Harris mountains, but the islands also allowed for some to nest on small, remote, and not so remote, locations. On one day I had to brake hard in the car as a snipe dashed across in front of me closely followed by an eagle. The snipe dived into the heather, but it didn't escape, the eagle crashed in after it, barely 50 metres from the road, and emerged victorious, the snipe clutched in one set of talons. I knew that eagle, it nested little more than a kilometre from where it was that day on a peat hag, the jumble of heather stalks that formed its nest just a pile on the ground that the sheep had to walk around while it was in use. That bird fledged its youngster in the first year, but the nest was burnt out in 1994. Whether it was a deliberate act or whether the muirburn had crept in that direction I couldn't tell, but the eagles moved to a crag nest that was on little more than a wall in the second year and failed.

Other nests were equally accessible, and just beyond the merlin square that held four pairs there was a fifth that reared twin chicks in 1993. It was the first such nest I'd had easy access to, and a late visit saw both youngsters out of the nest and seemingly unable to fly. I'd had that experience before, but this time it was something different. One of the juveniles flapped away with difficulty as I approached, but the second struggled even more and couldn't get off the ground. I'd noticed the problem in the nest and had assumed that it would be solved naturally, but when I caught up with the second bird, I found that the blades of its tail feathers still hadn't emerged from their sheaths. Instead of 12 beautiful black-and-white plumes, the eagle had what looked like 12 knitting needles projecting from its rear end. The other bird was similarly embarrassed, but after a quick bout of rough-and-tumble in the heather, the sheaths started to break, and on a later visit I saw both youngsters on the wing.

As with the others, this pair of eagles 1994 breeding attempt also failed, but it wasn't due to either deliberate or accidental human interference. The 1993 nest was reused, but when it was clear that they'd failed I went in to remove the eggs for analysis. I received quite a shock when I looked into the nest: first, there was only one egg and not two, but what stopped me was the shape of the egg. Eagle eggs could be described as being bluntly ovate, in other words the shape at one end isn't too dissimilar from the other, but that didn't apply here. The egg I saw was shaped like that of a guillemot: it was broad and blunt at one end but narrowed sharply so that the other end almost came to a point. I'd never seen anything like it in an eagle's nest before.

Those were another two successful years with the RSPB, but when I left the islands in August 1994 I already knew that I wouldn't be going back, there was no winter work for me this time, and I knew in my heart that the RSPB wouldn't be re-employing me for the 1995 season. It didn't matter how well I performed my tasks, my face just didn't fit in with what they wanted.

CHAPTER 15

Investigating food supply

When I returned to the Lake District in the late summer of 1994 I was already aware that I hadn't missed a great deal during my absence. The eagles hadn't reared chicks in 1993 or 1994, and after laying fertile eggs in each of the 13 years from 1980 (and fledging nine young in that time), both of the most recent clutches were infertile. It was the first time the eagles here had failed in consecutive years since the mid 1970s, and was the first time they'd ever laid infertile eggs in successive years.

There was already talk of the eagles, and more especially the male, being too old to breed successfully, but I dismissed that as speculation rather than a credible theory. The birds' ages were unknown, and no one knew to what age eagles could breed. It was only possible to ascribe them minimum ages based on the length of time they'd been in the pair plus five years to allow for them being in adult plumage at the time they arrived. This gave age estimates at the end of 1994 of 22 years for the male and 17 years for the female. Having seen the female's arrival myself and seen her early plumage, the estimate for her age was likely to be fairly accurate, but the male had arrived before my time, and I couldn't be certain that he wasn't older than estimated. Too little was known about eagle longevity and site occupancy for any safe conclusions to be reached, and, in fact, the information being collected at Haweswater was probably the most reliable of all that was available. It can be very difficult to identify a change of eagle if the site isn't closely monitored.

Ringing recoveries were also of little help as too few British eagles had been ringed and most of those recovered were still juveniles. There hadn't been a recovery of an adult eagle in the UK that matched the minimum ages of the birds in Riggindale. The Lakeland birds could have been old, in their prime or just youngsters, there was no way of knowing and so there was no reason to assume that they were too old.

There were other considerations to be taken into account when thinking about the breeding failures, which appeared to have been overlooked, particularly food supply. I'd already linked a change in live prey availability with the changed development of the later juveniles, but there were also other issues with food. The autumn changes and the regular June shortages obviously weren't going to affect breeding performance, but changes in the winter diet had become evident some years before and this could be influential. Supplementary feed blocks to maintain the health of the sheep during the late winter period were first used in 1982, and this was followed by a reduction in flock size, resulting in fewer carcasses for the eagles when they most needed them to survive the late winter, attain breeding condition and see the female ready to produce fertile eggs.

When I started to talk along these lines my ideas were dismissed as being too subjective. It seemed that people didn't want to know about anything other than the age theory, which was even more subjective than my idea and based on no evidence whatsoever. There was only one solution to the impasse: I would have to investigate food availability in the home range. I knew my results would be seen as biased and that a single-site study was of limited value to eagles in general, but my concern was for the Haweswater eagles. If I discovered a measurable difference in food availability between years that could be linked to breeding performance, then this situation could be resolved in the eagles' favour.

It was difficult to know where to start; while eagles' food requirements had been estimated in the past the results were little more than guesswork and usually based on captive birds, which made them thoroughly unrealistic. No one knew what the requirements were or at what level they became critical to survival or to breeding performance. For a species that Leslie Brown had described in 1976 as being 'intimately known', there was a great deal about the golden eagle that the experts didn't know.

I had some idea of the eagles' eating habits from watching many hundreds of feeds, and when I photographed the birds in 1986 I counted the number of pieces they pulled from the carcass and later simulated the feed with stewing steak to get an idea of the weight consumed. That, plus knowledge of the length of feeds, the time it took the eagles to feed on different items and the relative distension of their crops after each feed, led me to dismiss the previous estimates of food requirements as being far too low. That was useful information, but what I needed to know was how much food was available to the eagles. I had to start from scratch, so the first thing I needed was to have some idea of the amount of prey in the home range. That was a challenge in itself; I'd already estimated the range to cover about 50 sq km, and it would have been impossible for me to collect accurate data over such a large area, so I concentrated on the core area of the range, the area in which I already knew the eagles to spend most of their time (there were many days during the year when neither eagle left it) and on which they relied for the bulk of their diet. On 28 September 1994 I set out to see if there was a problem with the eagles' food supply.

It seemed obvious that it would be the late-winter period, the last few weeks before egg laying, that would most directly influence breeding performance, but I wanted to get an idea of what might be happening before that most important time arrived. So I started in the autumn to get an idea of the number of crows, ravens and rabbits in the area and to see how many sheep and deer carcasses were available before the pre-laying period began in February. There were other potential prey species, but the ones I selected were the most important, and by counting the number of fresh carcasses that became available and the maximum number of potential live prey items, I was certain I'd be able to produce comparable annual data for the most important 25 per cent of the home range. It was another long-term project, of course, and I expected to be engaged in this one for at least five years, so I just had to hope that the eagles survived and performed in a way that would allow whatever results I produced to be applied to their future.

I walked the valley floors, zigzagged back and forth across the screes and boulder fields, clambered up and down the ridges and searched the high tops over an area of about 12 sq km and wasn't at all surprised that I didn't find any carcasses that first month. Most mammals were fit and healthy at that time of year and basked in the autumnal sun rather than cowered from the winter storms. It was pretty much the same during the next two months as well, but I knew that sheep mortality would peak towards the eagles' laying date and that deer mortality came even later than that, in April and May, when they gorge on the fresh sweet grass and are capable of literally eating themselves to death. Crows and ravens abounded, but I found few rabbits, and they were mostly at the public access point to Riggindale where the eagles had to hunt in the twilight to avoid the disturbance caused by hillwalkers and birdwatchers. There'd always been rabbits there during my time, but their numbers were low, and I felt sure the eagles would be relying on carrion more than anything else.

I decided that the pre-laying period began with the onset of nest refurbishment and amended my monthly searches into a weekly transect from the beginning of February until the laying date. The route I followed took me through the rabbit warren, all the way around the valley at scree level and then on into the second valley. It was a basic trek of about 20 km, though the meanderings, back-tracking and diversions to check-out uncertainties must have added a few more on to that. The late-winter route was chosen deliberately because of something I was already aware of. I'd realised in earlier years that, though I was likely to find a dead sheep almost anywhere, there were, in fact, locations in which sheep tended to die more often than anywhere else, and I had to visit these to be certain of the numbers and the eagles' activities. When tested statistically, one such location in Riggindale was found to be significantly more likely to hold a carcass than any other comparable part of the core area. The same was true of red deer, but their graveyard was in the second valley, and so the transect had to include that as well.

As far as was possible I undertook these walks at the same time of day (starting each in the morning twilight when most rabbits were still active), in similar weather conditions (although the amount of snow and depths of frosts varied considerably from year to year) and seven days apart. I searched and scanned everywhere, found and checked every carcass and plotted its location onto maps for future comparisons, and counted the live rabbits, crows and ravens. I also collected pellets to see if they revealed the eagles to be foraging further afield. It was a long and difficult task, but I enjoyed every moment of being out before dawn in whatever winter weather came my way.

Checking the roosts and perches wasn't a job I undertook lightly, it involved repeat-edly climbing and descending the ridges when even a slightly misplaced foot on the icy rocks could result in a long fall to the screes below. And I had to do the rounds three times each year in winter conditions for this project, once in late January to remove winter pellets and then again at the end of February and in the third week of March to ensure that I was collecting pellets from the pre-laying period. I checked the perches throughout the year, and it wasn't just in the winter that I had a few scary moments: a foothold slipping just as I put my weight on it or a bunch of heather uprooting as I pulled up on it. I'd slipped and slid from many of the perches over the years, but some were by far more dangerous than others, and the winter increased the risk to almost unacceptable levels at some locations. Most of the perches appeared to be easily accessible when viewed from the valley floor, but all had their individual characteristics, and the approach to most had a sting in the tail. Some roosts could be reached simply by walking along the hillside (such as *KB* and *lbHC3*) while others required a short scramble up a muddy bank (the main roost), on rocks (*lxWR1*) or with a twisting squirm as I struggled through a tree growing too close to a crag to be avoided (*the new cross tree*). Others required a long step across a near vertical chimney through the ridge (*hER1*) and some were precipitously inaccessible (*hAGr* and *the flying pin*) with the pellets being collected from a safe position below the perch, but all had to be visited in late January, whatever the weather conditions, to ensure there was no mix-up over the dates the pellets were cast.

And the two most used day perches at that time could be the worst of all. From the security of the RSPB hide *the ledge* appeared to be easy and *the hole* seemed to be just above it, and with an eagle on each the scale didn't appear daunting, but after struggling up the ever-steepening ridgeside there was a twist and a shuffle to reach the ledge and a need to reverse out again. *The hole*, apparently so close when seen from below, was a different matter; it could only be reached with one foot on tiptoes on the icy or muddy edge of *the ledge* while the nails of one hand clawed for some purchase as the other arm reached fully up and over the bulge to grope blindly on the spot where the female stood. It looked no distance when viewed from the hide, but there was a 2.5-m gap between the male's perch and the female's, and a 10-m drop behind as you reach up and around for the pellets.

But worst of all was *SR*, an innocuous-looking jumble of rocks surrounded by grass. The perch itself looked easily accessible from one side, but the problems came after this. The perch was a rock on a ledge beneath a jutting triangular overhang that looked like bedrock but was, in fact, an enormous boulder. I tried accessing the ledge from all possible directions at first and eventually decided on an approach from the left, but one day I knelt on a sharp stone and started upwards. Using my left hand to balance as I rubbed the stinging knee with the other, I did no more than apply the gentlest of upwards pressure, and yet the entire rock moved as I knelt below it. I wasn't there for long after that, and the thought of having about 5 tonnes of rock crash down on top of me, when no one knew where I was or when I was due back, didn't encourage me to stay or return. It may well have seen me ending my time as eagle food, but I wasn't quite ready for that. I've been wary of the rock ever since but knew that I'd have to crawl beneath it at least three times every year during this project. And to add to the discomfort of each visit was the knowledge that, one winter, I found myself here scrambling up ground frozen rock-hard, without a depth of snow to kick my boots into, the slope increasing to the near vertical above me and with the growing realisation that I couldn't go down safely and going up only made the route more dangerous. Collecting pellets wasn't always fun!

By the end of the seven-week period in 1995, I'd found the fresh carcasses of three sheep and one deer and had mean seasonal counts of six rabbits and five corvids. My pellet analysis didn't add a great deal, with only a single example of rabbit and vole illustrating how little these species were taken at that time of year. The numbers didn't appear to amount to much but it equated to an available biomass of about 104 kg during the seven weeks. One expert source suggested that eagles only required about 250 g of meat per day, so what I'd found available in seven weeks would be sufficient to feed both eagles for about seven months; if only it was that easy! Foxes, crows and ravens would eat the carrion as well as the eagles, but even with only one data set, it didn't really look as though food supply would prove to be the problem.

The eagles laid their eggs in the top nest that year, starting on 24 March, but neither hatched and both proved to be infertile. The male was another year older, and there was nothing they could do about it. The question of age became common knowledge, and it was an accepted fact that the male eagle was too old by the time I started my rounds again in February 1996.

I checked above the top nest as I did my preliminary rounds of the perches on 21 January 1996, and while I didn't find an egger's spike I was shocked to find a boot print and what appeared to be evidence of someone trying to insert a spike. I thought there was little point in relaying the information, so I just stuck my boot print on top of the holes to show that someone knew about them and went on my way. There appeared to be fresh sticks on that nest, so I was surprised when Stefan told me on 3 February that the birds were building a new nest on the crag above the hide site. The hide was no longer left standing over winter, so the eagles possibly didn't associate the location with the human activity. I'd seen both eagles in flight display on the 2nd, with flight-rolls and dips, and I'd heard the male calling from the next crag down the valley, but this building was a real surprise. The new nest was in an exposed location, though set in a small recess, and would have been the most difficult of all for eggers to reach.

There was snow falling and lying during my visit on the 13th, but I saw more flight-displays and watched the female fly to the new nest with some heather in her talons at 10.10 a.m. Six minutes later, however, I saw the male take material onto the top nest and stay to adjust it for three minutes. He took material to the new nest 92 minutes after that and then added another eight pieces during the next 45 minutes. He was obviously taken by the new site but was still attached to the preferred one, and I didn't see the female add material again until two minutes after the male's last piece, but then she'd been preoccupied. Prior to the male first visiting the new nest he had collected and delivered a sheep's leg to his mate. There'd been more examples of the male provisioning the female in the years since I first recorded it in 1988, but it was interesting to see how the actions developed over the years. On this occasion the female had reached her perch on the other side of the valley two minutes after taking her first material to the new nest, and there she waited for more than an hour while the male visited the top nest and then disappeared into the corrie. When he returned it was just like watching him delivering food to a juvenile.

He swept past the female to land about 20 metres away, and she flew down to claim the food. The male flew at once but returned 22 minutes later before busying himself with building the new nest. For her part, the female ate for 32 minutes and then sat watching for 17 before getting up to display with her mate in a pursuit flight, roll and parallel glide past the middle nest. Nest material was taken to the new site throughout February, and by 20 March it was built up and partly lined as if ready for the eggs. But when I passed the top nest, on a roost-checking day, I noticed that it too was in good condition with fresh material on it, even though the building activity hadn't been seen.

My 1996 transects showed an increase in the apparent food supply, the potential biomass rising from 104 kg in 1995 to 160 kg in 1996 with the increase almost entirely due to the amount of carrion I found. From three sheep and one deer in 1995 it went to three sheep and three deer in 1996. There was also an increase of four rabbits on the mean count although corvid numbers remained stable, as would be the case throughout my project. The pellets produced two rabbit entries (but no voles), a fox and an increase of corvid-pellets from three to seven. It was the deer that came as a surprise when I found them; it was very early in the year for this degree of deer mortality, but not least because all three, a hind and two yearlings, had died in their sleep rather than in falls from crags. When I approached the first of these I even impressed myself with my stalking technique as I crept in with camera at the ready, so I was a little disappointed when the deer didn't even move when I gave it a kick.

The deer carcass was lying close to the valley floor and out of sight of the RSPB watch point, so I thought I'd do them a favour and move it into view but when I returned the next day even Stefan obstructed me and told me that I couldn't progress beyond his position. It was as if I was someone who wasn't known and who'd never been there before, and I had to remind Stefan that the eggs hadn't been laid, that he was standing under the nest that was being built and that I was going to move the carcass whatever he thought.

It was a great brute of a beast and, ungralloched, it took some shifting through the boulder fields, but I wasn't simply moving it for the RSPB's benefit. As well as the graveyards, I'd realised some time earlier that the eagles wouldn't feed on all of the carcasses that became available, even when they were in secluded locations that saw little human activity, and I knew this brute to be in the wrong place. I struggled on; on some steps I had to stand above the carcass, take a leg in each hand and swing it like a pendulum to increase the momentum before heaving it up, past and behind me and onto the next step up. It was an icy morning, but the steam was rising by the time I'd lugged the beast up to a position I knew would suit the eagles. I knew it would suit because I'd had an audience for part of the time. Soon after I'd started moving the carcass the female eagle came sweeping in to settle in a tree about 50 metres above me. She glowered down at me, impatient to begin her meal, her amber-yellow eyes burning into the back of my neck as I puffed and panted beneath her. The job complete, I gave the eagle a friendly wave and exited straight down the slope; she was on the carcass and feeding before I reached the valley floor. It was incredible to see that the eagle had no fear of me and would fly in and perch close by and accept my efforts to help her.

Having seen the condition of the top nest, I wasn't at all surprised when the new nest was abandoned and incubation began in the top one on 24 March. New nests are often started and abandoned before incubation, but on this occasion the eagles had the added impetus to move once they saw the RSPB erect their garden shed in the usual place, directly below the new nest crag, before incubation began. I wondered if it was a deliberate attempt to make the eagles use the top site, even though this meant moving the birds from a really awkward nest into an easily accessible one that everyone knew had been targeted by eggers in the past. There was nothing I could do about it, the eagles were expected to lay infertile eggs, so from that point of view, it didn't matter.

The incubation period continued apace, and everything appeared to be running smoothly, but the knives were out for the eagles. Even though the birds were still in-cubating their eggs it came as no surprise to see an article in the *Daily Express* entitled 'Is Lakeland's eagle past it at 24?' While the RSPB spokesman didn't say that the male was too old that was the clear implication. It was claimed that they'd removed previous eggs for analysis (Geoff, who had removed them, was an employee of Oxfam at the time, but that didn't seem to matter), and given the lack of chemical residues in the eggs, 'That is what leads us to believe that the male could be infertile'. There was no mention of problems with the food supply or habitat quality, the factors that most affect eagles throughout Scotland. I let the eagles do the talking, and after confirming that the first egg hadn't hatched I found myself on the ridge above the nest on 11 May and saw the newly hatched eaglet from the second egg, born in spite of its father being 'too old'!

It was far too early to reach any conclusions about food supply, but 104 kg in 1995 resulted in a breeding failure, and 160 kg in 1996 saw a breeding success. The food-supply project then went on the back burner as I prepared to follow a juvenile instead. Geoff ringed the chick on 14 June, but it seemed to be a long wait between then and the first fall/jump/flight of the juvenile. The late hatching date meant that an average nestling period would take the birds into late July, but this youngster was happy to stay on the nest into August. It was active and noisy, but I wasn't the only person to miss it leaving the nest; that happened during the evening of the 4th while low cloud shrouded the crags. It didn't go far, though, and I found it the next morning on the *bilberry peaks*, so it probably hadn't flown more than 20 metres. After three years without young, it was fascinating to see the juvenile soon find its way to *the dome* and behave just as its predecessors had done.

It was exhilarating to watch a juvenile again and to see so many similarities with the earlier birds. It was flying strongly by mid-month, but as with the others, it could be lazy, and after it fell asleep at 10.58 a.m. on the 16th, I gave up waiting for more action when it still hadn't moved again by 4.30 p.m. The juveniles had little to fill the still, long, hot days of August, and this one seemed to be settling into the pattern of the live-prey birds, though it survived on carrion supplemented by whatever the male caught rather than depending entirely on live prey. There were times when it showed its inexperience as well, and on the 23rd it seemed to have trouble landing in trees. It tried to join the female below the middle nest at 10.35 a.m. but crashed into the canopy without seeming to aim for any particular branch and fell through the tree with the female standing by and watching. The female changed trees, and the juvenile tried to follow, struggling into the tree at 10.47 a.m. using its wings for extra leverage. Two minutes later it was up to make a clumsy pass at a large lamb, and the next time the female moved the juvenile took the easy option and just landed on the ground beside it.

I first saw the juvenile leave the valley on 10 September, 35 days after leaving the nest, and this bird as good as disappeared. I didn't see it or the adults in Riggindale again until the 27th, when the female was perched in *the hole*, and both adults were in the valley without the juvenile on the 30th. I searched the surrounding hills, but sightings were few and far between; the juvenile was already wandering far afield, another sign that the food supply was failing. I started in Riggindale on 5 October, but while there were fresh droppings on *the ledge* and in *the hole* there were no birds to be seen. As I scanned around the valley my eyes fell on an unusually late red deer calf, still in its spotted coat. I thought it had little chance of surviving the winter, but it would be food for the birds when it fell. I walked to the top of Castle Crag and from there was delighted to find the juvenile eagle perched on one of the adults' favourite sites, and above it sat the female – so it was still around and being tolerated – but it remained in place when the old bird returned to Riggindale. On 7 and 8 October the juvenile was in valleys to the south-east of the site, but then it was gone and it didn't return. There were fresh sticks on the top nest and a second ledge on the crag later that month to confirm its departure, and material was added to the middle nest in November.

There were regular sheep carcasses this late autumn, so I was pleased to know that the birds would be feeding well, but the carrion attracted other scavengers as well, another indication of the lack of food in the range. There were two sheep carcasses in the valley head on 6 December, but when the eagles approached them they were hounded to distraction. A flock of 63 ravens had reached the carcasses first, and the eagles couldn't get near them; 20 or 30 ravens chased and dive-bombed them on every approach. The ravens worked as a pack and so heavily outnumbered the eagles that some continued to feed while the eagles were overhead, safe in the knowledge that the others would protect them. Some ravens even perched and watched, taking over the feeding as the opportunity arose, and after 40 minutes of almost continuous harassment the eagles turned tail, abandoned the meat to the ravens and left the valley in search of easier pickings, driven from their home by the marauding corvids. I had to wonder how the juvenile would fare if two adult eagles couldn't defend food in their own nesting valley.

Buoyed by the 1996 breeding success, and hoping that the old-age theory had been put to rest, I had great expectations for 1997 and soon began to count the available food. I thought the late autumn carcasses might have led to an overwinter abundance, but I didn't find a single fresh carcass until 24 February, even the late deer calf survived the mild winter, and I found no other carcasses until 21 March. From a biomass figure of

160 kg in 1996, the 1997 counts produced only 98 kg. Rabbit numbers had doubled, but I found only three pellets that contained their remains. The first egg was laid in the top nest on 25 March, and although the incubation period progressed as it should, and I saw two eggs in the nest on 12 May, I knew they wouldn't be hatching. It was a tremendous disappointment, and when Geoff and I climbed up to retrieve the infertile eggs for analysis on the 22nd, it was the first time the birds had deserted before we reached the nest crag.

The year rolled slowly by after that with the eagles displaying and visiting their nests, but they had little to fill their time. Sheep carrion was less abundant that year, and by the autumn the eagles were hunting rabbits in the twilight and in places I'd never seen them before. As I drove to the site on 19 November, I was amazed to find the male hunting low down and close to the road, and I watched as he flapped heavily across the lake and back to his valley having failed to make a kill. When I caught up with him again he was on a ledge close to the acacia nest, and the birds would build here this year – it was the eleventh such site on which I'd seen a new nest started even though they'd only ever used the two established nests during my years and, from 1995, would only ever use the top site. The weather was almost continuously wet towards the end of the year, and while that's good for producing carrion, it made it harder for the eagles to forage.

The eagles refurbished the top nest as usual during the 1998 pre-laying period, but my food transects produced a biomass figure of only 78 kg. I found only two sheep carcasses during the seven weeks, and rabbit numbers had remained stable. The rabbit warren was moving further into Riggindale, which made it easier for the eagles to hunt and that year I found 12 pellets (out of 23) that contained their remains. There were stoats in two pellets but also two with red grouse remains. That was always a bad sign; the eagles were feeding on grouse when their numbers were lowest and were feeding on the breeding stock when their population was in decline. I saw, and also found more evidence of, the male provisioning his mate, but I now saw this as a bad sign as well, not just as the male's attentiveness to his mate. The provisioning suggested that food, and especially carrion, was not as easily found as it had been in the past and that the eagles were having to rely on the limited numbers of live prey species.

The eagles mated and the top nest was lined and ready for eggs by 17 March, but I waited. The birds mated at 3.22 p.m. on the 24th, and the male took material to the nest; the female was largely inactive as if in pre-laying lethargy, but at 4 p.m. I saw something that I thought I'd never see. Both eagles were circling with a peregrine close to the top nest crag when the male suddenly broke away, stooped down and caught the peregrine in open flight. It was as easy as that. The 'fastest bird in the world' had learnt the errors of its ways – you don't outfly a golden eagle on a mission.

Stefan saw the female on the nest for 58 minutes on 30 March, but we were now beyond the latest known laying date and things didn't look good. The next day Stefan saw the male deliver a rabbit to the female, but March turned into April without an egg being laid. The display flights, matings and material collection continued; the female made long visits to the nest and was seen breasting the cup and then, at last, an egg was laid and incubation began on 12 April. I checked the nest on the 21st, but it still only contained a single white egg. Incubation continued as usual after that, and I even saw the female bathing again on 12 May, but she stopped sitting on the 19th, and in spite of the male's best efforts the prospective hatching date was passed. The infertile egg was removed and another failure was recorded.

My 1999 transects recorded an increase in available food, the weight going to 114 kg. There were still only three carcasses to be counted, but rabbits had increased again, though I found them in fewer pellets and the total weight was still well below the 1996 figure. I predicted another failure, and I wasn't pleased to be proved correct. The eagles didn't even lay any eggs in 1999; it was the first year since 1968 that there hadn't been eagle eggs in the Lake District. I was desperately disappointed.

The talk was all of the male's age; I was told that this time he really was too old, but five years of counts had shown me how the food supply varied. The eagles had laid one egg in 1998 with a lower total biomass than in 1999 when they laid none, but I noticed that while food availability had increased towards the laying date during the first four years of my counts it had declined in 1999. I'd been measuring availability during a seven-week period for convenience in the lack of any information to guide me, but now I wondered if that wasn't too long. Reduced to the last three weeks before the mean laying date, the comparative carrion figures for the five years became 48, 98, 44, 24 and 24 kg respectively, producing two infertile eggs, a chick, two eggs, one egg and no eggs. I was aware that the results might be coincidental, but it was a strong coincidence, and I now had the opportunity for yet another new project.

I'd long been thinking about introducing a supplementary feeding project to help the eagles but knew that I had to assess the natural food supply before I could propose such a scheme, that's why I performed the transects. It's obviously vital to know the natural situation before you interfere with it, if for no other reason than you can't determine the effects of your efforts unless you know what went before. Providing food still wouldn't be the solution to a problem food supply, but it might answer a question: if food supply was the problem (and there seemed to be a link between food and breeding) could increasing food availability improve breeding performance?

If that worked it would then be a matter of habitat and stock management, and perhaps even managing the rabbits to ensure there was live prey available throughout the year. With the eagles now definitely 'too old' and no eggs being laid, there was nothing to lose, so I pushed hard for the project and wrote a proposal that went to the RSPB and the landowners, United Utilities (U U). There was opposition from the outset, and I was never invited to present the case in person. All I could do when they objected was remind the wardens that the RSPB were involved with a feeding project for hen harriers at Langholm in the Scottish Borders, they were releasing and feeding red kites across the country, and that, on their behalf, I'd fed white-tailed eagles on Mull; I could see no logical reason for their objections to feeding golden eagles in England. U U took their eagle advice from the RSPB, and the RSPB said the eagles were too old. But Laurie, the head ranger, was keen to try something, and as UU donated money for the eagle scheme they had some influence. I wanted to start the project in February 2000, but the RSPB's delaying tactics held us back, and I had to kick my heels in the valley until the experts finally made a decision.

There were still sights to see, of course, and sights to be seen for the first time, even after 22 years of observations. The birds were quite active on 7 March, with calling and a mating being noted, but then, at 5.41 p.m., with the female already at her roost, the male dropped to the screes below the middle nest and began to feed. I don't know how long he was there as he was still at the carcass when it became too dark for me to see him, even though he was less than 500 metres away. I'd seen late feeds before, but this was the first to go into such poor light which meant that I didn't see him go to roost. He must have flown in almost total darkness.

It wasn't until 10 March that Tony, the stalker, and I set out to start the scheme. We chose an old red deer stag that was past his prime, Tony moved in and felled the beast with a single shot. Gralloched, we moved the carcass into a suitable location and left the eagles to it. The female had been in *the hole* during the stalk but didn't fly to the deer before we left. I wasn't concerned, I was absolutely certain that the eagles would use the carcass, and indeed, I saw both birds feeding from it the next day. The wardens also saw it and reported that the eagles used the deer carcass for the best part of a week. That was perfect, but we could only put out one more carcass as our late start took us too close to the expected laying date, and I didn't want to be leaving piles of deer carcasses about the valley. I'd also decided there was no point in continuing after that as the eagles couldn't be guaranteed to lay eggs, and we could find ourselves shooting deer for no reason at all.

Tony and I were back on the hill on the 18th. It was a more difficult stalk this time with a bad crosswind making for an awkward approach, and the scattered hinds gave warning snorts as we picked our way across the slope, but the stag fell to the gun. We left the gun, our scopes, binoculars, bait-bags and other paraphernalia with the dog at a safe distance and moved in to prepare the carcass. As we did, the head that had been lying with a lolling tongue was lifted, and then the stag stood up. The three of us looked at one another, Tony and I had a gralloch knife between us, and we stood less than 3 metres from a stag at bay, a solid 8-point 14-stoner. The stag took a step towards us, stumbled in the marshy ground and went down again. We were on it in a flash; I grabbed its antlers and used all my weight and strength to heave back its head while Tony administered the *coup de grâce*. It would have been dead within a few minutes in any case, but we wanted the kill to be as quick as possible in respect for the quarry. It was still a risky business, and many a stalker has been slashed by a wounded stag.

The female eagle was feeding from the carcass when I arrived the next afternoon, and both birds were still using it on the 25th, but we were into the laying dates by then without seeing any evidence of the eggs. Perhaps I'd been wrong about the influence of the food supply or perhaps we'd started the project too late in the year. I didn't know, and all I could do was wait.

There was some confidence to be gained from the male's activities – and more than ever before – as he set to the task of feeding his mate after we'd put out the second carcass. Even the wardens saw him catching and delivering rabbits to the female, and she had developed specific perches on which she waited. These were akin to the juveniles' safe perches, and on a daily basis the male may have taken the hint to get involved by the female arriving at one of them. With the most commonly used perch being on the opposite side of the valley to the rabbit warren, it was quite a sight to see the kill, the carry and the delivery, but it didn't seem to be having much impact, and I felt defeated until the first egg was laid on 13 April.

The elation that followed the onset of incubation that year was greater than any I'd felt before. The stags had increased the March carrion figure to 84 kg, and while still below that of 1996, the total was much better than the next best of 48 kg, and I knew that the eagles had utilised the meat we provided. The 'too old' eagles had laid eggs again after a year without eggs, and the coincidence with the manipulated food supply seemed too strong to be denied. The eagles had deserted their clutch after laying on the 12th in 1998, so I wasn't really expecting a breeding success from an even later laying date, but when I saw two eggs in the nest on the 24th, I felt certain I'd be able to instigate a full-blown supplementary feeding project the next year.

The incubation period progressed, but it soon became a repetition of 1998, and the female had effectively stopped trying by the last week of May. The male continued to incubate by himself for a few days, and even though he may have sat overnight at this time, he had to leave the nest to feed and he stopped rushing back. I couldn't blame the female, she was used to having chicks by 5 May, so perhaps with a better instinct for these things than the male she knew that there was no hope of the eggs hatching. We collected the eggs on 5 June, and unsurprisingly, they proved to be infertile.

I knew in my heart that seeing eggs in the nest would be insufficient evidence to convince the ageists that food was the problem; we had to see a chick. I was confident that the eggs would give me sufficient leverage to continue the project, and we'd start earlier the next time and put out more food. Even so I couldn't be confident that the immediate effect would be to see a chick, but I felt that even moving the laying date back into March, where it should have been, would be a degree of success that would allow me to continue with the work. I rewrote my feeding proposal and submitted it again, but, as usual, I heard nothing, so I watched the eagles and kept an eye on the deer herd for the remainder of the year to pick out likely candidates to be shot. There was little to report from the valley; I found goosander as eagle prey on 6 October and noted that I wasn't seeing many rabbits. There were pheasant pluckings on 2 November that suggested one of the birds, presumably the male, was still carrying food, and the pair were displaying with chases and talon-grappling on the 21st. There was the usual number of carcasses about the core area, and two magpies were in the valley on 7 December, so I began to anticipate really helping the eagles in 2001.

I found new material on the middle nest on 4 January, a fresh deer carcass on the 12th to give them a kick-start, and my food transects began with a sheep carcass on 4

February. It was looking good. There were always more than 50 deer from which we only needed to select four or five, but just when I decided to call in the stalkers foot-and-mouth disease struck, and even though it didn't reach the farms around the village, the fells around the lake or the eagles' valley, the access restrictions were applied, and I couldn't go to the hill again that year.

CHAPTER 16

The end of an era

I didn't return to Riggindale until 4 January 2002 when I watched the eagles go to roost from the lower hide site. The morning frost hadn't lifted, and it was setting hard again as I watched the female fly along the ridge to perform her checks before turning and long-dropping into the usual location for the night. The male was keeping to the gloom in the valley head but followed her part way down to circle and then, to my surprise, drop in to roost high in the *acacia* gully at 4.08 p.m. I'd never seen him roost there before and thought it odd that he hadn't joined his mate on the perch they'd shared since 1982.

I was back in the valley on the 8th and found the female on the ground below the middle nest crags, by the sheep graveyard, but she soon flew across the valley and settled low down on the north side. I wandered up to the top sheepfold and settled in; the female hadn't moved, so I fixed the telescope on her and began to scan for the male through binoculars. It was 20 minutes before I noticed an eagle crossing over down-valley of my position, so I checked the female and then watched the male with the naked eye until he swung up along the ridgeside, looking through binoculars as he landed quite low down below the middle nest. We stood in line abreast across the valley: eagle, man, eagle. His plumage looked quite wet, so I checked the female and then switched the telescope onto the male. I saw a dark eagle! I couldn't believe that I'd made such a basic error of identification and went back to the first bird; it was dark, it was the female. I went to the second one again; it was dark, but it wasn't the female. Still disbelieving, I turned the scope back on the first one, and as I did the female took off and flew across the valley, passing no more than 100 metres above me, to settle on the rocks barely 2 metres from the second bird. Through the telescope I could now see two dark eagles standing side by side without either showing any animosity towards the other. It was as if the female had deliberately flown across the valley to tell me that my eyes weren't deceiving me, she *did* have a new partner.

How I cursed sheep, farmers and foot-and-mouth disease! The three had conspired to prevent me from visiting the valley for 10 months and had guaranteed that I didn't know about the change of eagles possibly until long after it had happened. All I'd been able to do during those long months was confirm that a breeding attempt didn't take place and scan for the eagles from the road. The birds were visible when flying above the skyline or when perched on *the ledge*, almost 4 km from the road, but they were more difficult to see when perched elsewhere or flying in the valley head. I could check the second valley from the road as well if the birds weren't in Riggindale, but if they were in neither I was stuck. In 2001 I couldn't just head off over the hills or speed round to the grouse moors to watch them there.

When I checked my logbooks that evening I realised that there were more gaps in the record than I remembered, but there were confirmed records of both the eagles I knew throughout much of the year. I was always careful not to make assumptions with distant observations, so I knew my records were reliable and I'd been seeing the old male for much of that year. I knew I'd seen him on 28 October, chasing ravens with his mate before settling beside her in the middle of what was usually a busy public footpath. The gap in my notes that followed was the most interesting; it lasted until 14 December, and during that time I only recognised the female eagle. I saw one bird on 18 November but wasn't confident of its identity, and I started to see two birds again after mid-December. The record was still a little sketchy after that because of the generally damp and gloomy weather, but I have no doubt that the male was lost and replaced within the space of six weeks, and probably in less time than that.

It seemed incredible that a replacement eagle could find its way to Haweswater in such a short space of time. The next nearest breeding site was more than 50 km away and didn't have a good breeding record, and excluding juveniles, I hadn't seen another eagle in the Lake District for almost 10 years. But then again, the new bird was an adult, and so must have been wandering for at least four years before arriving at Haweswater. But then I remembered the accursed foot-and-mouth disease. The access restrictions had prevented me from venturing onto the hill, but they'd also stopped 12 million other people from swarming over the fells in 2001. The coincidence of the male's loss at that time couldn't have been better planned; the new bird wandered into the Lakes when there was no one to disturb him or harry him from place to place, he would have had more freedom from humanity here than anywhere in Scotland, and he found his way to Haweswater just when he was needed. Foot-and-mouth disease probably saved the eagles for another year, and it was a demonstration of what could happen were it not for human activity.

The plumage differences between the two old birds were very distinct and could be relied on for identification at almost any distance, but with a dark male now present that would become much more difficult. I scrutinised the new bird's plumage to look for any pointers. I hadn't seen any of the immature white on him as he crossed the valley or flew in to land, but his darkness suggested that he was a very young adult. This was proven after the next moult when he took on his full adult, paler, patterning. He didn't become as pale as the old male but was distinct enough from the female to make their separation somewhat easier. He also had a more ragged appearance than the female and that also suggested that he was a young bird. As I stared at the two eagles standing together, I noted that the paler patch on the male's closed wing was lower down than it was on the female and that proved to be the best pointer at this early stage. I also noted that the male had particularly pale undertail coverts, a feature that often leads to such eagles being described as subadults, but it is also quite common in old adults. The male was smaller than his mate, of course, but such a distinction would be meaningless if I only saw one bird or saw it at a distance.

I was back in the valley early the next morning to see if the new bird was still about or if the old male had returned. I'd seen the female flying and displaying with spare males in the past when her mate was otherwise engaged and didn't want to announce the new arrival until I could be sure that he was a member of the pair, and I began to have some doubts; I only saw the female on the 9th and saw no eagles at all on the 12th or 13th. I returned to the valley on the 17th with the intention of waiting until darkness had fallen but had to wait no longer than the time it took me to set up before I picked out the new male perched on the highest point of the north ridge. He was flying at 2.16 p.m., crossed the valley, swung down to land in the sheep graveyard and 10 minutes later stepped onto a fresh carcass. A magpie joined him, and the female eagle flew in to stand and watch two minutes later. He was definitely in the pair.

A fox stalked towards him after 20 minutes, with its tail held aloft, a second magpie appeared and then a second fox, and even the female came closer, but he completed his 68-minute feed at his own pace before flying to perch above the middle nest, allowing the female to take over to eat for 40 minutes. All seemed to be well with the pairing, and on the 27th I watched the two eagles talon grappling and tumbling as their first pre-nuptial displays began.

When I announced the new bird's presence to the Raptor Study Group on the 24th there was some disbelief because none of the wardens had noticed the change, and one wouldn't be convinced for some time. But there was no question of a mistake; as well as the plumage differences between the two males there were also behavioural differences that did more than support my announcement. There was the new male roosting near *the acacia tree* on the 4th (and subsequently on most other nights), and before he was entirely au fait with the valley, there were also changes to the day perches being used. Sites such as the *HC trees* were ignored along with the *mWK1* and *lbHC1, 2 and 3*, and it became commonplace to find the new male using a *rock band* on the north ridge, the *ht ledge* in the valley head, and he even took a liking to *the niche* that had held the food cache in 1982. Most surprising of all, he also used *the old cross tree* near *the ledge*, a perch favoured by the 1980 female. I hadn't seen it used since her loss, and I never saw the old male perch in it. The changes of location may have been individual choice or down to the uncertainty of a new bird pairing with a larger and dominant partner, but some of these habits didn't change in the following years. The new bird was, perhaps especially with his choice of roost, still keeping his distance and was, in spite of the flight displays, still uncertain of his position in the valley as late as 2 April when I watched him crouch in readiness to defend himself as the female approached in a sweeping flight. She flew straight past him, though, and he relaxed, knowing he'd been accepted.

The male was definitely part of the pair, and during another afternoon to nightfall watch on 28 February, I had further new experiences to record. There were dip displays, flight-rolls and talon grappling before a thick snow shower stopped their activity at 2.52 p.m. for 25 minutes. Afterwards, as if I needed any further proof of his identity,

I watched the male flying where I'd never seen the old male fly during the previous 22 years. He circled low over the old barn near the mouth of the valley and flapped out and around, rather than over, the ridge end before returning barely 10 metres above the lake shore. Flapping over the water at the mouth of the valley, he continued between the hawthorns and birch trees that surround the public footpath and then turned up-valley, increased his speed and flew directly to the top nest. The old male simply didn't make flights like that. He spent the next 40 minutes displaying, chasing peregrines and casually sailing about with the female before going to roost in the *acacia* gully at 4.45 p.m. after he'd watched his mate drop into her usual site at 4.32 p.m. as if familiarising himself with her habits, just as the old male had done in 1982 when the female was new.

I was well into my food transects by that date, but I failed to find any fresh carrion during February, even though there'd been three carcasses in January. Rabbit numbers had also fallen to barely a third of their peak in 1999, and so, while the pellets revealed badger and stoat in the diet, the natural situation didn't look too promising. I'd already made my annual proposal to increase the available food, citing the 2000 eggs as evidence of the value of the work when compared to the non-laying years of 1999 and 2001, but I'd forgotten something vital. The problem with the eagles was seen to be the age of the male, and so with a new male in the pair, that problem had been removed and there was no need to help the birds! The March food total was 48 kg with less live prey available than before, and it came as no surprise that, even with the new male, the eagles didn't lay any eggs in 2002. And that breeding failure was easily explained by the female by then being 'too old to breed'. I was wasting my breath trying to argue the point and I knew it; the excuse for poor breeding had been concocted in 1994, and it wasn't going to change.

The eagles added to the top nest throughout the spring, and when I did an early morning check before the wardens were awake on 26 July I found they'd also been carrying material to two new sites, one close to the middle nest and one close to the top site. It was always encouraging to know that the birds were still interested in such matters, and the freshness of the pairing allowed me to watch the eagles flight-rolling on 1 September. Just as happened throughout the years with the old male, the pair were in the second valley on the 13th, and they settled on ledges and called as if prospecting new nest sites and chased peregrines, kestrels and ravens as if defending these sites from potential competitors. I also found a fresh sheep carcass beneath the crag that had held a nest in 1968, but what had taken me to this valley wasn't the eagles this time or anything else to be pleased or encouraged by.

As I drove along the road on the opposite side of the lake, I could see shining out like beacons about 50 large white sacks that I knew would be full of rocks. The Lake District National Park Authority was generating a tremendous amount of publicity for itself with its footpath repairs, but I couldn't believe they'd be doing it in that valley. The bags had to be carried by helicopter one at a time, and yet they were barely 200 metres from one of the eagles' nest crags. There were a similar number of bags close to the road end, and the potential for disturbing the eagles increased with each one. Not even crows or ravens had been on the sheep carcass when I found it, so it was perfect for the eagles, but I wondered what chance they'd have of feeding from it once the helicopter flights began.

I made my thoughts known to the park authority at the earliest possible moment and pointed out that not only would the operation almost certainly prevent the eagles from feeding on what proved to be the only fresh carrion in the core area that September, but the proximity of the first set of bags to the various nest sites, and what we could expect the eagles to be doing at that time of year, would, technically, be in breach of the Wildlife and Countryside Act; it would be reckless disturbance of a Schedule 1 species while it was in the act of nest-building.

My comments fell on deaf ears; I was informed that the RSPB and English Nature (now Natural England) were aware of the operation and had both approved it. I was told that my comments had been noted, but the helicopter flights would take place as planned. I was also patronised with an observation about how frustrating it must be to be left out of the consultation loop. It was frustrating, the person who made those remarks and left me out of the loop, the National Park Area Manager, was also Chair of the Raptor Study Group that included the RSPB and EN. In fact, it seemed as though I was the only person not consulted about the operation, and I was the eagle specialist in that raptor group. Having my specialist knowledge excluded from the process didn't really surprise me, the organisations involved all knew I'd object to the flights, and they knew they wouldn't be able to counter my arguments without saying that the eagles didn't matter anymore.

I checked the sheep carcass on the 18th (the eagles hadn't been to it), and the morning of the 19th found me in that area again, but this time tucked away in the crags to watch the helicopter. The one assurance the National Park Authority had given me was that the helicopter would only fly over the lake (which was highly unlikely given the location of most footpaths), and it duly arrived at 9.42 a.m. by flying down the watercourse between the eagles' two valleys before swinging past one of the peregrine sites, above the eagles' 1968 nest crag, past me, past the sheep carcass and past the favourite perches the female had used so many times before. On each flight the helicopter picked up the bag of stones swung out and then back in towards the nest crags before sweeping over the ridge and on to the dumpsite. The helicopter had to be refuelled at less than hourly intervals, so it was flown back past the crags and across Riggindale to the lake-head before returning and continuing as before.

It took the helicopter most of the day to ferry the bags to their intended location, and not once did I see the eagles during that time. It was a similar tale the next day when the bags were collected from near the car park. The helicopter carried in its fuel from the south, returned in that direction and then, obviously after flying a circuit, flipped over High Street to hover inside Riggindale. It spent the day flying up and down along the nest ridge and sometimes crossing Riggindale to follow the route it had used the day before. The eagles were absent again, but they hadn't moved to their other valley to feed on the sheep carcass; that still lay untouched by anything and would remain unused by the eagles. I checked it for two weeks until it was torn apart by foxes. Such a carcass would never have gone unused in the past, but that was an irrelevance to the experts.

I watched the helicopter make more than 200 low-level flights during those days, each one of them in the core area of the eagles' range. I saw it flying close to the eagle nests, over the food and over the valleys that had formed the eagles' safe haven for the previous 33 years, but what I didn't see was anyone from the RSPB monitoring the procedure. And nor did that come as any surprise; I could already hear their arguments: it wasn't the breeding season, the eagles were too old anyway, they could go somewhere else to feed, it was only for two days and, besides, the most important part of England's only golden eagle territory was obviously the only place in the Lake District from which stones could be collected for footpath repairs!

I could do little more to help the eagles. I'd been intimately involved with the birds and had studied their lives for 24 years, but my knowledge counted for nothing. I'd learnt over the years that egg collectors weren't really trying to steal the eggs; the birds were too old before they'd stopped breeding successfully; and the drastically depleted food supply couldn't possibly have any relevance to the eagles' lives. The call of the eagle had become an unheeded plea for help.

The birds were about Riggindale on most of my visits that autumn, but I only found two more fresh sheep carcasses in the core area, and a series of evening roost watches in late November told me that they were foraging further afield for their food. I failed to see either bird come to roost on three consecutive visits and couldn't find them on the moors during the daytime, so I knew their ranging area was changing in response to the lack of food. They were exiting the valley to the west far more frequently than in the past, but the foraging was limited in that direction and I failed to find them during my searches; the birds were obviously wandering far beyond the area that had sustained the range since the 1960s. I had little hope for their future and knew that I wouldn't be allowed to supplement their diet when the time for nest-building came around again. The eagles were back by early December, and I watched them sky-dancing and flight-rolling on the 17th, but I wondered about how many more glorious flight displays I'd see in this valley.

Both eagles sky-danced on 8 January 2003, and the female visited the top nest for a minute from 9.59 a.m., but snow was lying down to the valley floor, and if there were any carcasses they'd be buried and out of reach to the birds. There were some more displays, but I didn't see another nest visit and failed to see the eagles in Riggindale between 27 January and 24 February. That wasn't too unusual or a cause for concern in itself, they'd long struggled to find food at that time of year, and snow lay with heavy frosts for much of that time, but the lack of nest refurbishment did concern me. The middle nest hadn't been touched, and while the top nest had been added to, it was roughly made with sticks and heather and showed no signs of the soft material that would hold the eggs. The nest still hadn't been fully lined by 2 April, and this was the year in which I recorded the least nesting activity of all.

My 2003 food transects produced a biomass figure of only 37 kg, the next lowest being the 64 kg of the year before, and the March figure was only 24 kg, the same as in 1999, the first year in which no eggs were laid, and in stark contrast to the 98 kg of 1996 when the birds last bred successfully. Even the live prey figure was down as the rabbit population fell away again, 13 kg being the lowest since 1995.

The year rolled by with the eagles doing little more than occupying the valley. The female was on the top nest on 2 May but hadn't laid eggs, and I saw few flight displays that spring. The eagles were absent from the valley on my first three visits in August, but September and October saw them back in the core area, and a carcass below the top nest crag on 17 November gave them something to keep them at home. With both birds settled on *the ledge*, I decided to check the carcass for signs of use and received quite a shock on arriving and looking up to the crag. There, on an edge and out of sight from down-valley, was a new nest. It wasn't lined, but it was a brand new structure and was in a reasonable position. It proved yet again that the valley, and everywhere else in the home range, had to be searched on a regular basis if any idea of the eagles' activities was to be gleaned. Relying on what was being seen from a garden shed, halfway along the floor of the nesting valley during the breeding season, told you nothing at all.

All seemed to be as normal during the early part of 2004, so I set off to clean the roosts and perches of pellets and map the locations of existing carcasses on 25 January. It was an unusual morning with both frost and drizzle as I entered the valley at 8.20 a.m. There was only a handful of rabbits on show as I worked my way through the warren, but I flushed a woodcock on the walk and was pleased to find a sheep carcass below the middle nest. There was no sign of the eagles, so I sat for a cup of tea at 9.20 a.m. before breaking away from the screes and into the more open terrain. It was my usual habit on these cleaning trips, giving me time to search for the eagles so I could amend my route if necessary, and I always took the opportunity to scan the valley and count the deer. As with the rabbits, the deer numbers fluctuated over the years; from a normal count of 26 animals during the early years of my involvement, their numbers had increased until 60 was by no means uncommon (often with 15 or 16 calves being born per year), but numbers had dropped again and I only counted 29 that morning.

I repacked my sack after a 15-minute break, stood and looked behind me, both to check that I hadn't left anything and to look through the screes above me. The outcrops, gullies, boulders and trees made that area difficult to work, and I had to be certain of what I recorded, so I had to check all sides of anything that might conceal a carcass. And it wasn't only the ground I checked; as I'd noted in earlier years deer could be found hanging in trees, and I'd once found a sheep nicely lodged in the fork of a tree as if a big cat was on the prowl. As I scanned I noticed some wool, part of a fleece from an earlier carcass, among the rocks, but as I made a note of its location something urged me to look again, an image was burning into the back of my eyes, and when I did take another look it was a double take. It wasn't obvious at first, but beside the fleece, half hidden by rocks, was the female eagle; she was no more than 30 metres from where I stood.

I knew she hadn't flown in while I'd been there (even though she clearly didn't fear me, and this was where I dumped the deer carcass in 1996 when she'd flown in to perch above me and barely wait for me to leave before flying down to feed), so I had to ask why my arrival hadn't disturbed her. She wasn't feeding or watching me, and through binoculars I could see that her head was tucked into her scapulars as if she was in a deep sleep. It was a worry; an eagle shouldn't have been so drowsy on the ground – if I could blunder in so close without rousing her a fox would have been able to grab her with ease. I was devastated and didn't want to face the obvious conclusion, so I took a photograph for the record and hoped she'd fly away before I did anything else.

I had to take a closer look at the bird but didn't want to startle her by charging straight up the slope, so I cut off in a semi-circle with the intention of approaching her from the side, so she'd have a clear flight out from the slope. Halfway there I kicked a loose stone, and her head came up, but at that range I didn't need binoculars to see that her third eyelids were closed. I was standing in front of her but she still didn't know I was there. I was becoming fairly distraught but tried to be optimistic; I'd stalked this close to a wild eagle in the past, but I knew this to be an entirely different situation. As I moved in, I didn't even think about photography, the closer I approached the more likely it seemed as though I'd be carrying the eagle home with me, so the camera was forgotten about in my hand. I edged closer to the eagle and finally, at about 5 metres, her eyes opened fully and we stared at each other. She wasn't to be caught, however; she turned her head away and casually leapt into the air to swing away down-valley and drop out of sight behind a bluff where she was immediately mobbed by crows.

The flight raised my spirits a little; she seemed steady on her wings, so I began to make excuses for her: perhaps she was just dozy that morning, perhaps she wasn't too bothered because she'd chosen to come that close to me in the past and had known me and seen me help her since 1982, or perhaps she just couldn't be bothered to react until I ventured too close to her. Two years earlier as I checked the perches I found her perched on *the old cross tree*, but as I approached she simply flew across to the *SR* perch. I scrabbled about at the tree and then pressed on for *the ledge* before dropping down to *SR* as the three perches formed a triangle. The female was still there, so I stayed in view of her and when she decided the time was right she simply flew back to *the old cross tree*. I was never more than 200 metres from her and twice less than 50, but she hadn't flown out of the valley, performed a disturbance display or flown down to watch from some distant perch, she just avoided the nuisance she'd watched visit those same locations more than a hundred times before.

I pressed on with my searches, but my mind was elsewhere, and the next few perches went by in a daze. I visited the valley-head sites that had remained unused since the demise of the old male and scoured the ground for food that might encourage the eagles to breed, but not once that day did I see the male eagle. As I skirted the big screes I looked down-valley and saw the female fly across; she didn't make it to a favoured perch but dropped to land in a grassy hollow on the lower slopes of the ridge I was about to search. I continued on my way and was in and out of her sight as I scrambled about, but I'd marked her position and deliberately approached her from above, for once not showing her that I was there.

As I edged closer, knowing that the slope of the ground would conceal my body and allow me to peep into the hollow with only the top half of my head on view, I half expected to find her gone, but she was still there. She was standing flatly and looking out across the valley, watchful if not fully alert. As if to take my work full circle, I coughed and stepped forward to show myself, just as I'd done with the juvenile in 1979, and coughed again as she scanned around. Her head turned sharply towards me at the second cough, and we again faced each other. With me stationary, she soon looked away, defecated and launched into a flight that took her back across the valley to land among the boulders below the middle nest.

With each flight taking the female closer to the valley floor, I knew that her story was coming to an end. After all those years of watching her I was left with a simple choice: should I chase her down and catch her to see her die in a cage, be mounted and put on display in my living room or should I leave her where she was, untouched by human hand, to die in the valley she'd known as home for 22 years? I walked away, and when I turned my back I knew that I would never see her again.

Epilogue

As I write this late in 2008 the female eagle hasn't been replaced at Haweswater. The male has continued his lonely vigil in Riggindale for almost five years in the apparently vain hope of attracting a new mate. Each year he climbs high into the sky to perform his advertisement displays, but if there are other eagles to see him, he fails to attract a mate. Each year he repairs at least one of the nests he's never used, in readiness for that monumental occasion when the eggs are laid, but no female arrives to add to the Lakeland story. He displays and calls and prepares the site, but his ardour soon cools and he wanders away for days at a time. He always returns to his valley alone to spend the remainder of the year waiting for February when fresh hope arrives.

It looks like being a sad end to the story of the Lakeland eagles. Nineteen young were fledged during 30 years of breeding (16 from Riggindale), and I'd studied 13 of those eaglets, seeing six reared during my six years as the RSPB's eagle warden. No young have been reared since 1996, and no eggs have been laid since 2000. There hasn't even been a pair of birds since early in 2004.

I was very lucky to become involved when I did, during the eagles' most productive period, but I've had to watch their decline from two successful breeding pairs to a single bird. I believe that more could have been done to help the Lakeland eagles, but my investigative fieldwork was only grudgingly accepted, while speculation was treated as fact and negated the need for positive intervention or investigation. It's a situation that cannot now be reversed, and while conservationists are happy to reintroduce a variety of species across the country, what had been England's rarest resident species for the best part of four decades has been allowed to die out without any official help other than to stand and watch from a garden shed during the spring and summer.

I fear for the future of Scotland's eagles as well; although they are unlikely to become extinct in the foreseeable future I see the same attitudes there as I've seen in England – problems are discussed but not investigated or addressed. The results of the 2003 national survey tell us that only 145 pairs bred successfully (about 33 per cent of the population), so why did the other 297 pairs fail? Indeed, why did 180 pairs fail to even lay eggs? Perhaps they were all too old! While that is not actually a ridiculous possibility for the population overall, the most feasible answers in most cases relate to problems with habitat quality and food supply, just as we've seen in England. Worse still, in terms of future planning, conservationists have exaggerated the number of golden eagles in Scotland. We are told that there were 442 pairs in 2003 but there were not, that figure was reached by assuming a built-up nest was evidence of occupancy by a pair, but we know that single eagles build nests. Excluding the false pairs only makes a small change to the total figure, but I fail to understand why conservationists would artificially increase the numbers of such a rare species while simultaneously announcing that it is threatened.

In 1991 I predicted that the 1992 national eagle survey would find a similar number of pairs to the 1982 results but that productivity would be lower, and that is what happened. I cannot claim any great insight by saying this as the 1992 results were easily predictable, just as it was easy to predict that 2003 would again find a similar number of pairs and slightly better productivity. The simple figures produced by the surveys suggest that productivity is sufficient to maintain the population at about its current level, but it is clearly too low to allow eagles to spread into, or consolidate their numbers in, areas with few or no birds. Eagles returned to the Lake District during a period of range expansion, following their return to south-west Scotland and Northern Ireland, but they are now in decline in the former and have been lost from the latter.

The pioneering Lakeland birds lived through the pesticide problem that resulted in eggshell thinning and failed breeding in Scotland, but that may also have delayed successful breeding in England at a time when expansion and increase were still possible. It seems certain that the numbers of young eagles being reared annually in Scotland are now, and have been for some time, too few to support the fringe populations. Productivity is affected by a failing food supply that is influenced by habitat quality, land management policy and practice, and increased human activity in the uplands. The numbers of young reared may well sustain the population at present, but these factors, plus the severe levels of lethal persecution that prevents range occupancy and successful breeding in some parts of Scotland, may not only prevent eagles re-establishing in the Lake District but may begin the decline over a wider part of Scotland, and the decline could be rapid. The Haweswater birds moved from successful breeding through failures, non-breeding and to one bird in only eight years; the period between national surveys is 10 years.

In spite of its aura of regal aloofness and the passion it inspires in many people, I think the golden eagle is the forgotten species of English conservation. With the attitudes I've witnessed here being mirrored in Scotland, its description of being a 'usually silent' species will be proven correct, and no more will we be summoned to the Lakeland fells by the call of the eagle.

Flight of the Wild Geese

Graham Uney

The sight of strings of wild Barnacle geese flying overhead, with a noisy chorus of honking, will be a familiar sight to many. However, following their migration, little is known about the lives of these sociable geese. *Flight of the Wild Geese* tells the story of the winter wildlife of the Solway Firth, that wonderfully wild estuary set between the rugged hills of Cumbria and the rolling farmland, moors and forests of Dumfries and Galloway. It explores the links that these beautiful places share with the most remote islands of the North Atlantic, and with the stunning landscapes of the high Arctic. This is a book of birds, of people, and of places.

The author's sea journey takes in a number of remote islands, beginning with the two Scottish outliers of North Rona and Sula Sgeir, then venturing ever northwards via the stunning rocky coasts of the Faroe Islands, the black-sand volcanics of Jan Mayen, and the great sea bird colonies of Bear Island before encountering pack ice in the vast sea channel of the Storfjorden. Here, in Svalbard's Arctic waters, ivory gulls roamed the ice islands searching for food, while seals hunted the open flats between. Arctic wildlife filled every space, backed by an array of glistening snow peaks, their glaciers carving rivers of ice down to the sea. This was the author's first view of Svalbard – Kingdom of the Ice Bear.

The author also reflects on his life as a writer, photographer and environmental surveyor. Growing up in the flatlands of East Yorkshire where his love of wildlife was instilled, he yearned to know more about where the winter-visiting birds went during the summer. He learnt a great deal about waders, ducks, geese and swans at the Humber Estuary but, once these birds had migrated to cooler climes in the summer, their lives were a mystery. Later in life and with the Solway Firth on his doorstep, where some of the largest numbers of geese are to be found, he decided to find out.

" a fine travel tale, mixed with natural history and keen observation en route. ...this is the perfect book to read ..." *Waterlife*

"This is a book written by a birder and a birder's book ... if you enjoy reading about birds and their homes you'll enjoy this book." *Habitat*

*ISBN 978-1904445-54-8   240 × 170mm   softback   liberally illustrated
176pp + 16pp colour section   £16.99*

Bestseller! Bestseller! Bestseller! Bestseller!

A life of Ospreys

Roy Dennis

roy dennis

Ospreys are one of our best known and best loved birds and Roy Dennis is synonymous with the successful return of the osprey to Scotland. From the time he saw his first osprey, back in 1960, Roy has worked to help this magnificent raptor establish itself once more in a country where it had been hounded and persecuted to near-extinction over hundreds of years.

A Life of Ospreys tells the story not only of the osprey, but of the osprey watcher, following the bird's fortunes in Scotland, seeing its numbers rise from that single pair in the 1950s to close to 200 pairs today. It traces the osprey's history in Scotland and the rest of the UK – including the bad old days of egg thieves and the shooting of birds as specimens – to the present day, with satellite radios allowing us to follow the every move of the osprey on its migration to Africa and back.

With many personal anecdotes and insights, the book covers the ecology and conservation of the osprey from Roy pioneering the building of artificial nests – instrumental in increasing their numbers and range – to starting the first European translocation of chicks from their nests in the Highlands and releasing them at Rutland Water Nature Reserve in the Midlands.
Included in this book are Roy's personal diary entries, written at a time when no one knew whether or not his lifetime's work would succeed, and which add a unique sense of history to this very personal tale.

"Everything one could ever wish to know about these birds seems to be covered in this book." *John Muir Trust Journal*

"The book is delightful, lavishly and intelligently illustrated containing much factual data and is highly readable. ...Buy it." *ECOS*

"one of the most arresting nature books this year... His book has excellent photographs and also information on where to see the osprey eyries." The Times

ISBN 978-1904445-26-5 240 × 170 mm   softback   240pp , full colour throughout, liberally illustrated with photographs, maps, graphs and tables. £18.99

Whittles Publishing • Dunbeath • Caithness • Scotland UK • KW6 6EY
Tel: +44(0)1593-731 333; Fax: +44(0)1593-731 400;
e-mail: info@whittlespublishing.com; www.whittlespublishing.com